SAGEMATH CRYPTOGRAPHY AND NETWORK SECURITY

DR. AMOL PRAKASH BHAGAT | FAIZAN SHAH RAMJU SHAH | KIRAN NAMDEV KHAKARE | AND CHETAN RAMESH INGOLE

Copyright © Dr. Amol Prakash Bhagat, Faizan Shah Ramju Shah, Kiran Namdev Khakare, and Chetan Ramesh Ingole
All Rights Reserved.

This book has been self-published with all reasonable efforts taken to make the material error-free by the author. No part of this book shall be used, reproduced in any manner whatsoever without written permission from the author, except in the case of brief quotations embodied in critical articles and reviews.

The Author of this book is solely responsible and liable for its content including but not limited to the views, representations, descriptions, statements, information, opinions and references ["Content"]. The Content of this book shall not constitute or be construed or deemed to reflect the opinion or expression of the Publisher or Editor. Neither the Publisher nor Editor endorse or approve the Content of this book or guarantee the reliability, accuracy or completeness of the Content published herein and do not make any representations or warranties of any kind, express or implied, including but not limited to the implied warranties of merchantability, fitness for a particular purpose. The Publisher and Editor shall not be liable whatsoever for any errors, omissions, whether such errors or omissions result from negligence, accident, or any other cause or claims for loss or damages of any kind, including without limitation, indirect or consequential loss or damage arising out of use, inability to use, or about the reliability, accuracy or sufficiency of the information contained in this book.

Made with ♥ on the Notion Press Platform
www.notionpress.com

For every reader ....

who breathe life into these pages..............

Contents

Foreword	*vii*
Preface	*ix*
Acknowledgements	*xi*
Prologue	*xiii*
1. Computer And Network Security Concepts	1
2. Conventional Encryption Model / Classical Encryption Techniques	13
3. Encryption And Decryption	27
4. Symmetric Key Encryption And Public Key Encryption	38
5. IP Security: IP Sec	65
6. IP Security Policy	76
7. Threats And Malwares In Network	92
8. Network Security Controls	98
9. Web And System Security	105
10. Security Features In Operating System	128

Demonstrations In SageMath And Other Tools

11. Practical Introduction To Cryptography And Network Security Tools	139
12. SageMath Installation And Configuration	144
13. Linear Algebra, Matrix Multiplication, And Classical Encryption With SageMath	148
14. Block Cipher And Data Encryption Standard With SageMath	154
15. Digital Signature With SageMath	160
16. Public-Key Cryptography And RSA With SageMath	165
17. Advanced Encryption Standard With SageMath	169
18. Password -based Authentication With JAVA	174
19. Activation Of Firewall On Windows Operating System	176
20. Detecting Trojans By Using -Netstat And TCP View	182
21. Scanning For Vulnerabilities	192

Foreword

Within the vast tapestry of cyberspace, threads of vulnerability and resilience intertwine. **Cryptography**, the art of concealment, stitches a narrative of secrecy, integrity, and authentication. As you embark on this exploration of hidden realms and encoded messages, prepare to be captivated by the elegance and power woven into the fabric of **network security**.

Information pirouettes through cyberspace, **cryptography** stands as the maestro orchestrating a symphony of **security**. Join us on a journey where algorithms become guardians, and **networks** transform into fortresses, as we delve into the fascinating realm of **cryptography and network security**.

In the digital age, where information is both currency and vulnerability, the key to safeguarding our virtual realms lies in the intricate dance of algorithms and protocols. **Cryptography** is the guardian of this dance floor, ensuring that only the right partners waltz through the corridors of data. Join us as we unveil the secrets behind the locks and keys that secure our connected world.

Preface

What topics covered in this book

Introduction : OSI Security Architecture, Security Attacks: Threats, Vulnerability and Controls, Security Services: Confidentiality, Integrity, Availability, Introduction to Cryptography, Conventional Encryption: Conventional encryption model - classical encryption techniques

    Encryption and Decryption: Characteristics of Good Encryption Technique: Properties of Trustworthy Encryption Systems; Types of Encryption Systems: Based on Key, Based on Block; Confusion and Diffusion; Cryptanalysis

    Symmetric Key Encryption and Public Key Encryption: Data Encryption Standard (DES) Algorithm: Double and Triple DES, Security of the DES; Advanced Encryption Standard (AES) Algorithm, DES and AES Comparison, RSA Technique, Digital Signature

    IP Security: Overview of IP Security (IPSec); IP Security Architecture; Modes of Operation; Security Associations, Security Parameter Index (SPI), SA Management, Security Policy: Authentication Header (AH); Encapsulating Security Payload (ESP); Internet Key Exchange

    Network Security: Network Concepts; Threats in Networks, Threats in Transit: Eavesdropping and Wiretapping, Protocol Flaws, Impersonation; Network Security Controls: Architecture, Encryption, Virtual Private Networks, Public Key Infrastructure (PKI) and Certificates

    Web and System Security: Web Security: Secure socket layer and transport layer security, Secure Electronic transaction, System Security: Intruders, Viruses and related threads; Network Security Controls: Architecture, Security Features of Trusted Operating Systems

With demonstrations of

Cryptography and Network Security Tools
    SageMath Installation and Configuration
    Linear Algebra, Matrix Multiplication, and Classical Encryption
    Block Cipher and Data Encryption Standard
    Digital Signature
    Public-Key Cryptography and RSA
    Advanced Encryption Standard
    Authentication Using Password
    Activation of Firewall and Settings
    Detecting Trojans by using -Netstat
    Steganography using image hide techniques
    Scanning for vulnerabilities using (Angry IP, HPing2, IPScanner)

Acknowledgements

In the labyrinth of bytes and the ever-expanding corridors of cyberspace, this endeavor to unravel the mysteries of cryptography and network security has been an odyssey of collective effort and shared wisdom. To those who laid the groundwork with their pioneering research and timeless contributions, we extend our deepest appreciation. Your dedication to the ever-evolving field of security has been the beacon guiding our exploration.

A heartfelt nod to the tireless guardians of the digital realm—cybersecurity professionals and experts—who continually strive to outwit the unseen adversaries. Your vigilance inspires our pursuit of a safer, more resilient online world.

Family and friends, who provided unwavering support during the peaks and valleys of this literary journey, your patience and encouragement have been the bedrock upon which this work stands.

Lastly, to the readers who embark on this exploration of cryptographic realms, may the knowledge within these pages empower you to navigate the digital seas with confidence and understanding.

Prologue

As we stand on the precipice of this cybernetic frontier, a question echoes through the corridors of code:

How do we secure the delicate balance between innovation and vulnerability?

Welcome to the Prologue of "**SageMath Cryptography and Network Security**" This tome is not just a guide; it's a lantern illuminating the cryptic realms where algorithms and networks weave their intricate patterns. Here, we embark on a quest to demystify the arcane arts of **cryptography and network security**, unraveling the enigma that guards our digital domain.

In the vast expanse of the digital ether, where information pulses like the lifeblood of our interconnected world, shadows linger. They are the echoes of potential threats, the footprints of unseen intruders, and the whispers of data waiting to be uncovered.

Peer into the shadows with us, where encryption becomes a shield, and protocols stand guard at the gates of information. Together, let us navigate the twists and turns of this cybernetic labyrinth, where every byte tells a story, and every security measure is a chapter in the epic saga of safeguarding the virtual frontier.

The journey begins, and the shadows await your scrutiny. Dare you step into the realm where secrecy meets scrutiny, and security is both an art and a science?

Brace yourself for a voyage through **SageMath Cryptography and Network Security**.

CHAPTER ONE

Computer and Network Security Concepts

1.1 NETWORK AND INTERNET SECURITY

Measures to deter, prevent, detect, and correct security violations that involve the transmission of information
- Covers a host of possibilities
- Examples of security violations

1. User A transmits a file to user B. The file contains sensitive information (e.g., payroll records) that is to be protected from disclosure. User C, who is not authorized to read the file, is able to monitor the transmission and capture a copy of the file during its transmission.
2. A network manager, D, transmits a message to a computer, E, under its management. The message instructs computer E to update an authorization file to include the identities of a number of new users who are to be given access to that computer. User F intercepts the message, alters its contents to add or delete entries, and then forwards the message to computer E, which accepts the message as coming from manager D and updates its authorization file accordingly.
3. Rather than intercept a message, user F constructs its own message with the desired entries and transmits that message to computer E as if it had come from manager D. Computer E accepts the message as coming from manager D and updates its authorization file accordingly.
4. An employee is fired without warning. The personnel manager sends a message to a server system to invalidate the employee's account. When the invalidation is accomplished, the server is to post a notice to the employee's file as confirmation of the action. The employee is able to intercept the message and delay it long enough to make a final access to the server to retrieve sensitive information The message is then forwarded, the action taken, and the confirmation posted. The employee's action may go unnoticed for some considerable time.
5. A message is sent from a customer to a stockbroker with instructions for various transactions. Subsequently, the investments lose value and the customer denies sending the message.

1.1.1 COMPUTER SECURITY

NIST Computer Security Handbook [NIST95] . Computer Security: The protection afforded to an automated information system in order to attain the applicable objectives of preserving the integrity, availability, and confidentiality of information system resources (includes hardware, software, firmware, information/data, and telecommunications).

Confidentiality :-

- Data Confidentiality: Assures that private or confidential information is not made available or disclosed to unauthorized individuals

- Privacy: Assures that individuals control or influence what information related to them may be collected and stored and by whom and to whom that information may be disclosed.

Integrity :-

- Data integrity: Assures that information (both stored and in transmitted packets) and programs are changed only in a specified and authorized manner
- System integrity: Assures that a system performs its intended function in an unimpaired manner, free from deliberate or inadvertent unauthorized manipulation of the system

Availability : Assures that systems work promptly and service is not denied to authorized users
CIA triad :-
Fundamental security objectives for both data and for information and computing services
NIST standard FIPS 199 (Standards for Security Categorization of Federal Information and Information Systems)
Three security objectives for information and for information systems.
Requirements and the definition of a loss of security in each category :-

- **Confidentiality :-** Preserving authorized restrictions on information access and disclosure, including means for protecting personal privacy and proprietary information. A loss of confidentiality is the unauthorized disclosure of information.
- **Integrity:-** Guarding against improper information modification or destruction, including ensuring information nonrepudiation and authenticity. A loss of integrity is the unauthorized modification or destruction of information.
- **vailability:-** Ensuring timely and reliable access to and use of information. A loss of availability is the disruption of access to or use of information or an information system. [The NIST Computer Security Handbook [NIST95]]

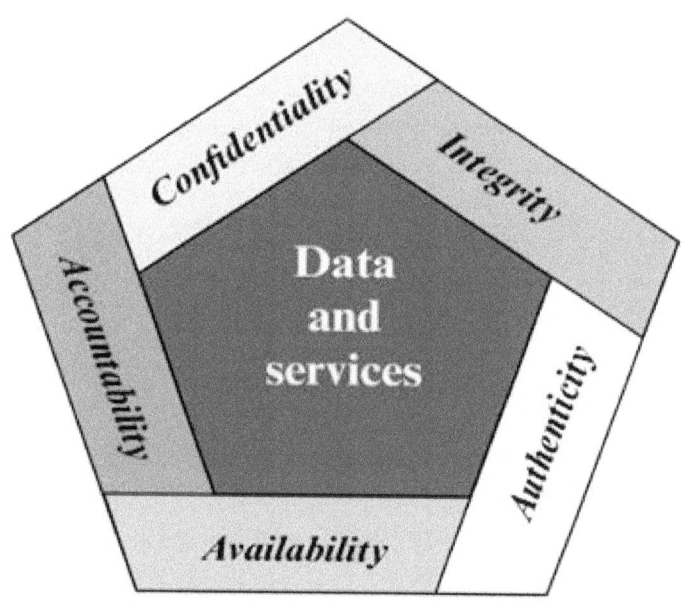

Figure 1.1: Essential Network and Computer Security Requirements

Essential Network and Computer Security Requirements
A] Confidentiality

B] Integrity
C] Accountability
D] Authenticity
E] Availability

Authenticity:- The property of being genuine and being able to be verified an trusted; confidence in the validity of a transmission, a message, or message originator. This means verifying that users are who they say they are and that each input arriving at the system came from a trusted source.

Accountability: Requirement for actions of an entity to be traced uniquely to that entity. Nonrepudiation, deterrence, fault isolation, intrusion detection and prevention, and afteraction recovery and legal action. Truly secure systems are not yet an achievable goal. Trace a security breach to a responsible party. Systems must keep records of their activities to permit later forensic analysis to trace security breaches or to aid in transaction disputes.

1.2 OSI Security Architecture

- Assess effectively the security needs of an organization and to evaluate and choose various security products and policies.
- Difficult enough in a centralized data processing environment; with the use of local and wide area networks.
- ITU-T Recommendation X.800, Security Architecture for OSI
- OSI security architecture is useful to managers
- Architecture was developed as an international standard, computer and communications vendors have developed security features for their products and services that relate to this structured definition of services and mechanisms.
- Focuses on security attacks, mechanisms, and services

Security attack: Any action that compromises the security of information owned by an organization.

Security mechanism: A process (or a device incorporating such a process) that is designed to detect, prevent, or recover from a security attack

Security service: A processing or communication service that enhances the security of the data processing systems and the information transfers of an organization. The services are intended to counter security attacks, and they make use of one or more security mechanisms to provide the service.

Threat and attack RFC 4949, Internet Security Glossary

- **Threat:-** A potential for violation of security, which exists when there is a circumstance, capability, action, or event that could breach security and cause harm. That is, a threat is a possible danger that might exploit a vulnerability.

- **Attack:-** An assault on system security that derives from an intelligent threat; that is, an intelligent act that is a deliberate attempt (especially in the sense of a method or technique) to evade security services and violate the security policy of a system.

The security of an organization is the greatest concern of the people working at the organization. Safety and security are the pillars of cyber technology. It is hard to imagine the cyber world without thinking about security. The architecture of security is thus a very important aspect of the organization. The OSI (Open Systems Interconnection) Security Architecture defines a systematic approach to providing security at each layer. It defines security services and security mechanisms that can be used at each of the seven layers of the OSI model to provide security for data transmitted over a network. These security services and mechanisms help to ensure the confidentiality, integrity, and availability of the data.

OSI architecture is internationally acceptable as it lays the flow of providing safety in an organization.
OSI Security Architecture focuses on these concepts :-
A] Security Attack
B] Security Mechanism
C] Security Service

OSI Security Architecture is categorized into three broad categories namely **Security Attacks, Security mechanisms, and Security Services.**

1.2.1 Security Attacks

Attack :- An assault on system security that derives from an intelligent threat; that is, an intelligent act that is a deliberate attempt (especially in the sense of a method or technique) to evade security services and violate the security policy of a system. X.800 and RFC 4949. There are tow main types of a Security Attacks such as Passive attacks and Active Attacks.

A] PASSIVE ATTACKS :- In Passive attack only read a massage observe the massage do not modify the massage. A Passive attack attempts to learn or make use of information from the system but does not affect system resources. Passive Attacks are in the nature of eavesdropping on or monitoring transmission. The goal of the opponent is to obtain information that is being transmitted. Passive attacks involve an attacker passively monitoring or collecting data without altering or destroying it. Examples of passive attacks include eavesdropping, where an attacker listens in on network traffic to collect sensitive information, and sniffing, where an attacker captures and analyzes data packets to steal sensitive information. Types of Passive attacks are as follows :-

- The release of message content
- Traffic analysis

The release of message content :–

- Telephonic conversation, an electronic mail message, or a transferred file may contain sensitive or confidential information.
- We would like to prevent an opponent from learning the contents of these transmissions.

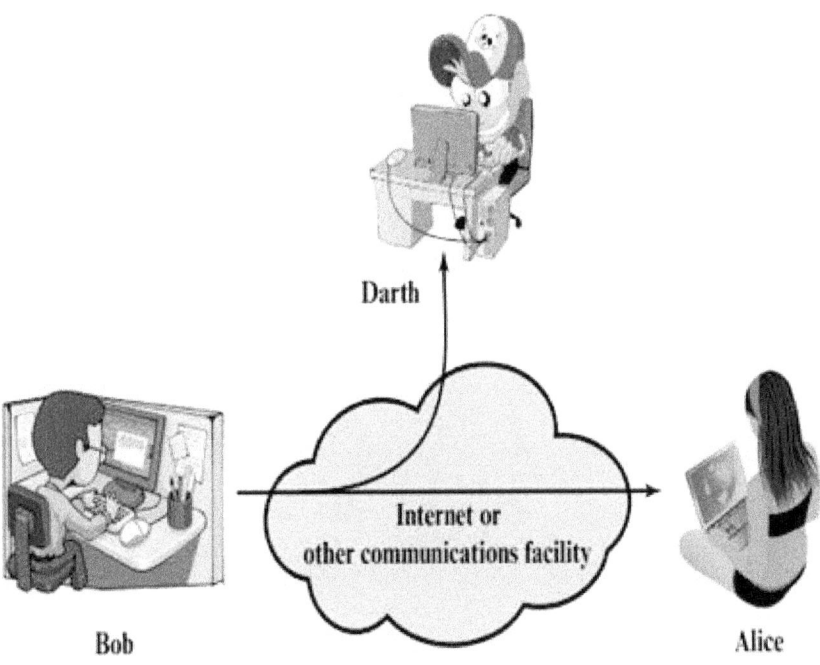

Figure 1.2: Passive Attacks

Traffic analysis :-

- Masking the contents of messages or other information traffic
- Opponent could determine the location and identity of communicating hosts and could observe the frequency and length of messages being exchanged
- Passive attacks are very difficult to detect

B] ACTIVE ATTACKS :- Active attacks are a type of cybersecurity attack in which an attacker attempts to alter, destroy, or disrupt the normal operation of a system or network. Active attacks involve the attacker taking direct action against the target system or network, and can be more dangerous than passive attacks, which involve simply monitoring or eavesdropping on a system or network. Types of active attacks are as follows:

- Masquerade
- Modification of messages
- Repudiation
- Replay
- Denial of Service

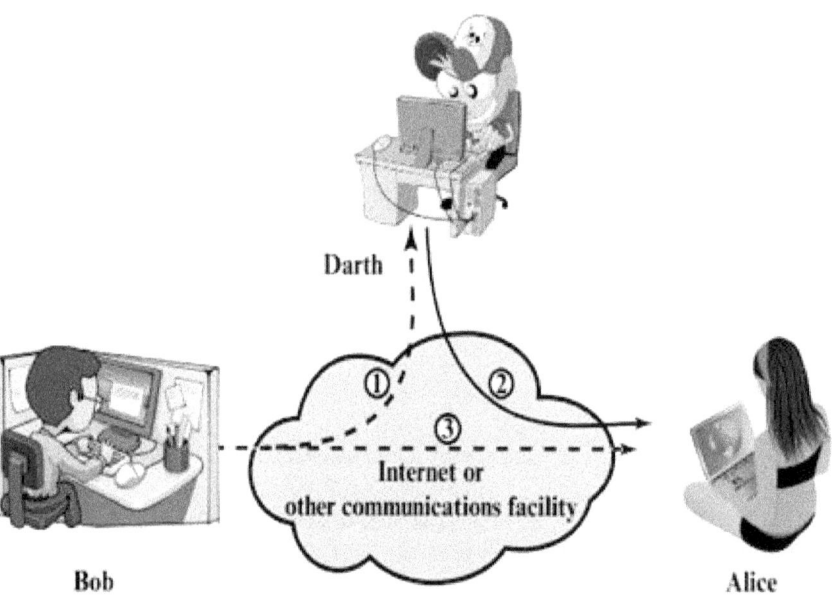

Figure 1.3: Active Attacks

Masquerade – Masquerade is a type of cybersecurity attack in which an attacker pretends to be someone else in order to gain access to systems or data. This can involve impersonating a legitimate user or system to trick other users or systems into providing sensitive information or granting access to restricted areas. There are several types of masquerade attacks, including:

- **Username and password masquerade:** In a username and password masquerade attack, an attacker uses stolen or forged credentials to log into a system or application as a legitimate user.
- **IP address masquerade:** In an IP address masquerade attack, an attacker spoofs or forges their IP address to make it appear as though they are accessing a system or application from a trusted source.
- **Website masquerade:** In a website masquerade attack, an attacker creates a fake website that appears to be legitimate in order to trick users into providing sensitive information or downloading malware.
- **Email masquerade:** In an email masquerade attack, an attacker sends an email that appears to be from a trusted source, such as a bank or government agency, in order to trick the recipient into providing sensitive information or downloading malware.

Modification of messages – It means that some portion of a message is altered or that message is delayed or reordered to produce an unauthorized effect. Modification is an attack on the integrity of the original data. It basically means that unauthorized parties not only gain access to data but also spoof the data by triggering denial-of-service attacks, such as altering transmitted data packets or flooding the network with fake data. Manufacturing is an attack on authentication. For example, a message meaning "Allow JOHN to read confidential file X" is modified as "Allow Smith to read confidential file X".

Repudiation –Repudiation attacks are a type of cybersecurity attack in which an attacker attempts to deny or repudiate actions that they have taken, such as making a transaction or sending a message. These attacks can be a serious problem because they can make it difficult to track down the source of the attack or determine who is responsible for a particular action.There are several types of repudiation attacks, including:

- **Message repudiation attacks:** In a message repudiation attack, an attacker sends a message and then later denies having sent it. This can be done by using spoofed or falsified headers or by exploiting vulnerabilities in the messaging system.
- **Transaction repudiation attacks:** In a transaction repudiation attack, an attacker makes a transaction, such as a financial transaction, and then later denies having made it. This can be done by exploiting vulnerabilities in the transaction processing system or by using stolen or falsified credentials.
- **Data repudiation attacks:** In a data repudiation attack, an attacker modifies or deletes data and then later denies having done so. This can be done by exploiting vulnerabilities in the data storage system or by using stolen or falsified credentials.

Replay –It involves the passive capture of a message and its subsequent transmission to produce an authorized effect. In this attack, the basic aim of the attacker is to save a copy of the data originally present on that particular network and later on use this data for personal uses. Once the data is corrupted or leaked it is insecure and unsafe for the users.

Denial of Service –Denial of Service (DoS) is a type of cybersecurity attack that is designed to make a system or network unavailable to its intended users by overwhelming it with traffic or requests. In a DoS attack, an attacker floods a target system or network with traffic or requests in order to consume its resources, such as bandwidth, CPU cycles, or memory, and prevent legitimate users from accessing it. There are several types of DoS attacks, including:

- **Flood attacks:** In a flood attack, an attacker sends a large number of packets or requests to a target system or network in order to overwhelm its resources.
- **Amplification attacks:** In an amplification attack, an attacker uses a third-party system or network to amplify their attack traffic and direct it towards the target system or network, making the attack more effective.

To prevent DoS attacks, organizations can implement several measures, such as:-

1. Using firewalls and intrusion detection systems to monitor network traffic and block suspicious activity.
2. Limiting the number of requests or connections that can be made to a system or network.
3. Using load balancers and distributed systems to distribute traffic across multiple servers or networks.
4. Implementing network segmentation and access controls to limit the impact of a DoS attack.

Difference between Active Attack and Passive Attack:
Active Attacks:

- In an active attack, Modification in information takes place.
- Active Attack is a danger to Integrity as well as availability.
- In an active attack, attention is on prevention.
- Due to active attacks, the execution system is always damaged.
- In an active attack, Victim gets informed about the attack.
- In an active attack, System resources can be changed.
- Active attack influences the services of the system.
- In an active attack, information collected through passive attacks is used during execution.
- An active attack is tough to restrict from entering systems or networks.
- Active attack can be easily detected.
- The purpose of an active attack is to harm the ecosystem.
- In an active attack, the original information is modified.
- The duration of an active attack is short.
- The prevention possibility of active attack is High

- Complexity is High.

Passive Attacks:

- Passive attack, Modification in the information does not take place.
- Danger to Confidentiality.
- Attention is on detection.
- There is no harm to the system.
- Victim does not get informed about the attack.
- System resources are not changing.
- Information and messages in the system or network are acquired.
- Passive attacks are performed by collecting information such as passwords, and messages by themselves
- Passive Attack is easy to prohibit in comparison to active attack.
- Very difficult to detect.
- The purpose of a passive attack is to learn about the ecosystem.
- In passive attack original information is Unaffected.
- The duration of a passive attack is long.
- The prevention possibility of passive attack is low.
- Complexity is low.

1.3 Security Services

Security services refer to the different services available for maintaining the security and safety of an organization. They help in preventing any potential risks to security.

X.800: a service that is provided by a protocol layer of communicating open systems and that ensures adequate security of the systems or of data transfers

RFC 4949: a processing or communication service that is provided by a system to give a specific kind of protection to system resources; security services implement security policies and are implemented by security mechanisms

X.800 divides these services into five categories and fourteen specific services

Authentication is the process of verifying the identity of a user or device in order to grant or deny access to a system or device.

- Assurance that the communicating entity is the one that it claims to be
- Peer Entity Authentication: Used in association with a logical connection to provide confidence in the identity of the entities connected
- Data-Origin Authentication: In a connectionless transfer, provides assurance that the source of received data is as claimed

Access control involves the use of policies and procedures to determine who is allowed to access specific resources within a system. The prevention of unauthorized use of a resource (i.e., this service controls who can have access to a resource, under what conditions access can occur, and what those accessing the resource are allowed to do)

Data Confidentiality is responsible for the protection of information from being accessed or disclosed to unauthorized parties.

- The protection of data from unauthorized disclosure
- **Connection Confidentiality:** The protection of all user data on a connection

- **Connectionless Confidentiality:** The protection of all user data in a single data block
- **Selective-Field Confidentiality:** The confidentiality of selected fields within the user data on a connection or in a single data block
- **Traffic-Flow Confidentiality:** The protection of the information that might be derived from observation of traffic flows

Data integrity is a security mechanism that involves the use of techniques to ensure that data has not been tampered with or altered in any way during transmission or storage.

- The assurance that data received are exactly as sent by an authorized entity (i.e., contain no modification, insertion, deletion, or replay)
- **Connection Integrity with Recovery:-** Provides for the integrity of all user data on a connection and detects any modification, insertion, deletion, or replay of any data within an entire data sequence, with recovery attempted
- **Connection Integrity without Recovery:-** Provides only detection without recovery
- **Selective-Field Connection Integrity:** Provides for the integrity of selected fields within the user data of a data block transferred over a connection and takes the form of determination of whether the selected fields have been modified, inserted, deleted, or replayed.

Non- repudiation involves the use of techniques to create a verifiable record of the origin and transmission of a message, which can be used to prevent the sender from denying that they sent the message. Provides protection against denial by one of the entities involved in a communication of having participated in all or part of the communication

- **Nonrepudiation, Origin:** Proof that the message was sent by the specified party
- **Nonrepudiation, Destination:** Proof that the message was received by the specified party

AVAILABILITY SERVICE

X.800 and RFC 4949 define availability to be the property of a system or a system resource being accessible and usable upon demand by an authorized system entity, according to performance specifications for the system (i.e., a system is available if it provides services according to the system design whenever users request them).

1.4 SPECIFIC SECURITY MECHANISMS

The mechanism that is built to identify any breach of security or attack on the organization, is called a security mechanism. Security Mechanisms are also responsible for protecting a system, network, or device against unauthorized access, tampering, or other security threats. Security mechanisms can be implemented at various levels within a system or network and can be used to provide different types of security, such as confidentiality, integrity, or availability.

Some examples of security mechanisms include :-

- **Encipherment (Encryption)** involves the use of algorithms to transform data into a form that can only be read by someone with the appropriate decryption key. Encryption can be used to protect data it is transmitted over a network, or to protect data when it is stored on a device.
- **Digital signature** is a security mechanism that involves the use of cryptographic techniques to create a unique, verifiable identifier for a digital document or message, which can be used to ensure the authenticity and integrity of the document or message.
- **Traffic padding** is a technique used to add extra data to a network traffic stream in an attempt to obscure the true content of the traffic and make it more difficult to analyze.

- **Routing control** allows the selection of specific physically secure routes for specific data transmission and enables routing changes, particularly when a gap in security is suspected.
- **Notarization:** The use of a trusted third party to assure certain properties of a data exchange
- **Authentication Exchange:** A mechanism intended to ensure the identity of an entity by means of information exchange
- **Data Integrity:** A variety of mechanisms used to assure the integrity of a data unit or stream of data units

PERVASIVE SECURITY MECHANISMS

- Mechanisms that are not specific to any particular OSI security service or protocol layer
- **Trusted Functionality:** That which is perceived to be correct with respect to some criteria (e.g., as established by a security policy)
- **Security Label:** The marking bound to a resource (which may be a data unit) that names or designates the security attributes of that resource
- **Event Detection:** Detection of security-relevant events
- **Security Audit Trail:** Data collected and potentially used to facilitate a security audit, which is an independent review and examination of system records and activities
- **Security Recovery:** Deals with requests from mechanisms, such as event handling and management functions, and takes recovery actions.

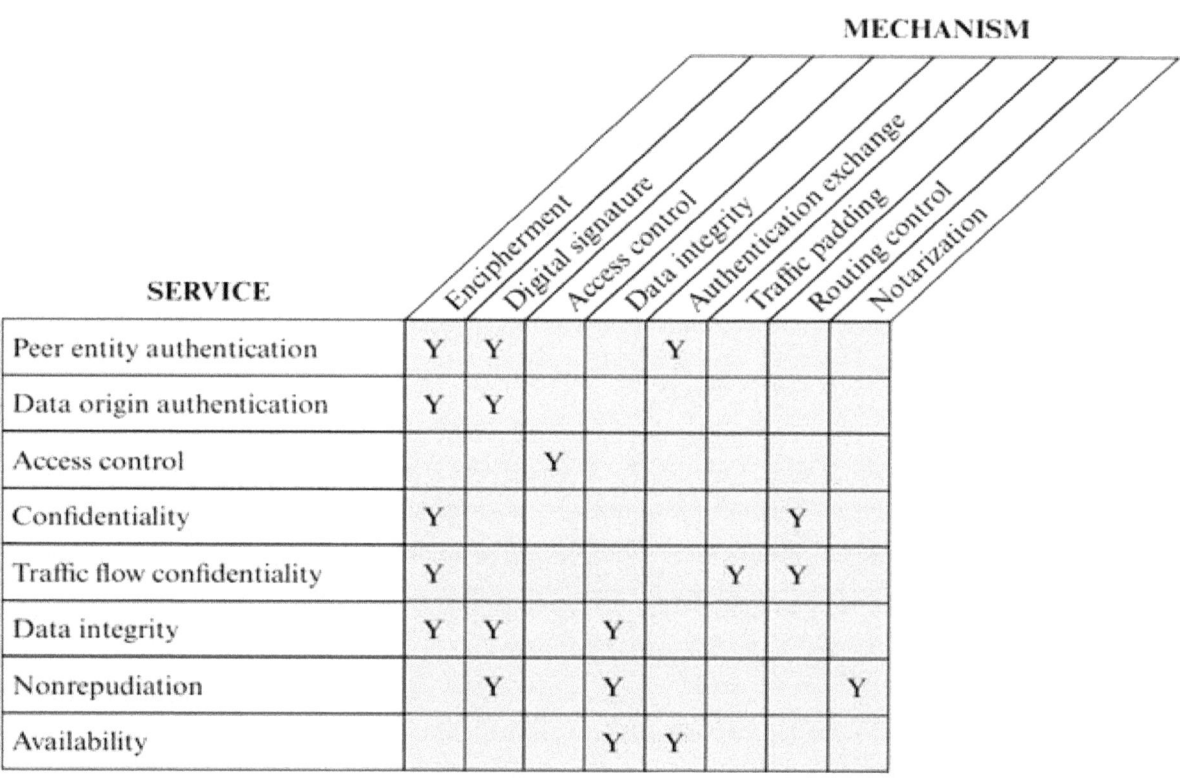

Figure 1.4: Security Services and Security Mechanisms

1.5 Introduction to Cryptography

Cryptography is the study and practice of techniques for secure communication in the presence of third parties called adversaries. It deals with developing and analyzing protocols that prevents malicious third parties from retrieving information being shared between two entities thereby following the various aspects of information security. Secure Communication refers to the scenario where the message or data shared between two parties can't be accessed by an adversary. In Cryptography, an Adversary is a malicious entity, which aims to retrieve precious information or data thereby undermining the principles of information security. Data Confidentiality, Data Integrity, Authentication and Non-repudiation are core principles of modern-day cryptography.

1. **Confidentiality** refers to certain rules and guidelines usually executed under confidentiality agreements which ensure that the information is restricted to certain people or places.
2. **Data integrity** refers to maintaining and making sure that the data stays accurate and consistent over its entire life cycle.
3. **Authentication** is the process of making sure that the piece of data being claimed by the user belongs to it.
4. **Non-repudiation** refers to the ability to make sure that a person or a party associated with a contract or a communication cannot deny the authenticity of their signature over their document or the sending of a message.

Consider two parties Alice and Bob. Now, Alice wants to send a message m to Bob over a secure channel. So, what happens is as follows. The sender's message or sometimes called the Plaintext, is converted into an unreadable form using a Key k. The resultant text obtained is called the Ciphertext. This process is known as Encryption. At the time of received, the Ciphertext is converted back into the plaintext using the same Key k, so that it can be read by the receiver. This process is known as Decryption.

Alice (Sender) Bob (Receiver)

$C = E(m, k) \longrightarrow m = D(C, k)$

Here, C refers to the Ciphertext while E and D are the Encryption and Decryption algorithms respectively. Let's consider the case of Caesar Cipher or Shift Cipher as an example. As the name suggests, in Caesar's Cipher each character in a word is replaced by another character under some defined rules.

Types of Cryptography:

There are several types of cryptography, each with its own unique features and applications. Some of the most common types of cryptography include:

1. Symmetric-key cryptography: This type of cryptography involves the use of a single key to encrypt and decrypt data. Both the sender and receiver use the same key, which must be kept secret to maintain the security of the communication.

2. Asymmetric-key cryptography: Asymmetric-key cryptography, also known as public-key cryptography, uses a pair of keys – a public key and a private key – to encrypt and decrypt data. The public key is available to anyone, while the private key is kept secret by the owner.

Hash functions: A hash function is a mathematical algorithm that converts data of any size into a fixed-size output. Hash functions are often used to verify the integrity of data and ensure that it has not been tampered with.

Applications of Cryptography:

Cryptography has a wide range of applications in modern-day communication, including:

- **Secure online transactions:** Cryptography is used to secure online transactions, such as online banking and e-commerce, by encrypting sensitive data and protecting it from unauthorized access.
- **Digital signatures:** Digital signatures are used to verify the authenticity and integrity of digital documents and ensure that they have not been tampered with.

- **Password protection:** Passwords are often encrypted using cryptographic algorithms to protect them from being stolen or intercepted.

Military and intelligence applications: Cryptography is widely used in military and intelligence applications to protect classified information and communications.

Challenges of Cryptography:

While cryptography is a powerful tool for securing information, it also presents several challenges, including :-

- **Key management:** Cryptography relies on the use of keys, which must be managed carefully to maintain the security of the communication.
- **Quantum computing:** The development of quantum computing poses a potential threat to current cryptographic algorithms, which may become vulnerable to attacks.
- **Human error:** Cryptography is only as strong as its weakest link, and human error can easily compromise the security of a communication.

CHAPTER TWO

Conventional Encryption Model / Classical Encryption Techniques

2.1 CLASSICAL/ CONVENTIONAL ENCRYPTION

Symmetric encryption, also referred to as conventional encryption or single-key encryption

- Public key encryption 1970s
- Most widely used of the two types of encryption
- An original message is known as the plaintext
- The coded message is called the ciphertext
- Process of converting from plaintext to ciphertext is known as enciphering or encryption
- Restoring the plaintext from the ciphertext is deciphering or decryption
- Many schemes used for encryption constitute the area of study known as cryptography
- Such a scheme is known as a cryptographic system or a cipher
- Techniques used for deciphering a message without any knowledge of the enciphering details fall into the area of cryptanalysis
- Cryptanalysis is what the layperson calls "breaking the code"
- Areas of cryptography and cryptanalysis together are called cryptology

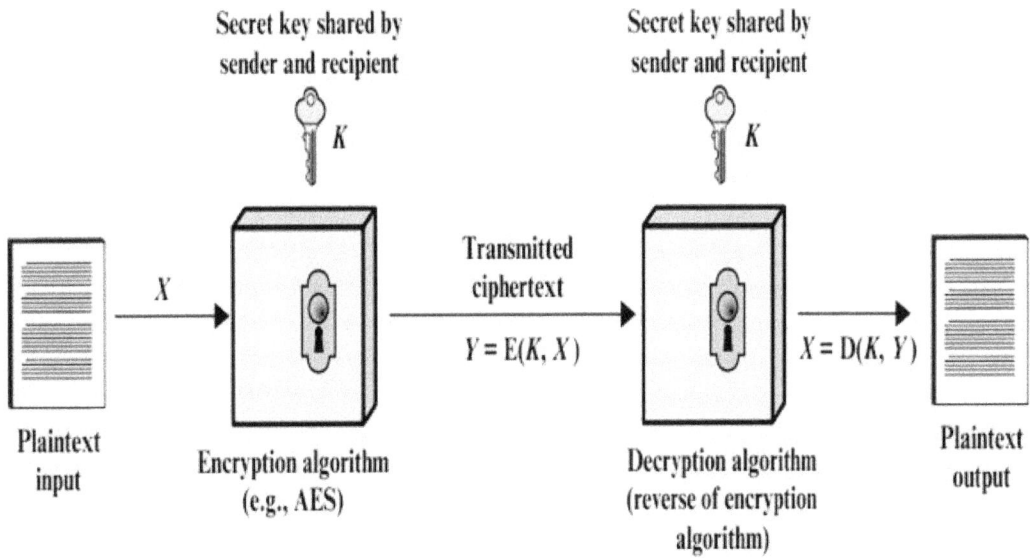

Figure 2.1: Symmetric Cipher Model

A symmetric encryption scheme has five ingredients (as shown in the figure 2.1):

- **Plaintext**: This is the original intelligible message or data that is fed into the algorithm as input.
- **Encryption algorithm**: The encryption algorithm performs various substitutions and transformations on the plaintext.
- **Secret key**: The secret key is also input to the encryption algorithm. The key is a value independent of the plaintext and of the algorithm. The algorithm will produce a different output depending on the specific key being used at the time. The exact substitutions and transformations performed by the algorithm depend on the key.
- **Ciphertext**: This is the scrambled (unintelligible) message produced as output. It depends on the plaintext and the secret key. For a given message, two different keys will produce two different ciphertexts.
- **Decryption algorithm**: This is essentially the encryption algorithm run in reverse. It takes the ciphertext and the secret key and produces the original plaintext.

Encryption Requirements
There are two requirements for secure use of conventional encryption:

- The encryption algorithm must be strong.

1. At a minimum, an opponent who knows the algorithm and has access to one or more ciphertexts would be unable to decipher the ciphertext or figure out the key.
2. In a stronger form, the opponent should be unable to decrypt ciphertexts or discover the key even if he or she has a number of ciphertexts together with the plaintext for each ciphertext.

- Sender and receiver must have obtained copies of the secret key in a secure fashion and must keep the key secure. If someone can discover the key and knows the algorithm, all communication using this key is readable.

Why not keep the encryption algorithm secret
We assume that it is impractical to decrypt a message on the basis of the ciphertext plus knowledge of the encryption/decryption algorithm. This means we do not need to keep the algorithm secret; we need to keep only the key secret. This feature of symmetric encryption makes low-cost chip implementations of data encryption algorithms widely available and incorporated into a number of products. With the use of symmetric encryption, the principal security problem is maintaining the secrecy of the key.

Model of Symmetric Cryptosystem
The essential elements of a symmetric encryption scheme is described in the figure 2.2.

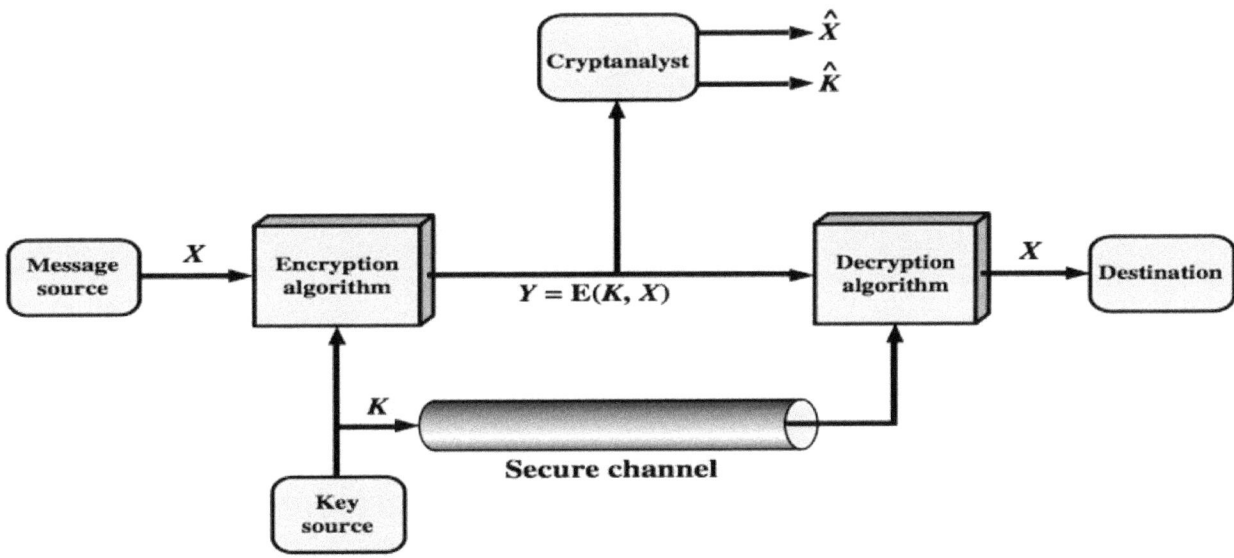

Figure 2.2: Essential Elements of Symmetric Encryption.

A source produces a message in plaintext, X=[X1,X2,…,XM]. A key of the form K=[K1,K2,…,KJ] is generated. If the key is generated at the message source, then it must also be provided to the destination by means of some secure channel. Alternatively, a third party could generate the key and securely deliver it to both source and destination. The ciphertext Y=[Y1,Y2,…,YN] is produced by the encryption algorithm with the message *X* and the encryption key *K* as input.

The encryption process is:
$$Y=E(K,X)$$
This notation indicates that *Y* is produced by using encryption algorithm E as a function of the plaintext *X*, with the specific function determined by the value of the key *K*.

The intended receiver with the key is able to invert the transformation:
$$X=D(K,Y)$$
An opponent, observing *Y* but not having access to *K* or *X*, may attempt to recover *X* or *K* or both. It is assumed that the opponent knows the encryption (E) and decryption (D) algorithms. The opponent may do one of the following:

- Recover *X* by generating a plaintext estimate $X^\wedge$, if the opponent is interested in only this particular message.
- Recover *K* by generating an estimate $K^\wedge$, if the opponent is interested in being able to read future messages.

Cryptography
Cryptographic systems are characterized along three independent dimensions:

1. **Type of operations for transforming plaintext to ciphertext.** All encryption algorithms are based on two general principles:

- **Substitution**: each element in the plaintext (bit, letter, group of bits or letters) is mapped into another element,
- **Transposition**: elements in the plaintext are rearranged. The fundamental requirement is that no information be lost (all operations are reversible). *Product systems* involve multiple stages of substitutions and transpositions.

2. **Number of keys used.**

- If both sender and receiver use the same key, the system is referred to as symmetric, single-key, secret-key, or conventional encryption.
- If the sender and receiver use different keys, the system is referred to as asymmetric, two-key, or public-key encryption.

3. **How the plaintext is processed.**

- A <u>block cipher</u> processes the input one block of elements at a time, producing an output block for each input block.
- A <u>stream cipher</u> processes the input elements continuously, producing output one element at a time, as it goes along.

Cryptanalysis and Brute-Force Attack

The objective of attacking an encryption system is to recover the key in use rather than simply to recover the plaintext of a single ciphertext. There are two general approaches to attacking a conventional encryption scheme:

- **Cryptanalysis** (cryptanalytic attacks): This attack relies on the nature of the algorithm plus some knowledge of the general characteristics of the plaintext or some sample plaintext–ciphertext pairs. It exploits the characteristics of the algorithm to attempt to deduce a specific plaintext or to deduce the key being used.

- **Brute-force attack**: The attacker tries every possible key on a piece of ciphertext until an intelligible translation into plaintext is obtained. On average, half of all possible keys must be tried to achieve success.

If either type of attack succeeds in deducing the key, then future and past messages encrypted with that key are compromised.

Type of Attack	Known to Cryptanalyst
Ciphertext Only	▪ Encryption algorithm ▪ Ciphertext
Known Plaintext	▪ Encryption algorithm ▪ Ciphertext ▪ One or more plaintext–ciphertext pairs formed with the secret key
Chosen Plaintext	▪ Encryption algorithm ▪ Ciphertext ▪ Plaintext message chosen by cryptanalyst, together with its corresponding ciphertext generated with the secret key
Chosen Ciphertext	▪ Encryption algorithm ▪ Ciphertext ▪ Ciphertext chosen by cryptanalyst, together with its corresponding decrypted plaintext generated with the secret key
Chosen Text	▪ Encryption algorithm ▪ Ciphertext ▪ Plaintext message chosen by cryptanalyst, together with its corresponding ciphertext generated with the secret key ▪ Ciphertext chosen by cryptanalyst, together with its corresponding decrypted plaintext generated with the secret key

Figure 2.3: Types of Attacks on Encrypted Message

2.2 Substitution Techniques

It is the one in which the letter of plaintext are replaced by other letter or by number or symbol. Type of Substitution Techniques As Given Below ,

1. Caesar Cipher
2. Monoalphabetic Cipher
3. Polyalphabetic Cipher
4. Playfair Cipher

Caesar Cipher :- It is also called shift cipher or additive cipher , each letter in the plaintext is replaced by a letter Corresponding to a no. of shift in the alphabet.The earliest known, and the simplest, use of a substitution cipher was by Julius Caesar. Caesar cipher involves replacing each letter of the alphabet with the letter standing three places further down the alphabet Example as shown below ,
Plain : meet me after the toga party
Cipher : PHHW PH DIWHU WKH WRJD SDUWB
We can define the transformation by listing all possibilities, as follows:
plain: a b c d e f g h i j k l m n o p q r s t u v w x y z
cipher: D E F G H I J K L M N O P Q R S T U V W X Y Z A B C
Then the algorithm can be expressed as follows. For each plaintext letter p, substitute the ciphertext letter C:
$C = E(3, p) = (p + 3) \mod 26$
$C = E(k, p) = (p + k) \mod 26$
$p = D(k, C) = (C - k) \mod 26$
The encryption and decryption algorithms are known There are only 25 keys to try

The language of the plaintext is known and easily recognizable Triple DES algorithm makes use of a 168-bit key, giving a key space of 2168 or greater than 3.7 *1050 possible keys. It the cryptanalyst attacker knowns a ciphertext , then be can apply brute force technique to find the plaintext by using block all the possible keys.

	PHHW	PH	DIWHU	WKH	WRJD	SDUWB
KEY						
1	oggv	og	chvgt	vjg	vqic	rctva
2	nffu	nf	bgufs	uif	uphb	qbsuz
3	meet	me	after	the	toga	party
4	ldds	ld	zesdq	sgd	snfz	ozqsx
5	kccr	kc	ydrcp	rfc	rmey	nyprw
6	jbbq	jb	xcqbo	qeb	qldx	mxoqv
7	iaap	ia	wbpan	pda	pkcw	lwnpu
8	hzzo	hz	vaozm	ocz	ojbv	kvmot
9	gyyn	gy	uznyl	nby	niau	julns
10	fxxm	fx	tymxk	max	mhzt	itkmr
11	ewwl	ew	sxlwj	lzw	lgys	hsjlq
12	dvvk	dv	rwkvi	kyv	kfxr	grikp
13	cuuj	cu	qvjuh	jxu	jewq	fqhjo
14	btti	bt	puitg	iwt	idvp	epgin
15	assh	as	othsf	hvs	hcuo	dofhm
16	zrrg	zr	nsgre	gur	gbtn	cnegl
17	yqqf	yq	mrfqd	ftq	fasm	bmdfk
18	xppe	xp	lqepc	esp	ezrl	alcej
19	wood	wo	kpdob	dro	dyqk	zkbdi
20	vnnc	vn	jocna	cqn	cxpj	yjach
21	ummb	um	inbmz	bpm	bwoi	xizbg
22	tlla	tl	hmaly	aol	avnh	whyaf
23	skkz	sk	glzkx	znk	zumg	vgxze
24	rjjy	rj	fkyjw	ymj	ytlf	ufwyd
25	qiix	qi	ejxiv	xli	xske	tevxc

Figure 2.4: Brute-Force Cryptanalysis of Caesar Cipher

Figure 2.5: Compressed using ZIP

The third characteristic is also significant. If the language of the plaintext is unknown, then plaintext output may not be recognizable. Furthermore, the input may be abbreviated or compressed in some fashion, again making recognition difficult. For example, shows a portion of a text file compressed using an algorithm called ZIP. If this file is then encrypted with a simple substitution cipher (expanded to include more than just 26 alphabetic characters), then the plaintext may not be recognized when it is uncovered in the brute-force cryptanalysis.

Since it is a part of symmetric encryption same key is used for encryption & decryption.

$\rightarrow 1 =< K =< 25$

Encryption :-
Example :- Msg (Plaintext) $\rightarrow$ " HELLO ", Let Key = 4
H $\rightarrow$ C(H) = (P+K) mod 26
= (7+4) mod 26
= 11 = L
E $\rightarrow$ C(E) = (P+4) mod 26
= (4+4) mod 26
= 8 = I
L $\rightarrow$ C(L) = P
O $\rightarrow$ C(O) = S
Ciphertext $\rightarrow$ **LIPPS** .
Decryption :- Msg (Ciphertext) $\rightarrow$ LIPPS , Key = 4
P(L) = (L-4) mod 26
= (11-4) mod 26
= 7 = H
P(I) = E , P(P)=L & P(S) = O
Plaintext = HELLO.

Monoalphabetic Cipher :- A single cipher alphabet for each plain text alphabet is used throughout the process. With only 25 possible keys, the Caesar cipher is far from secure. A dramatic increase in the key space can be achieved by allowing an arbitrary substitution. Before proceeding, we define the term permutation. A permutation of a finite set of elements S is an ordered sequence of all the elements of S, with each element appearing exactly once .

For example, if S = {a, b, c}, there are six permutations of S:
abc, acb, bac, bca, cab, cba

In general, there are n! permutations of a set of n elements, because the first element can be chosen in one of n ways, the second in n - 1 ways, the third in n - 2 ways, and so on. Recall the assignment for the Caesar cipher:
plain: a b c d e f g h i j k l m n o p q r s t u v w x y z
cipher: D E F G H I J K L M N O P Q R S T U V W X Y Z A B C

If, instead, the "cipher" line can be any permutation of the 26 alphabetic characters, then there are 26! or greater than 4 * 1026 possible keys. This is 10 orders of magnitude greater than the key space for DES and would seem to eliminate brute-force techniques for cryptanalysis. Such an approach is referred to as a monoalphabetic substitution cipher, because a single cipher alphabet (mapping from plain alphabet to cipher alphabet) is used per message.

There is, however, another line of attack. If the cryptanalyst knows the nature of the plaintext (e.g., noncompressed English text), then the analyst can exploit the regularities of the language. To see how such a cryptanalysis might proceed, we give a partial example here that is adapted from one in [SINK09]

UZQSOVUOHXMOPVGPOZPEVSGZWSZOPFPESXUDBMETSXAIZ
VUEPHZHMDZSHZOWSFPAPPDTSVPQUZWYMXUZUHSX
EPYEPOPDZSZUFPOMBZWPFUPZHMDJUDTMOHMQ

P	13.33	H	5.83	F	3.33	B	1.67	C	0.00
Z	11.67	D	5.00	W	3.33	G	1.67	K	0.00
S	8.33	E	5.00	Q	2.50	Y	1.67	L	0.00
U	8.33	V	4.17	T	2.50	I	0.83	N	0.00
O	7.50	X	4.17	A	1.67	J	0.83	R	0.00
M	6.67								

Figure 2.6: Relative Frequency of Letters

Relative frequency of the letters can be determined and compared to a standard frequency distribution for English.

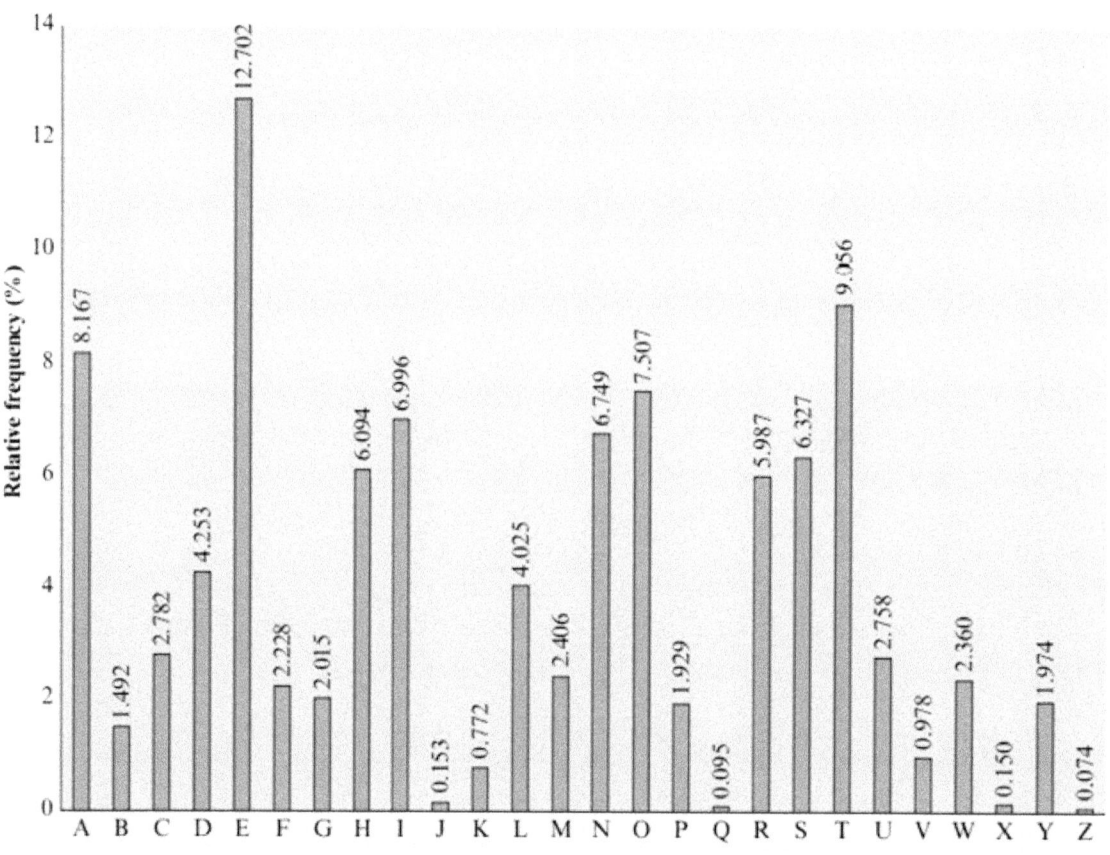

Figure 2.7: Relative Frequencies and Standard Frequencies

P and Z equivalents of e and t
- S, U, O, M, and H from the set {a, h, i, n, o, r, s}
- A, B, G, Y, I, J likely included in the set {b, j, k, q, v, x, z}

- A powerful tool is to look at the frequency of two-letter combinations, known as diagrams. Most common such digram is th, most common digram is ZW
- Make the correspondence of Z with t and W with h
- Equate P with e, ZWP as "the" ZWSZ form th_t

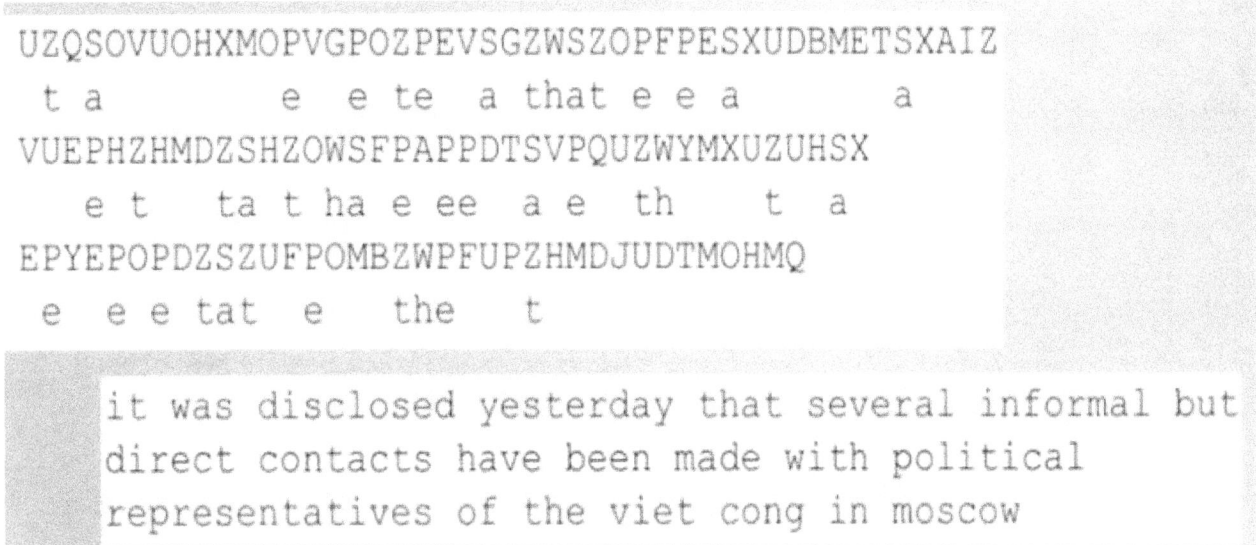

Figure 2.8: Decoded Message

Easy to break because they reflect the frequency data of the original alphabet. A countermeasure is to provide multiple substitutes, known as homophones, for a single letter. Letter e could be assigned a number of different cipher symbols, such as 16, 74, 35, and 21, Carl Friedrich Gauss devised an unbreakable cipher using homophones. Even with homophones, each element of plaintext affects only one element of ciphertext, and multiple-letter patterns (e.g., diagram frequencies) still survive in the ciphertext, making cryptanalysis relatively straightforward.

- Encrypt multiple letters of plaintext
- Use multiple cipher alphabets

Polyalphabetic Cipher :- There is no fixed substitutions each occurrence of a character may have a different substitution. i.e, We can more than 1 substitution for the same letter.
Eg:- MY NAME => NP OBXZ
The relationship between a character in the plaintext to a character in the ciphertext is one to many. There are two type of polyalphabetic cipher are, VIGENÈRE CIPHER and VERNAM CIPHER,

VIGENÈRE CIPHER :- It Designed by Blaise de vigenere [16th Century French mathematician], The best known, and one of the simplest, polyalphabetic ciphers is the Vigenère cipher. In this scheme, the set of related monoalphabetic substitution rules consists of the 26 Caesar ciphers with shifts of 0 through 25. Each cipher is denoted by a key letter, which is the ciphertext letter that substitutes for the plaintext letter a.

The encryption is done using a (26*26) matrix or table.
There are two types of method, first we solved problem using vigenere table select intersection value, using key letter.
Note :- Coloum à plaintext and row à key.
Second method will be, when the table is not given then calculate some for encryption as well as decryption equations as below,
$E_i = (P_i + K_i) \mod 26$,

$D_i = (E_i - K_i) \mod 26$.

VERNAM CIPHER :- The ultimate defense against such a cryptanalysis is to choose a keyword that is as long as the plaintext and has no statistical relationship to it. Such a system was introduced by an AT&T engineer named Gilbert Vernam in 1918. Vernam cipher working as below diagram.

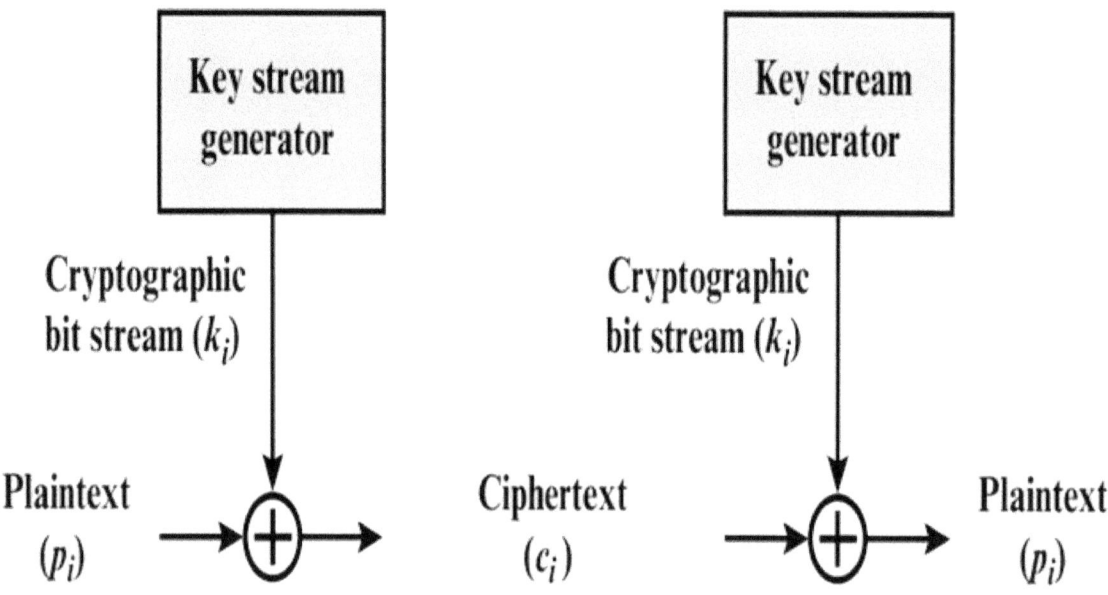

Figure 2.9: Vernam Cipher

Playfair Cipher :- The best-known multiple-letter encryption cipher is the Playfair

Treats diagrams in the plaintext as single units and translates these units into ciphertext diagrams. Playfair algorithm is based on the use of a 5 * 5 matrix of letters constructed using a keyword .Lord Peter Wimsey in Dorothy Sayers's Have His Carcase .The matrix is constructed by filling in the letters of the keyword (minus duplicates) from left to right and from top to bottom, and then filling in the remainder of the matrix with the remaining letters in alphabetic order

M	O	N	A	R
C	H	Y	B	D
E	F	G	I/J	K
L	P	Q	S	T
U	V	W	X	Z

Figure 2.10: Playfair Cipher

Repeating plaintext letters that are in the same pair are separated with a filler letter, such as x, so that balloon would be treated as ba lx lo on

Two plaintext letters that fall in the same row of the matrix are each replaced by the letter to the right, with the first element of the row circularly following the last. For example, ar is encrypted as RM.

Two plaintext letters that fall in the same column are each replaced by the letter beneath, with the top element of the column circularly following the last. For example, mu is encrypted as CM.

Otherwise, each plaintext letter in a pair is replaced by the letter that lies in its own row and the column occupied by the other plaintext letter. Thus, hs becomes BP and ea becomes IM (or JM, as the encipherer wishes).

Playfair cipher is a great advance over simple monoalphabetic ciphers. Whereas there are only 26 letters, there are 26 * 26 = 676 diagrams so that identification of individual diagrams is more difficult.

Relative frequencies of individual letters exhibit a much greater range than that of diagrams, making frequency analysis much more difficult. Playfair cipher was for a long time considered unbreakable. Used as the standard field system by the British Army in World War I, Considerable use by the U.S. Army and other Allied forces during World War II, Despite this level of confidence in its security, the Playfair cipher is relatively easy to break, because it still leaves much of the structure of the plaintext language.

2.3 Transposition Techniques

A very different kind of mapping is achieved by performing some sort of permutation on the plaintext letters. This technique is referred to as a transposition cipher. No replacement the characters, we will rearrange the characters position. i.e, We will apply sort of permutation one the plaintext letters.

There are Two types of transposition techniques, such as rail fence techniques and row/ column transposition cipher.

Rail Fence Techniques :- Plaintext is written down as a sequence of diagonals and then read off as a sequence of rows. To encipher the message "meet me after the toga party" with a rail fence of depth 2. In this plaintext is written down as a sequence of diagonals and then read off as a sequence of rows.

Ex:-

```
                    m e m a t r h t g p r y
                      e t e f e t e o a a t
```

The encrypted message is

MEMATRHTGPRYETEFETEOAAT

Figure 2.11: Rail Fence

This sort of thing would be trivial to cryptanalyze.

Row/ Column Transposition Cipher :- A more complex scheme is to write the message in a rectangle, row by row, and read the message off, column by column, but permute the order of the columns. The order of the columns then becomes the key to the algorithm. We write the massage in a rectangle row by row & read the massage of column by column but permute the order of column.

Ex:-

```
Key:            4 3 1 2 5 6 7
Plaintext:      a t t a c k p
                o s t p o n e
                d u n t i l t
                w o a m x y z
Ciphertext:     TTNAAPTMTSUOAODWCOIXKNLYPETZ
```

Figure 2.12: Transposition Cipher

A pure transposition cipher is easily recognized because it has the same letter frequencies as the original plaintext. For the type of columnar transposition, cryptanalysis is fairly straightforward and involves laying out the ciphertext in a matrix and playing around with column positions. Diagram and trigram frequency tables can be useful. The transposition cipher can be made significantly more secure by performing more than one stage of transposition. Result is a more complex permutation that is not easily reconstructed.

2.4 Rotor Machines

Multiple stages of encryption can produce a algorithm that is significantly more difficult to Cryptanalyze , Before the introduction of DES, the most important application of the principle of multiple stages of encryption was a class of systems known as rotor machines. Machine consists of a set of independently rotating cylinders through which electrical pulses can flow. Each cylinder has 26 input pins and 26 output pins, with internal wiring that connects each input pin to a unique output pin If we associate each input and output pin with a letter of the alphabet, then a single cylinder defines a monoalphabetic substitution. After each input key is depressed, the cylinder rotates one position, so that the internal connections are shifted accordingly

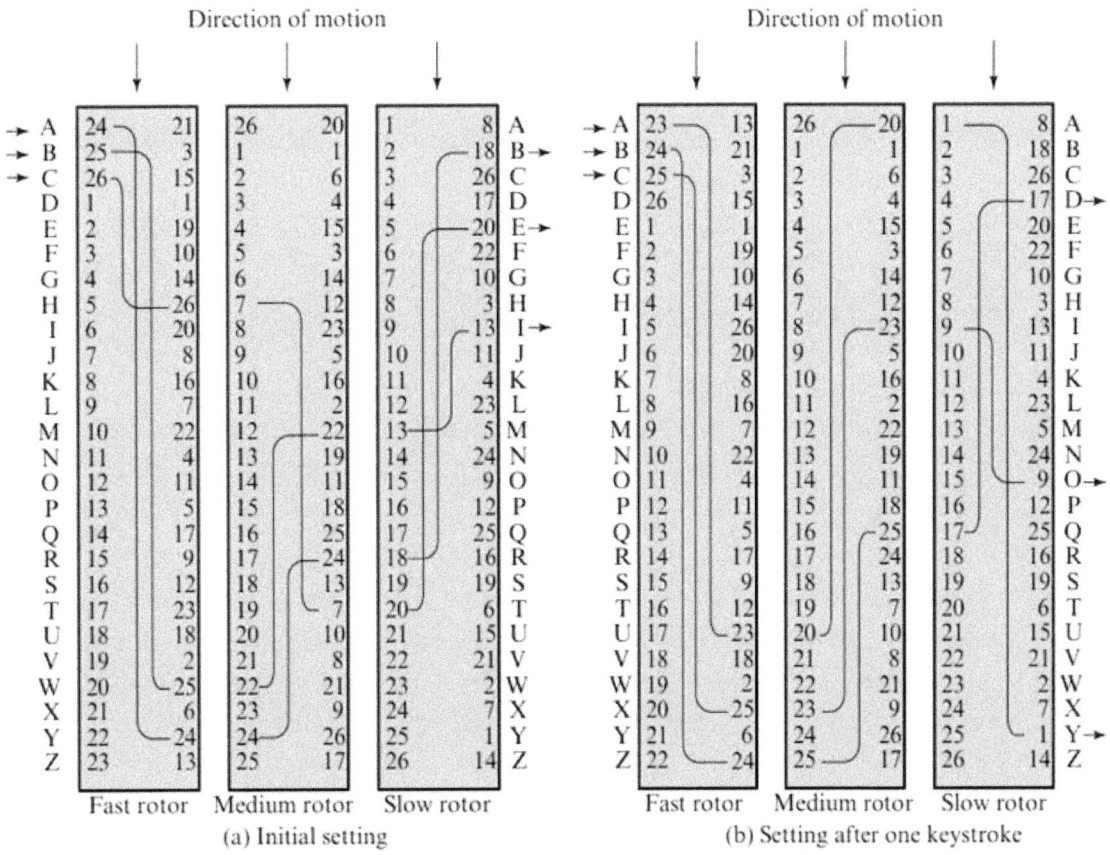

2.13: Rotor Machines

After 26 letters of plaintext, the cylinder would be back to the initial position.

A single-cylinder system is trivial and does not present a formidable cryptanalytic task .Power of the rotor machine is in the use of multiple cylinders, in which the output pins of one cylinder are connected to the input pins of the next, With multiple cylinders, the one closest to the operator input rotates one pin position with each keystroke.

For every complete rotation of the inner cylinder, the middle cylinder rotates one pin position. Finally, for every complete rotation of the middle cylinder, the outer cylinder rotates one pin position

26 * 26 * 26 = 17,576

The addition of fourth and fifth rotors results in periods of 456,976 and 11,881,376 letters (Vigenère cipher), respectively

2.5 Introduction to Steganography

A plaintext message may be hidden in one of two ways.

The methods of steganography conceal the existence of the message, whereas the methods of cryptography render the message unintelligible to outsiders by various transformations of the text.

A simple form of steganography, but one that is time-consuming to construct, is one in which an arrangement of words or letters within an apparently innocuous text spells out the real message.

The sequence of first letters of each word of the overall message spells out the hidden message.

Various other techniques have been used historically; some examples are the following [MYER91]

Character marking: Selected letters of printed or typewritten text are overwritten in pencil. The marks are ordinarily not visible unless the paper is held at an angle to bright light.

Invisible ink: A number of substances can be used for writing but leave no visible trace until heat or some chemical is applied to the paper.

Pin punctures: Small pin punctures on selected letters are ordinarily not visible unless the paper is held up in front of a light.

Typewriter correction ribbon: Used between lines typed with a black ribbon, the results of typing with the correction tape are visible only under a strong light

[WAYN09] proposes hiding a message by using the least significant bits of frames on a CD.

For example, the Kodak Photo CD format's maximum resolution is 3096 * 6144 pixels, with each pixel containing 24 bits of RGB color information

The least significant bit of each 24-bit pixel can be changed without greatly affecting the quality of the image.

```
                                                    3rd March
Dear George,

Greetings to all at Oxford. Many thanks for your
letter and for the Summer examination package.
All Entry Forms and Fees Forms should be ready
for final despatch to the Syndicate by Friday
20th or at the very latest, I'm told. by the 21st.
Admin has improved here, though there's room
for improvement still; just give us all two or three
more years and we'll really show you! Please
don't let these wretched 16+ proposals destroy
your basic O and A pattern. Certainly this
sort of change, if implemented immediately,
would bring chaos.

                                    Sincerely yours.
```

Figure 2.14: Steganography Example - Find the Hidden Message

The result is that you can hide a 130-kB message in a single digital snapshot. Steganography has a number of drawbacks when compared to encryption. It requires a lot of overhead to hide a relatively few bits of information, although using some scheme may make it more effective A message can be first encrypted and then hidden using steganography.

The advantage of steganography is that it can be employed by parties who have something to lose should the fact of their secret communication (not necessarily the content) be discovered.

Encryption flags traffic as important or secret or may identify the sender or receiver as someone with something to hide.

CHAPTER THREE

Encryption and Decryption

3.1 Characteristics of Good Encryption Technique

Good Cipher Characteristics In 1949 Shannon proposed the following characteristics for a good cipher

- The amount of secrecy needed should determine the amount of labor appropriate for the encryption and decryption This is just common sense in that why spend tons of money on protecting something that has little value?
- The set of keys and the enciphering algorithm should be free from complexity This implies that we should restrict neither the choice of keys nor the types of plaintext on which the algorithms can work. If the process is too complex, it will not be used. Furthermore, the key must be transmitted, stored, and remembered, so it must be short.
- The implementation of the process should be as simple as possible. This principle reflects the date when the characteristics were proposed. It references a hand implementation of an encryption algorithm. Today with the computational power that we have, we have very complex encryption algorithms. Still keeping it as simple as possible is a good idea.
- Errors in ciphering should not propagate and cause corruption of further information in the message. There are errors in the enciphering process, errors in computing, transmission, or human entry. One early error in the process should not throw off the entire remaining cipher.
- The size of the enciphered text should be no larger than the text of the original message. A ciphertext that expands dramatically in size cannot possibly carry more information than the plaintext, yet it gives the cryptanalyst more data from which to infer a pattern. Also a longer ciphertext implies more space for storage and more time to communicate.

Properties of Trustworthy Encryption Systems :-

- It is based on sound mathematics Good cryptographic algorithms are not just invented. They are derived from solid principles.
- It has been analyzed by competent experts and found to be sound Even the best cryptographic experts can think of only so many possible attacks. The developers may become too convinced of the strength of their own algorithm. A review by critical outside experts is essential.
- It has stood the "test of time". As a new algorithm gains popularity, people continue to review both its mathematical foundations and the way that it builds upon those foundations. Although a long period of successful use and analysis is not a guarantee of a good algorithm, the flaws in many algorithms are discovered relative soon after their release.
- We will be talking about several commercial grade data encryption algorithms later. Three algorithms are popular in the commercial world, namely DES (data encryption standard), RSA (Rivest-Shamir-Adelman), and AES (advanced encryption standard).

3.2 Types of Encryption Systems: Based on Key and Based on Block

Several important symmetric block encryption algorithms in current use are based on a structure referred to as a Feistel block cipher [FEIS73]

Stream Ciphers and Block Ciphers

Stream cipher encrypts a digital data stream one bit or one byte at a time. Classical stream ciphers are the autokeyed Vigenère cipher and the Vernam cipher. One-time pad version of the Vernam cipher would be used, in which the keystream (ki) is as long as the plaintext bit stream (pi). If the cryptographic keystream is random, then this cipher is unbreakable by any means other than acquiring the keystream. Keystream must be provided to both users in advance via some independent and secure channel.

3.2.1 STREAM CIPHER

Bit-stream generator must be implemented as an algorithmic procedure. Bit-stream generator is a key-controlled algorithm and must produce a bit stream that is cryptographically strong. It must be computationally impractical to predict future portions of the bit stream based on previous portions of the bit stream.

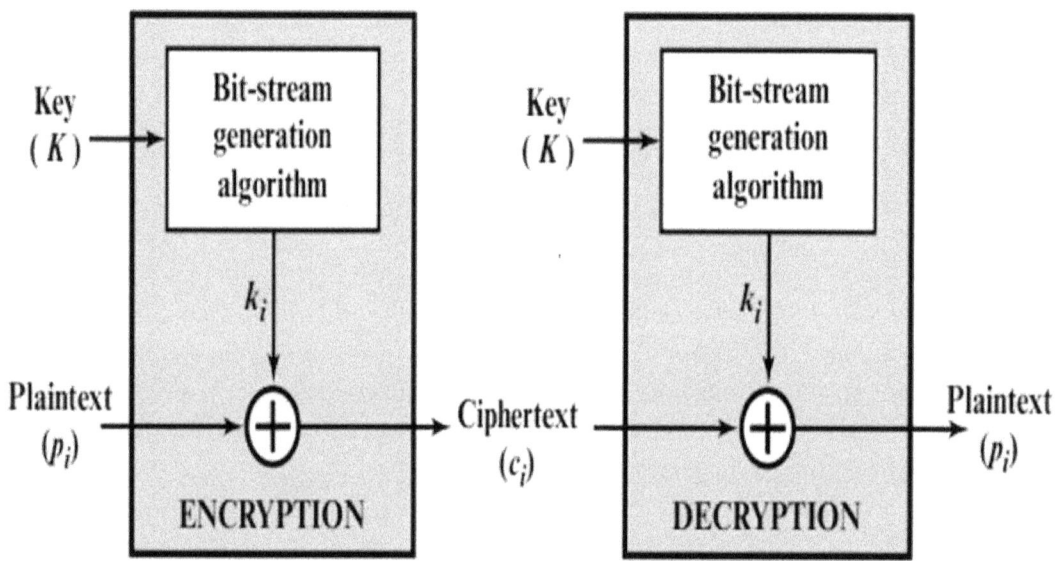

Figure 3.1: Stream Cipher

3.2.2 BLOCK CIPHER

Block cipher is one in which a block of plaintext is treated as a whole and used to produce a ciphertext block of equal length

- Block size of 64 or 128 bits is used
- Block cipher can be used to achieve the same effect as a stream cipher

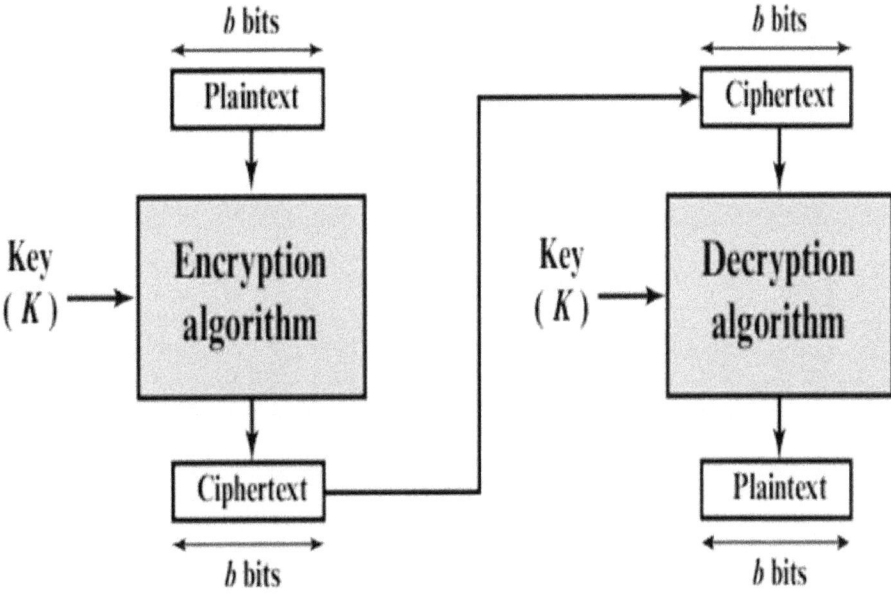

Figure 3.2: Block Cipher

3.3 FEISTEL CIPHER STRUCTURE

A block cipher operates on a plaintext block of n bits to produce a ciphertext block of n bits, 2^n possible different plaintext blocks and, for the encryption to be reversible (i.e., for decryption to be possible), each must produce a unique ciphertext block (reversible, or nonsingular).

Reversible Mapping		Irreversible Mapping	
Plaintext	Ciphertext	Plaintext	Ciphertext
00	11	00	11
01	10	01	10
10	00	10	01
11	01	11	01

Figure 3.3: Reverse and Irreversible Mapping

Ciphertext of 01 could have been produced by one of two plaintext blocks. Reversible mappings, the number of different transformations is 2^n, N =4.

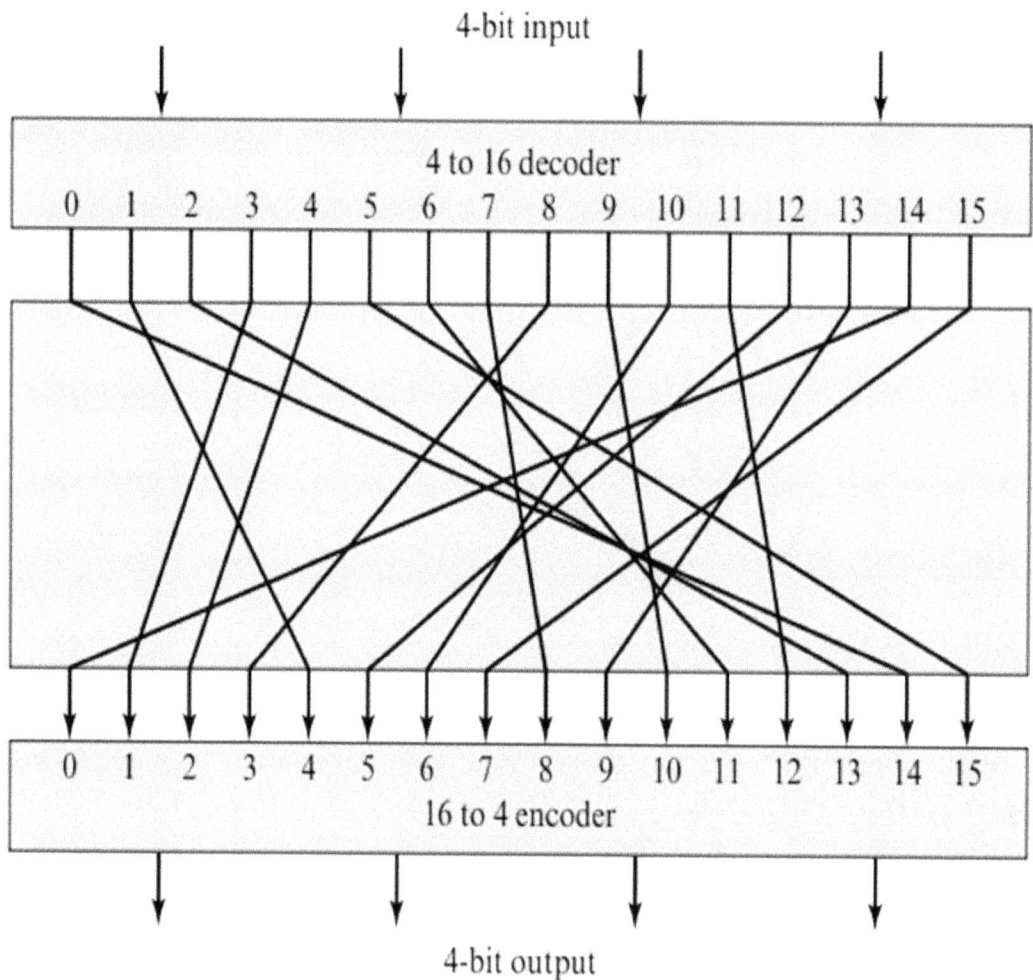

Figure 3.4: Plaintext-Ciphertext Transformation

Most general form of block cipher and can be used to define any reversible mapping between plaintext and ciphertext. Feistel refers to this as the ideal block cipher, because it allows for the maximum number of possible encryption mappings from the plaintext block. [FEIS75] Practical problem with the ideal block cipher: Small block size, system is equivalent to a classical substitution cipher. Vulnerable to a statistical analysis of the plaintext.

Plaintext	Ciphertext
0000	1110
0001	0100
0010	1101
0011	0001
0100	0010
0101	1111
0110	1011
0111	1000
1000	0011
1001	1010
1010	0110
1011	1100
1100	0101
1101	1001
1110	0000
1111	0111

Ciphertext	Plaintext
0000	1110
0001	0011
0010	0100
0011	1000
0100	0001
0101	1100
0110	1010
0111	1111
1000	0111
1001	1101
1010	1001
1011	0110
1100	1011
1101	0010
1110	0000
1111	0101

Figure 3.5: Plaintext-Ciphertext Mappings

If n is sufficiently larges.
Required key length is (4 bits) * (16 rows) = 64 bits
n * 2^n bits, For a 64-bit block 64 * 264 = 270 ≈ 1021 bits
The mapping in terms of a set of linear equations

$$y_1 = k_{11}x_1 + k_{12}x_2 + k_{13}x_3 + k_{14}x_4$$

$$y_2 = k_{21}x_1 + k_{22}x_2 + k_{23}x_3 + k_{24}x_4$$

$$y_3 = k_{31}x_1 + k_{32}x_2 + k_{33}x_3 + k_{34}x_4$$

$$y_4 = k_{41}x_1 + k_{42}x_2 + k_{43}x_3 + k_{44}x_4$$

Mapping in terms of Linear Equations

Feistel proposed [FEIS73] that we can approximate the ideal block cipher by utilizing the concept of a product cipher, which is the execution of two or more simple ciphers in sequence in such a way that the final result or product is cryptographically stronger than any of the component ciphers. Block cipher with a key length of k bits 2^k possible transformations. Block length of n bits 2n! transformations.

The use of a cipher that alternates substitutions and permutations.

- **Substitution:** Each plaintext element or group of elements is uniquely replaced by a corresponding ciphertext element or group of elements
- **Permutation:** A sequence of plaintext elements is replaced by a permutation of that sequence. No elements are added or deleted or replaced in the sequence, rather the order in which the elements appear in the sequence is changed.

The inputs to the encryption algorithm are a plaintext block of length 2w bits and a key K. Plaintext block is divided into two halves, LE_0 and RE_0. Two halves of the data pass through n rounds of processing and then combine to produce the ciphertext block Each round i has as inputs LE_{i-1} and RE_{i-1} erived from the previous round, as well as a subkey K_i derived from the overall K Subkeys K_i are different from K and from each other.

All rounds have the same structure. Substitution is performed on the left half of the data by applying a round function F to the right half of the data and then taking the exclusive-OR of the output of that function and the left half of the data. Round function has the same general structure for each round but is parameterized by the round subkey K_i.

F is a function of right-half block of w bits and a subkey of y bits, which produces an output value of length w bits: $F(RE_i, K_{i+1})$ Following this substitution, a permutation is performed that consists of the interchange of the two halves of the data.

Structure is a particular form of the SPN proposed by Shannon . parameterized by the round subkey K_i. F is a function of right-half block of w bits and a subkey of y bits, which produces an output value of length w bits: $F(RE_i, K_{i+1})$. Following this substitution, a permutation is performed that consists of the interchange of the two halves of the data Structure is a particular form of the SPN proposed by Shannon.

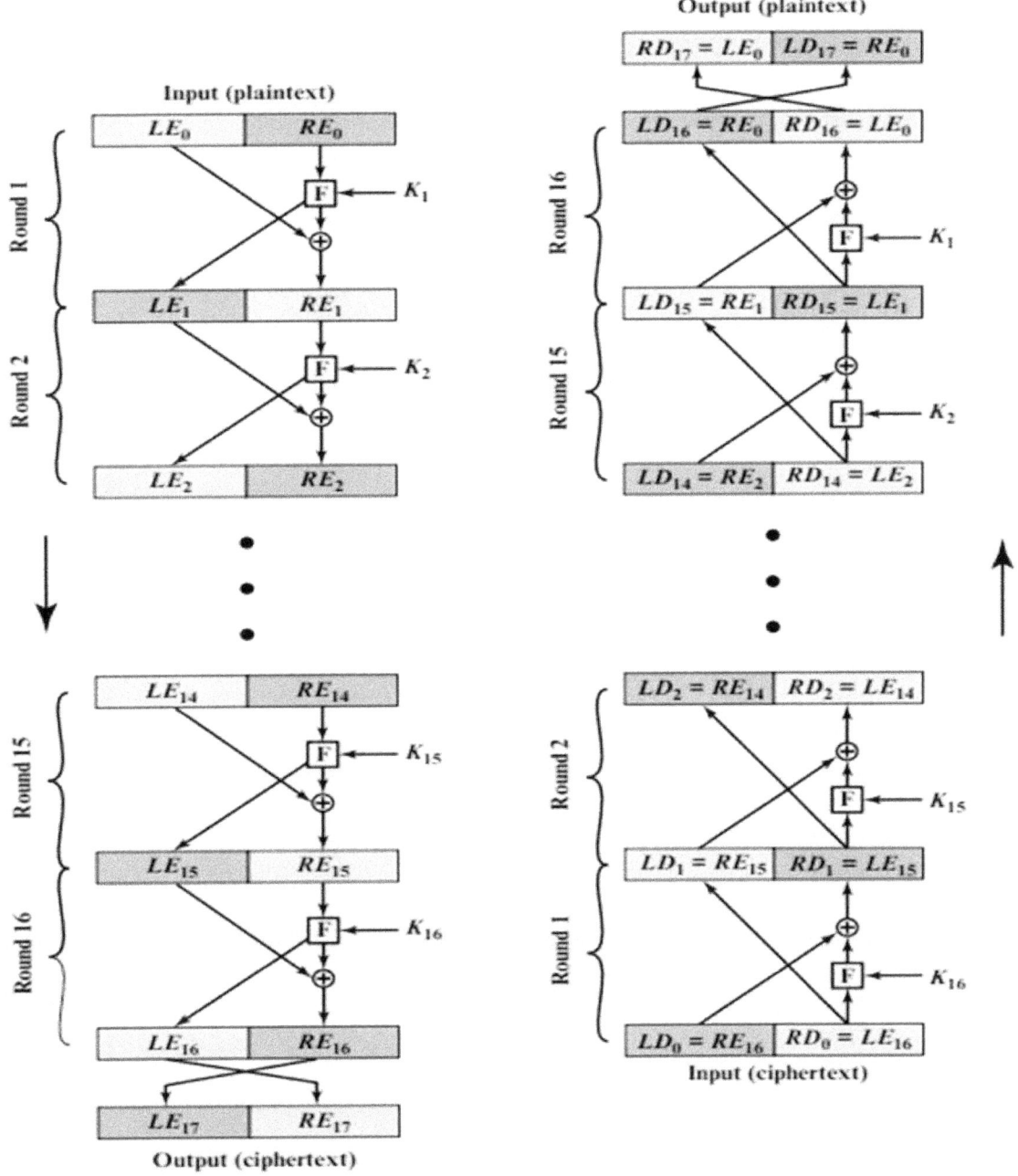

Figure 3.6: Feistel Encryption and Decryption (16 rounds)

The exact realization of a Feistel network depends on the choice of the following parameters and design features:

Block size:- Larger block sizes mean greater security (all other things being equal) but reduced encryption/ decryption speed for a given algorithm. The greater security is achieved by greater diffusion. Traditionally, a block size of 64 bits has been considered a reasonable tradeoff and was nearly universal in block cipher design. However, the new AES uses a 128-bit block size.

Key size:- Larger key size means greater security but may decrease encryption/ decryption speed. The greater security is achieved by greater resistance to brute-force attacks and greater confusion. Key sizes of 64 bits or less are now widely considered to be inadequate, and 128 bits has become a common size.

Number of rounds:- The essence of the Feistel cipher is that a single round offers inadequate security but that multiple rounds offer increasing security. A typical size is 16 rounds.

Subkey generation algorithm:- Greater complexity in this algorithm should lead to greater difficulty of cryptanalysis.

Round function F:- Again, greater complexity generally means greater resistance to cryptanalysis.

There are two other considerations in the design of a Feistel cipher:-

- **Fast software encryption/decryption:-** In many cases, encryption is embedded in applications or utility functions in such a way as to preclude a hardware implementation. Accordingly, the speed of execution of the algorithm becomes a concern.
- **Ease of analysis:-** Although we would like to make our algorithm as difficult as possible to cryptanalyze, there is great benefit in making the algorithm easy to analyze. That is, if the algorithm can be concisely and clearly explained, it is easier to analyze that algorithm for cryptanalytic vulnerabilities and therefore develop a higher level of assurance as to its strength. DES, for example, does not have an easily analyzed functionality.

Use the ciphertext as input to the algorithm, but use the subkeys K_i in reverse order. K_n in the first round, K_{n-1} in the second round, and so on, until K_1 is used in the last round.

The process of decryption with a Feistel cipher is essentially the same as the encryption process. The rule is as follows: Use the ciphertext as input to the algorithm, but use the subkeys K_i in reverse order. That is, use K_n in the first round, K_{n-1} in the second round, and so on, until K_i is used in the last round. This is a nice feature, because it means we need not implement two different algorithms; one for encryption and one for decryption.

To see that the same algorithm with a reversed key order produces the correct result, Figure shows the encryption process going down the left-hand side and the decryption process going up the right-hand side for a 16-round algorithm. For clarity, we use the notation LE_i and RE_i for data traveling through the encryption algorithm and LD_i and RD_i for data traveling through the decryption algorithm. The diagram indicates that, at every round, the intermediate value of the decryption process is equal to the corresponding value of the encryption process with the two halves of the value swapped. To put this another way, let the output of the ith encryption round be LE_i . RE_i (LE_i concatenated with RE_i). Then the corresponding output of the $(16 - i)^{th}$ decryption round is RE_i . LE_i or, equivalently, LD_{16-i} . RD_{16-i}.

Let us walk through Figure to demonstrate the validity of the preceding assertions. After the last iteration of the encryption process, the two halves of the output are swapped, so that the ciphertext is RE_{16} . LE_{16}. The output of that round is the ciphertext. Now take that ciphertext and use it as input to the same algorithm. The input to the first round is RE_{16} . LE_{16}, which is equal to the 32-bit swap of the output of the sixteenth round of the encryption process.

Now we would like to show that the output of the first round of the decryption process is equal to a 32-bit swap of the input to the sixteenth round of the encryption process. First, consider the encryption process. We see that,

$$LD_1 = RD_0 = LE_{16} = RE_{15}$$
$$RD_1 = LD_0 \oplus F(RD_0, K_{16})$$
$$= RE_{16} \oplus F(RE_{15}, K_{16})$$
$$= [LE_{15} \oplus F(RE_{15}, K_{16})] \oplus F(RE_{15}, K_{16})$$

$$[A \oplus B] \oplus C = A \oplus [B \oplus C]$$
$$D \oplus D = 0$$
$$E \oplus 0 = E$$

With reference to figure 3.6, the proces of encryption.

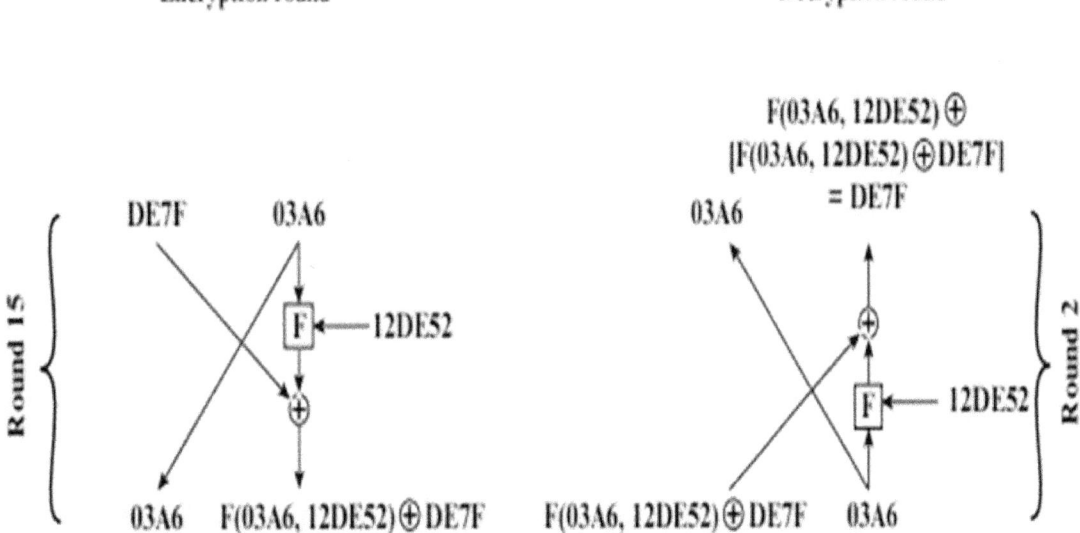

Figure 3.7: Encryption and Decryption Rounds

Now let's look at the decryption. We assume that $LD_1 = RE_{15}$ and $RD_1 = LE_{15}$, and we want to demonstrate that $LD_2 = RE_{14}$ and $RD_2 = LE_{14}$. So, we start with $LD_1 = F(03A6, 12DE52) \oplus DE7F$ and $RD_1 = 03A6$. Then, $LD_2 = 03A6 = RE_{14}$ and $RD_2 = F(03A6, 12DE52) \oplus [F(03A6, 12DE52) \oplus DE7F] = DE7F = LE_{14}$.

3.4 Confusion and Diffusion

Feistel's is a practical application of a proposal by Claude Shannon to develop a product cipher that alternates confusion and diffusion functions [SHAN49]. The Feistel cipher structure, which dates back over a quarter century and which is based on Shannon's proposal of 1945, is the structure used by a number of significant symmetric block ciphers currently in use Triple Data Encryption Algorithm (TDEA) and AES. NIST Format-preserving encryption. Camellia block cipher symmetric ciphers in TLS.

The terms diffusion and confusion were introduced by Claude Shannon to capture the two basic building blocks for any cryptographic system [SHAN49]. Shannon's concern was to prevent cryptanalysis based on statistical analysis.

Attacker has some knowledge of the statistical characteristics of the plaintext In a human-readable message in some language, the frequency distribution of the various letters may be known. There may be words or phrases likely to appear in the message.

If these statistics are reflected in the ciphertext, the cryptanalyst may be able to deduce the encryption key, part of the key, or at least a set of keys likely to contain the exact key.

Shannon refers to as a strongly ideal cipher, all statistics of the ciphertext are independent of the particular key used Shannon suggests two methods for frustrating statistical cryptanalysis.

In diffusion, the statistical structure of the plaintext is dissipated into long-range statistics of the ciphertext. Each plaintext digit affect the value of many ciphertext digits; generally, this is equivalent to having each ciphertext digit be affected by many plaintext digits.

$$y_n = \left(\sum_{i=1}^{k} m_{n+i} \right) \bmod 26$$

Adding k successive letters to get a ciphertext letter

Adding k successive letters to get a ciphertext letter y_n. Statistical structure of the plaintext has been dissipated. The letter frequencies in the ciphertext will be more nearly equal than in the plaintext; the diagram frequencies will also be more nearly equal. In a binary block cipher, diffusion can be achieved by repeatedly performing some permutation on the data followed by applying a function to that permutation; the effect is that bits from different positions in the original plaintext contribute to a single bit of ciphertext.

Block cipher involves a transformation of a block of plaintext into a block of ciphertext, where the transformation depends on the key.

Diffusion seeks to make the statistical relationship between the plaintext and ciphertext as complex as possible in order to thwart attempts to deduce the key.

Confusion seeks to make the relationship between the statistics of the ciphertext and the value of the encryption key as complex as possible, again to thwart attempts to discover the key.

Even if the attacker can get some handle on the statistics of the ciphertext, the way in which the key was used to produce that ciphertext is so complex as to make it difficult to deduce the key.

Achieved by the use of a complex substitution algorithm As [ROBS95b] points out, so successful are diffusion and confusion in capturing the essence of the desired attributes of a block cipher that they have become the cornerstone of modern block cipher design.

CHAPTER FOUR

Symmetric Key Encryption and Public Key Encryption

4.1 Data Encryption Standard (DES) Algorithm

Until the introduction of the Advanced Encryption Standard (AES) in 2001, the DES was the most widely used encryption scheme DES was issued in 1977 by the National Bureau of Standards, now the NIST, as Federal Information Processing Standard 46 (FIPS PUB 46) Algorithm is referred as the DEA. For DEA, data are encrypted in 64-bits blocks using a 56-bits key. Algorithm transforms 64-bit input in a series of steps into a 64-bit output Same steps, with the same key, are used to reverse the encryption. DES became the dominant symmetric encryption algorithm, especially in financial applications.

In 1994, NIST reaffirmed DES for federal use for another five year NIST recommended the use of DES for applications other than the protection of classified information In 1999, NIST issued a new version of its standard (FIPS PUB 46-3) that indicated that DES should be used only for legacy systems.

Triple DES (which involves repeating the DES algorithm three times on the plaintext using two or three different keys to produce the ciphertext) be used. Two inputs to the encryption function: the plaintext to be encrypted and the key Plaintext must be 64 bits in length and Key is 56 bits in length.

4.1.1 DES Encryption

The overall scheme for DES encryption is illustrated in Figure 4.1 below. As with any encryption scheme, there are two inputs to the encryption function: the plaintext to be encrypted and the key. In this case, the plaintext must be 64 bits in length and the key is 56 bits in length. Looking at the left-hand side of the figure, we can see that the processing of the plaintext proceeds in three phases. First, the 64-bit plaintext passes through an initial permutation (IP) that rearranges the bits to produce the permuted input.

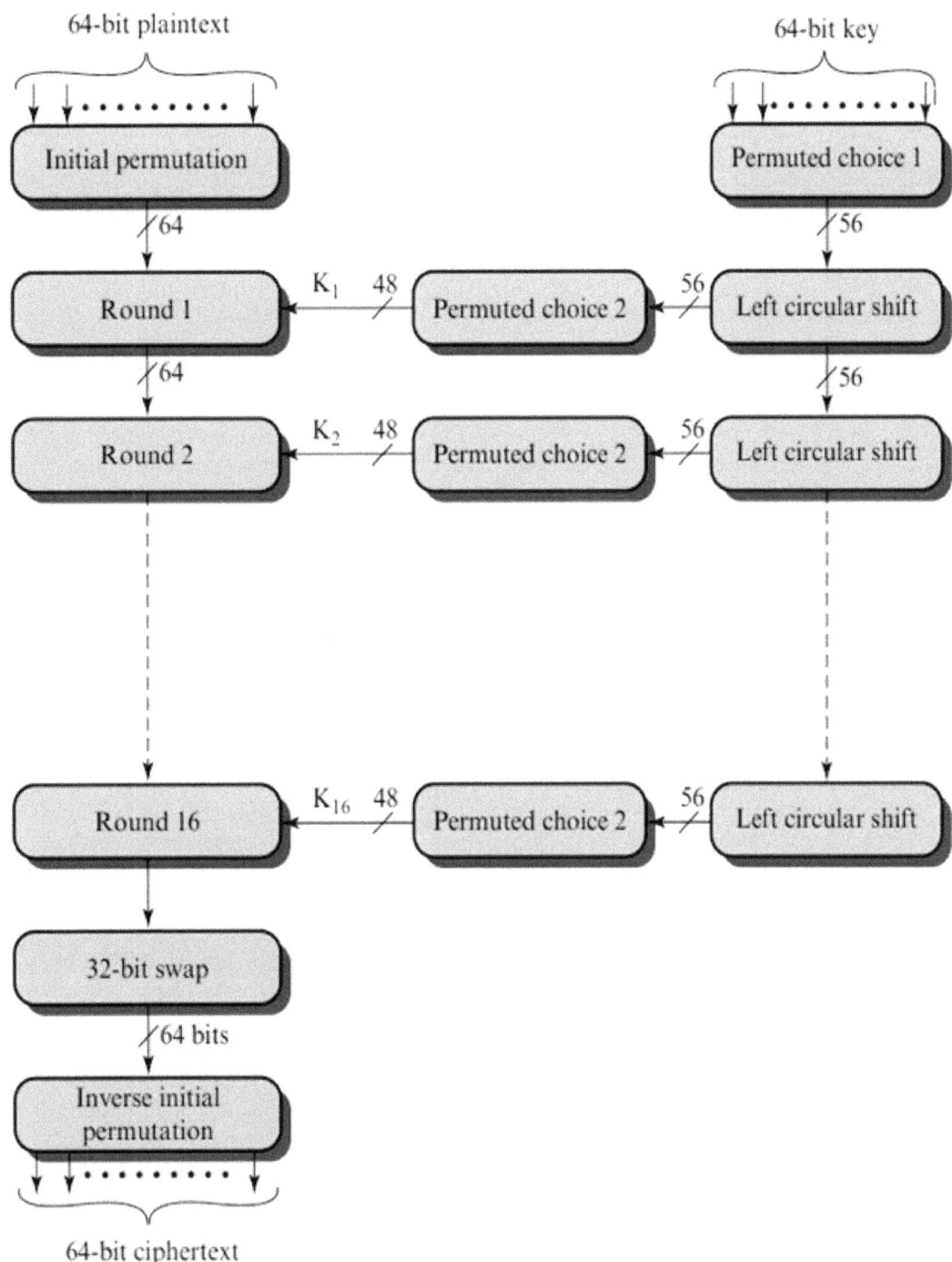

Figure 4.1: DES Encryption

This is followed by a phase consisting of sixteen rounds of the same function, which involves both permutation and substitution functions. The output of the last (sixteenth) round consists of 64 bits that are a function of the input plaintext and the key. The left and right halves of the output are swapped to produce the pre output. Finally, the pre output is passed through a permutation [IP^{-1}] that is the inverse of the initial permutation function, to produce the 64-bit ciphertext. With the exception of the initial and final permutations, DES has the exact structure of a Feistel cipher, as shown in Figure.

The right-hand portion of Figure shows the way in which the 56-bit key is used. Initially, the key is passed through a permutation function. Then, for each of the sixteen rounds, a subkey (K_i) is produced by the combination of a left circular shift and a permutation. The permutation function is the same for each round, but a different subkey is produced because of the repeated shifts of the key bits.

4.1.2 DES Decryption

As with any Feistel cipher, decryption uses the same algorithm as encryption, except that the application of the subkeys is reversed. Additionally, the initial and final permutations are reversed.

DES EXAMPLE :-

For this example, the plaintext is a hexadecimal palindrome. The plaintext, key, and resulting ciphertext are as follows:

Plaintext:	02468aceeca86420
Key:	0f1571c947d9e859
Ciphertext:	da02ce3a89ecac3b

Figure 4.2: DES Example

Round	K_i	L_i	R_i
IP		5a005a00	3cf03c0f
1	1e030f03080d2930	3cf03c0f	bad22845
2	0a31293432242318	bad22845	99e9b723
3	23072318201d0c1d	99e9b723	0bae3b9e
4	05261d3824311a20	0bae3b9e	42415649
5	3325340136002c25	42415649	18b3fa41
6	123a2d0d04262a1c	18b3fa41	9616fe23
7	021f120b1c130611	9616fe23	67117cf2
8	1c10372a2832002b	67117cf2	c11bfc09
9	04292a380c341f03	c11bfc09	887fbc6c
10	2703212607280403	887fbc6c	600f7e8b
11	2826390c31261504	600f7e8b	f596506e
12	12071c241a0a0f08	f596506e	738538b8
13	300935393c0d100b	738538b8	c6a62c4e
14	311e09231321182a	c6a62c4e	56b0bd75
15	283d3e0227072528	56b0bd75	75e8fd8f
16	2921080b13143025	75e8fd8f	25896490
IP^{-1}		da02ce3a	89ecac3b

Figure 4.3: Progression of DES Algorithm

Results :- Figure 4.3 shows the progression of the algorithm. The first row shows the 32-bit values of the left and right halves of data after the initial permutation. The next 16 rows show the results after each round. Also shown is the value of the 48-bit subkey generated for each round. Note that $L_i = R_{i-1}$. The final row shows the left- and right-hand values after the inverse initial permutation. These two values combined form the ciphertext.

The Avalanche Effect :-

A desirable property of any encryption algorithm is that a small change in either the plaintext or the key should produce a significant change in the ciphertext. In particular, a change in one bit of the plaintext or one bit of the key should produce a change in many bits of the ciphertext. This is referred to as the avalanche effect. If the change were small, this might provide a way to reduce the size of the plaintext or key space to be searched.

Round		δ
	02468aceeca86420 12468acccca86420	1
1	3cf03c0fbad22845 3cf03c0fbad32845	1
2	bad2284599e9b723 bad3284539a9b7a3	5
3	99e9b7230bae3b9e 39a9b7a3171cb8b3	18
4	0bae3b9e42415649 171cb8b3ccaca55e	34
5	4241564918b3fa41 ccaca55ed16c3653	37
6	18b3fa419616fe23 d16c3653cf402c68	33
7	9616fe2367117cf2 cf402c682b2cefbc	32
8	67117cf2c11bfc09 2b2cefbc99f91153	33

Round		δ
9	c11bfc09887fbc6c 99f911532ccd7d94	32
10	887fbc6c600f7e8b 2eed7d94d0f23094	34
11	600f7e8bf596506e d0f23094455da9c4	37
12	f596506e738538b8 455da9c47f6e3cf3	31
13	738538b8c6a62c4e 7f6e3cf34bc1a8d9	29
14	c6a62c4e56b0bd75 4bc1a8d91e07d409	33
15	56b0bd7575e8fd8f 1e07d4091ce2e6dc	31
16	75e8fd8f25896490 1ce2e6dc365e5f59	32
IP^{-1}	da02ce3a89ecac3b 057cde97d7683f2a	32

Figure 4.4: Avalanche Effect in DES: Change in Plaintext

Round		δ
	02468aceeca86420 02468aceeca86420	0
1	3cf03c0fbad22845 3cf03c0f9ad628c5	3
2	bad2284599e9b723 9ad628c59939136b	11
3	99e9b7230bae3b9e 9939136b768067b7	25
4	0bae3b9e42415649 768067b75a8807c5	29
5	4241564918b3fa41 5a8807c5488dbe94	26
6	18b3fa419616fe23 488dbe94aba7fe53	26
7	9616fe2367117cf2 aba7fe53177d21e4	27
8	67117cf2c11bfc09 177d21e4548f1de4	32

Round		δ
9	c11bfc09887fbc6c 548f1de471f64dfd	34
10	887fbc6c600f7e8b 71f64dfd4279876c	36
11	600f7e8bf596506e 4279876c399fdc0d	32
12	f596506e738538b8 399fdc0d6d208dbb	28
13	738538b8c6a62c4e 6d208dbbb9bdeeaa	33
14	c6a62c4e56b0bd75 b9bdeeaad2c3a56f	30
15	56b0bd7575e8fd8f d2c3a56f2765c1fb	27
16	75e8fd8f25896490 2765c1fb01263dc4	30
IP^{-1}	da02ce3a89ecac3b ee92b50606b62b0b	30

Figure 4.5: Avalanche Effect in DES: Change in Key

4.1.3 STRENGTH OF DES

The Use Of 56-BITS KEY :- Key size and the nature of the algorithm. Key length of 56 bits, there are 256 possible keys, which is approximately 7.2 * 1016 keys. Brute-force attack appears impractical , Half the key space has to be searched, a single machine performing one DES encryption per microsecond would take more than a thousand years to break the cipher 1977, Diffie and Hellman postulated that the technology existed to build a parallel machine with 1 million encryption devices, each of which could perform one encryption per microsecond [DIFF77]. Bring the average search time down to about 10 hours. Cost would be about $20 million.

With current technology, it is not even necessary to use special, purpose-built hardware. Speed of commercial, off-the-shelf processors threaten the security of DES. Seagate Technology [SEAG08] suggests that a rate of 1 billion (10^9) key. combinations per second is reasonable for today's multicore computers. Intel and AMD now offer hardware-based instructions to accelerate the use of AES.

Tests run on a contemporary multicore Intel machine resulted in a encryption rate of half a billion encryptions per second [BASU12], Contemporary supercomputer technology, a rate of 10^{13} encryptions per second is reasonable [AROR12].

Key Size (bits)	Cipher	Number of Alternative Keys	Time Required at 10^9 Decryptions/s	Time Required at 10^{13} Decryptions/s
56	DES	$2^{56} \approx 7.2 \times 10^{16}$	2^{55} ns = 1.125 years	1 hour
128	AES	$2^{128} \approx 3.4 \times 10^{38}$	2^{127} ns = 5.3×10^{21} years	5.3×10^{17} years
168	Triple DES	$2^{168} \approx 3.7 \times 10^{50}$	2^{167} ns = 5.8×10^{33} years	5.8×10^{29} years
192	AES	$2^{192} \approx 6.3 \times 10^{57}$	2^{191} ns = 9.8×10^{40} years	9.8×10^{36} years
256	AES	$2^{256} \approx 1.2 \times 10^{77}$	2^{255} ns = 1.8×10^{60} years	1.8×10^{56} years
26 characters	Monoalphabetic	$2! = 4 \times 10^{26}$	2×10^{26} ns = 6.3×10^9 years	6.3×10^6 years

Figure 4.6: Average Time Required for Exhaustive Key Search

NATURE OF DES ALGORITHM:- Exploiting the characteristics of the DES algorithm. Eight substitution tables, or S-boxes (Substitution Boxes), that are used in each iteration Design criteria for these boxes, and indeed for the entire algorithm, were not made public, there is a suspicion that the boxes were constructed in such a way that cryptanalysis is possible for an opponent who knows the weaknesses in the S-boxes. Over the years a number of regularities and unexpected behaviors of the S-boxes have been discovered. Despite this, no one has so far succeeded in discovering the supposed fatal weaknesses in the S-boxes.

TIMING ATTACKS :- Information about the key or the plaintext is obtained by observing how long it takes a given implementation to perform decryptions on various ciphertexts. An encryption or decryption algorithm often takes slightly different amounts of time on different inputs [HEVI99] reports on an approach that yields the Hamming weight (number of bits equal to one) of the secret key. DES appears to be fairly resistant to a successful timing attack but suggest some avenues to explore. Although this is an interesting line of attack, it so far appears unlikely that this technique will ever be successful.

4.1.4 BLOCK CIPHER DESIGN PRINCIPLES

NUMER OF ROUNDS :- Number of rounds, the function F, and the key schedule algorithm. The greater the number of rounds, the more difficult it is to perform cryptanalysis, even for a relatively weak F Number of rounds is chosen so that known cryptanalytic efforts require greater effort than a simple brute-force key search attack. Schneier [SCHN96] observes that for 16-round DES, a differential cryptanalysis attack is slightly less efficient than brute force differential cryptanalysis attack requires 255.1 operations, whereas brute force requires 255. If DES had 15 or fewer rounds, differential cryptanalysis would require less effort than a brute-force key search.

DESIGN OF FUNCTION F :- The heart of a Feistel block cipher is the function F, which provides the element of confusion in a Feistel cipher Difficult to "unscramble" the substitution performed by F. More nonlinear F, the more difficult any type of cryptanalysis will be. More difficult it is to approximate F by a set of linear equations, the more nonlinear F is Good avalanche properties. Strict avalanche criterion (SAC) [WEBS86], which states that any output bit j of an S-box should change with probability 1/2 when any single input bit i is inverted for all i, j . [WEBS86] Bit Independence Criterion (BIC), which states that output bits j and k should change independently when any single input bit i is inverted for all i, j, and k. SAC and BIC criteria appear to strengthen the effectiveness of the confusion function.

KEY SCHEDULE ALGORITHM :- Feistel block cipher, the key is used to generate one subkey for each round. Select subkeys to maximize the difficulty of deducing individual subkeys and the difficulty of working back to the main key. Adams suggests [ADAM94] that, at minimum, the key schedule should guarantee key/ ciphertext Strict Avalanche Criterion and Bit Independence Criterion.

4.2 Double and Triple DES

4.2.1 DOUBLE DES: ENCRYPTION :-

Double DES is quite simple to understand. Essentially, it does twice what DES normally does only once. Double DES uses two keys, say K1 and K2.

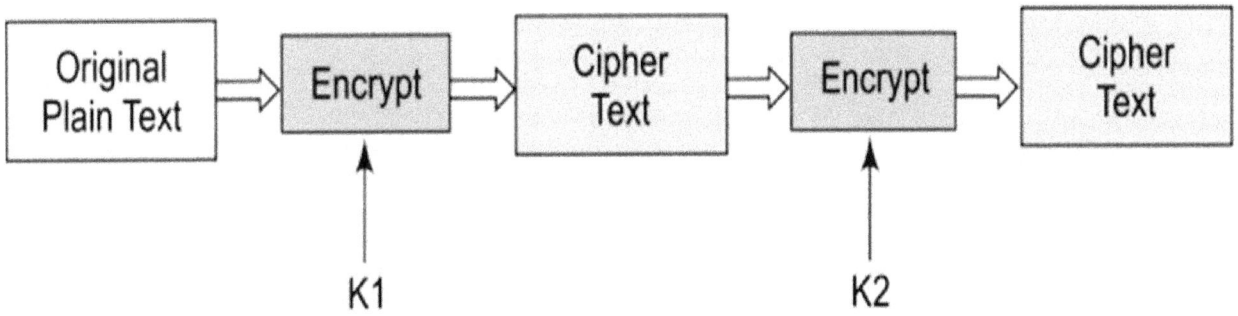

Figure 4.7: Doube DES

DOUBLE DES: DECRYPTION :- n-bit key, the cryptanalyst has to perform 2^n operations. Two different keys, each consisting of n bits, the cryptanalyst would need 2^{2n} attempts to crack the key. DES requires a search of 256 keys, Double DES would require a key search of (2^{2*56}), i.e. 2^{112} keys. Merkle and Hellman introduced the concept of the meet-in-the-middle attack.

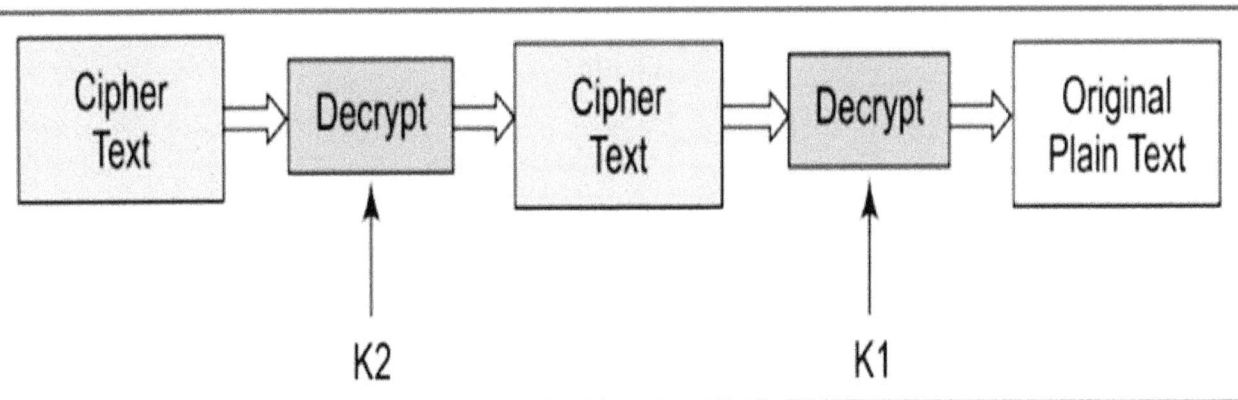

Figure 4.8: Double DES Decrypt

Attack involves encryption from one end, decryption from the other, and matching the results in the middle Cryptanalyst knows two basic pieces of information: P, and C for a message.

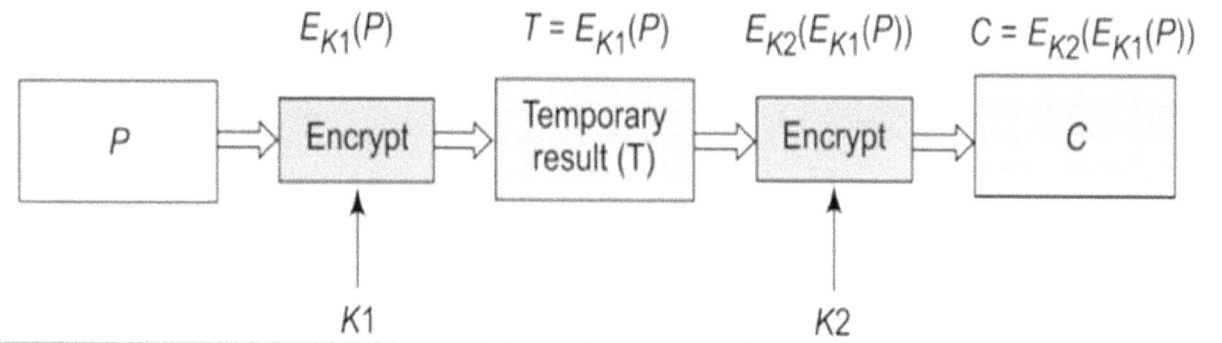

Figure 4.9: Double DES Process

Step 1: For all possible values (256) of key K1, the cryptanalyst would use a large table in the memory of the computer, and perform the following two steps:

- Encrypt the plain-text block P by performing the first encryption operation, i.e. $E_{K1}(P)$. That is, it will calculate T.
- Store the output of the operation $E_{K1}(P)$, i.e. the temporary cipher text (T), in the next available row of the table in the memory.

Step 2: At the end of the step 1, the cryptanalyst will have the table of cipher texts. Next, the cryptanalyst will perform the reverse operation. Now decrypt the known cipher text C with all the possible values of K2 [i.e. perform $D_{K2}(C)$ for all possible values of K2]. In each case, the cryptanalyst will compare the resulting value with all the values in the table of cipher texts, which were computed early.

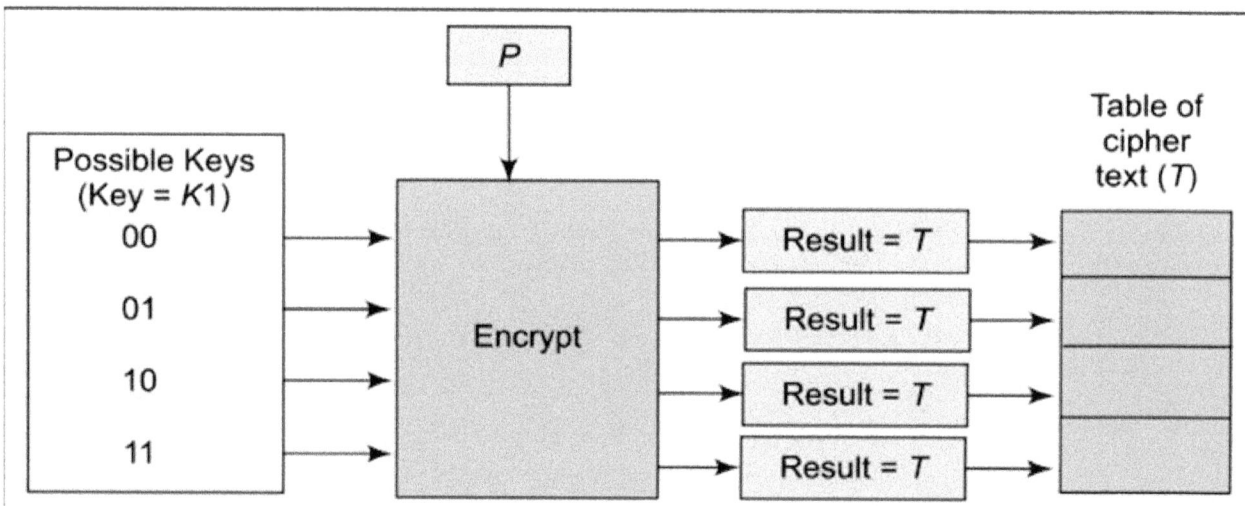

Figure 4.10: Encryption with Table Lookup

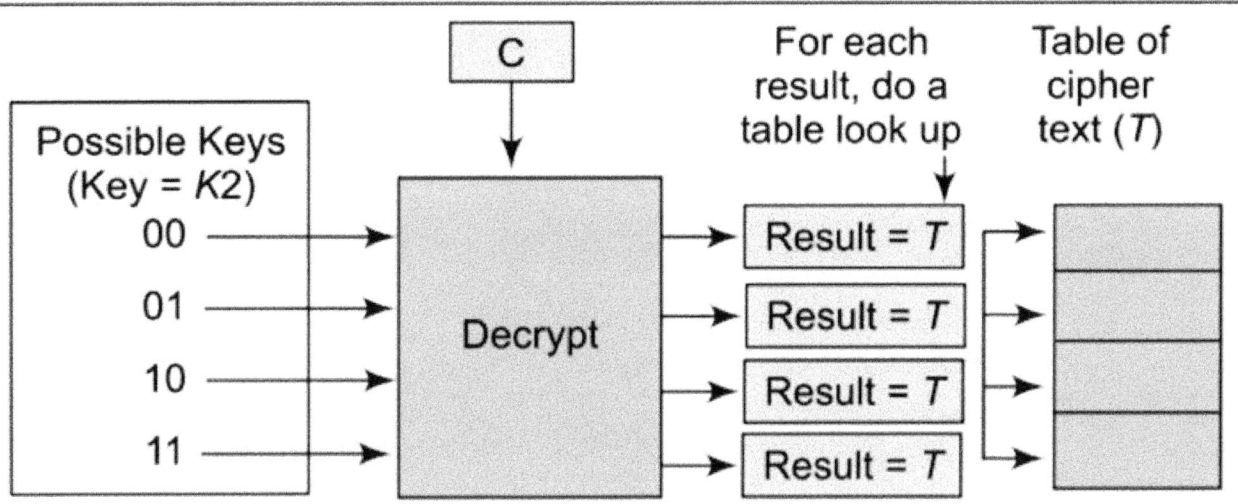

Figure 4.11: Decryption with Table Lookup

Temporary result (T) can be obtained in two ways, either by encrypting P with K1, or by decrypting C with K2. T = E_{K1} (P) = D_{K2} (C). If the cryptanalyst creates a table of E_{K1} (P) for all the possible values of K1, and then performs D_{K2} (C) for all possible values of K2 (i.e. computes T), there is a chance getting the same T in both the operations.

This attack is possible, but requires a lot of memory. For 64-bit plain-text blocks and 56-bit keys, 256 64-bit blocks require to store the table of T in memory. This is equivalent to 10^{17} bytes, which is too high for the next few generations of computers.

4.2.2 TRIPLE DES

Meet-in-the-middle attack on double DES is not quite practical yet, in cryptography, it is always better to take the minimum possible chances. Triple DES is DES three times. It comes in two kinds: one that uses three keys, and the other that uses two keys.

TRIPLE DES WITH THREE KEYS :-

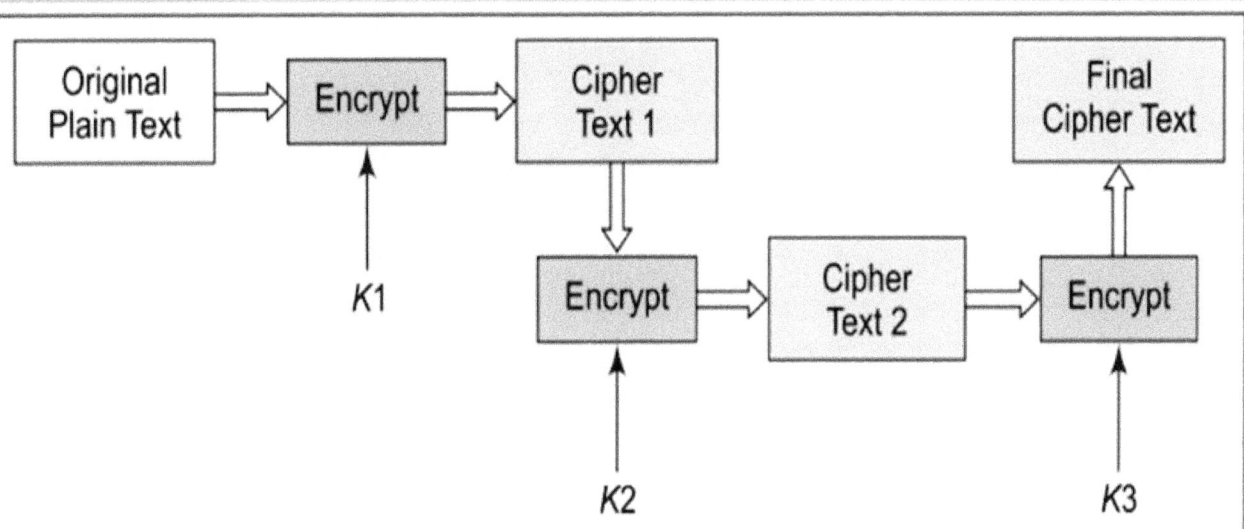

Figure 4.12: Triple DES

Triple DES with three keys is used quite extensively in many products, including PGP and S/ MIME. $P = D_{K1} (D_{K2} (D_{K3} (C)))$.

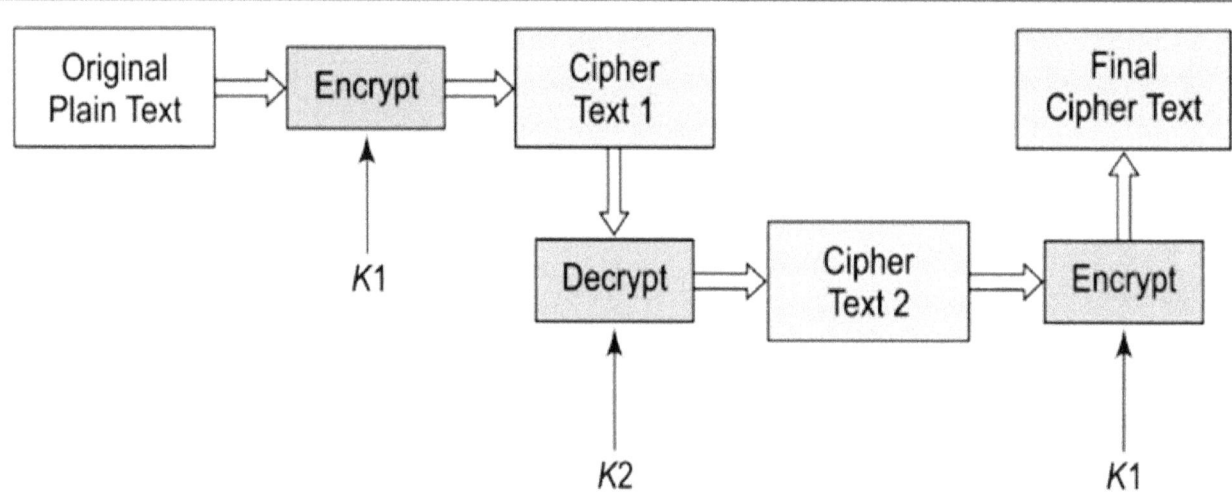

Figure 4.13: Triple DES with Two Keys

$C = E_{K3} (E_{K2} (E_{K1} (P)))$
$56 * 3 = 168$ bits
Tuchman uses just two keys for triple DES.
TRIPLE DES WITH TWO KEYS :-
$E_{K1} (P)$
$D_{K2} (E_{K1} (P))$
$E_{K1} (D_{K2} (E_{K1} (P)))$
$P = D_{K1} (E_{K2} (D_{K1} (C)))$

Encrypt-Decrypt-Encrypt (EDE) mode. Triple DES with two keys is not susceptible to the meet-in-the-middle attack, unlike double DES as K1 and K2 alternate here.

4.3 Advanced Encryption Standard (AES) Algorithm

In the 1990s, the US Government wanted to standardize a cryptographic algorithm Many proposals were submitted, and after a lot of debate, an algorithm called Rijndael was accepted Joan Daemen and Vincent Rijmen (Belgium) (Rijmen and Daemen). 56-bit keys of DES were no longer considered safe against attacks and the 64-bit blocks were also considered weak.

AES based on 128-bit blocks, 128-bit keys, June 1998, the Rijndael proposal was submitted to NIST as one of the candidates for AES. Out of the initial 15 candidates, only 5 were shortlisted in August 1999.

Rijndael (From Joan Daemen and Vincent Rijmen; 86 votes), Serpent (From Ross Anderson, Eli Biham, and Lars Knudsen; 59 votes), Twofish (From Bruce Schneier and others, 31 votes).

RC6 (From RSA Laboratories, 23 votes), MARS (From IBM, 13 votes)

October 2000, Rijndael was announced as the final selection for AES. November 2001, Rijndael became a US Government standard published as Federal Information Processing Standard 197 (FIPS 197).

4.3.1 AES MAIN FEATURES

- Symmetric and Parallel Structure, Adapted to Modern Processors, Suited to Smart Cards.
- Supports key lengths and plain-text block sizes from 128 bits to 256 bits, in the steps of 32 bits.
- Key length and the length of the plain-text blocks need to be selected independently.
- AES mandates that the plain-text block size must be 182 bits, and key size should be 128, 192, or 256 bits.
- Two versions of AES: 128-bit plain-text block with 128-bit key block, and 128- bit plain text block with 256-bit key block.
- Commercial standard: 128-bit plain text block and 128-bit key length 128 bits give a possible key range of 2^{128} or 3×103^8 keys.
- Even if NSA manages to build a machine with 1 billion parallel processors, each being able to evaluate one key per picosecond, it would take such a machine about 10^{10} years to search the key space.

4.3.2 AES OF OPERATION

Basics of Rijndael are in a mathematical concept called Galois field theory. Similar to the way DES functions, Rijndael also uses the basic techniques of substitution and transposition (i.e. permutation).

Key size and the plain-text block size decide how many rounds need to be executed. The minimum number of rounds is 10 when key size and the plain-text block size are each 128 bits. Maximum number of rounds is 14, One key differentiator between DES and Rijndael is that all the Rijndael operations involve an entire byte, and not individual bits of a byte. This provides for more optimized hardware and software implementation of the Algorithm.

(i) Do the following one-time initialization processes:

    (a) Expand the 16-byte key to get the actual *key block* to be used.

    (b) Do one time initialization of the 16-byte plain-text block (called *State*).

    (c) XOR the *state* with the *key block*.

(ii) For each round, do the following:

    (a) Apply S-box to each of the plain-text bytes.

    (b) Rotate row *k* of the plain-text block (i.e. *state*) by *k* bytes.

    (c) Perform a *mix columns* operation.

    (d) XOR the *state* with the *key block*

Figure 4.14: AES Operations

ONE-TIME INITIALIZATION PROCESS
Expand the 16-byte key to get the actual key block to be used:

- Inputs to the algorithm are the key and the plain text
- Key size is 16 bytes
- 16-byte key into 11 arrays, and each array contains 4 rows and 4 columns
- 16-byte key array is expanded into a key containing 11 * 4 * 4 = 176 bytes

One of these, 11 arrays are used in the initialization process and the other 10 arrays are used in the 10 rounds, one array per round. The terminology of word, in the context of AES means 4 bytes. 16-byte initial key (i.e. 16/4 = 4-word key) will be expanded into 176-byte key (i.e. 176/4 words, i.e. 44 words).

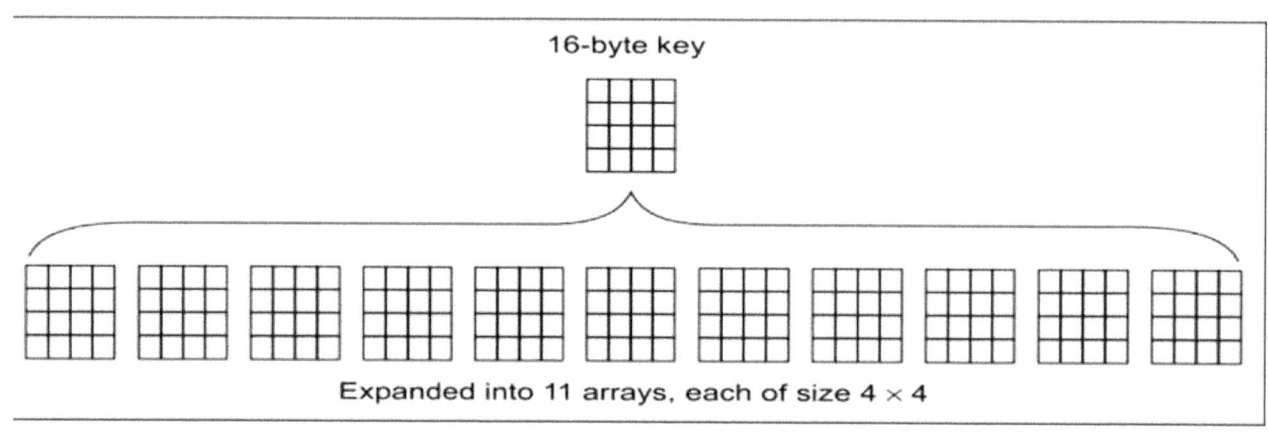

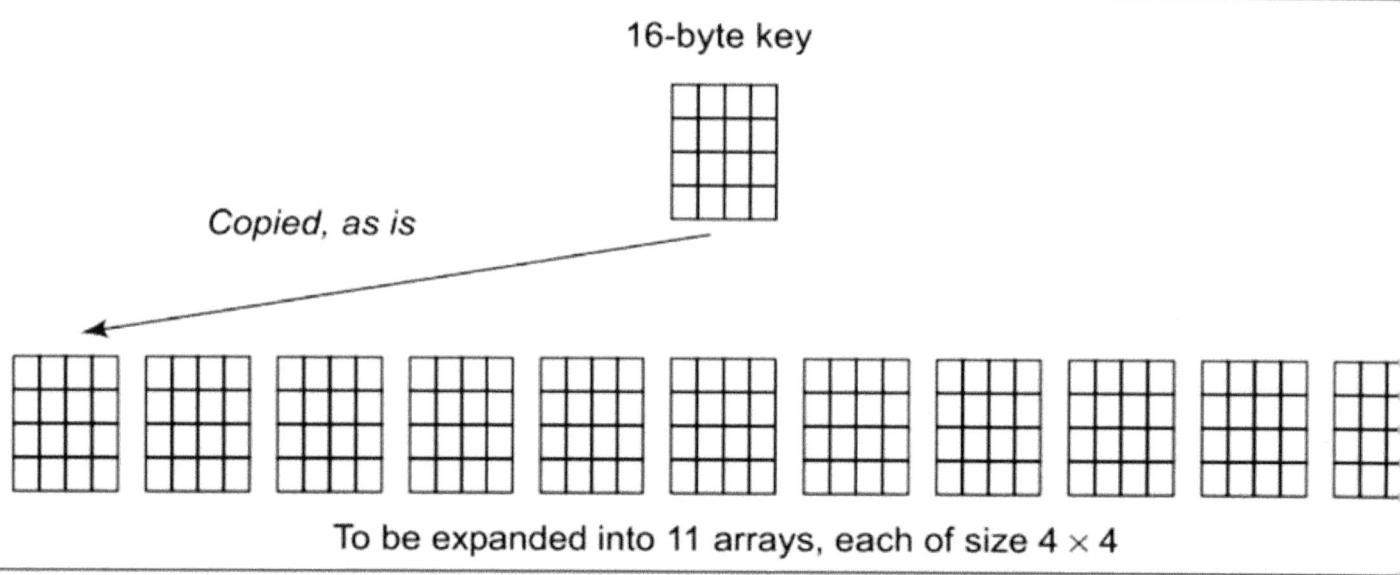

Figure 4.15: One Time Initialization Process

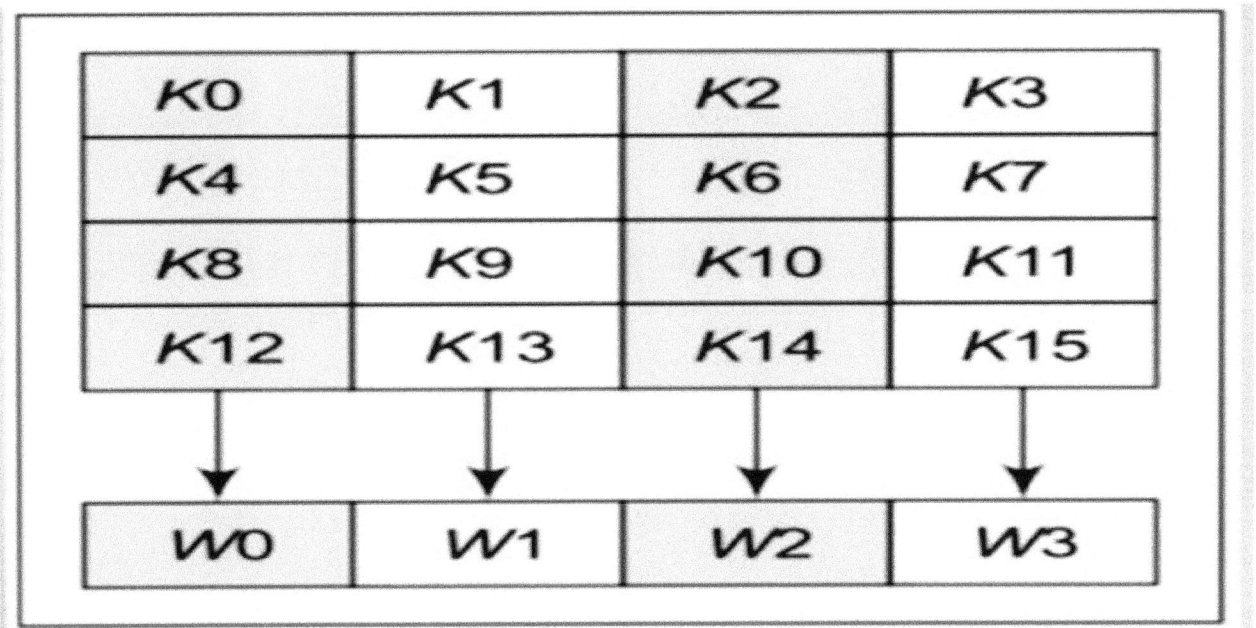

Figure 4.16: Copy Keys to Words

```
Expand Key (byte K [16], word W [44]) {
    word tmp;

    // First copy all the 16 input key blocks into first four words of output
    key
    for (i = 0; i < 4; i++) {
        W [i] = K [4*i], K [4*i + 1], K [4*i + 2], K [4*i + 3];
    }

    // Now populate the remaining output key words (i.e. W5 to W43)
    for (i = 4; i < 44; i++) {
        tmp = W [i-1];

        if (i mod 4 == 0)
            tmp = Substitute (Rotate (temp)) XOR Constant [i/4];

        w [i] = w [i-4] XOR tmp;
    }
}
```

Figure 4.17: Algorithm for Key Expansion

Do one-time initialization of the 16-byte plain-text block (called State)

- 16-byte plain-text block is copied into a two-dimensional 4 x 4 array called state
- Order of copying is in the column order
- That is, the first four bytes of the plaintext block get copied into the first column of the state array, the next four bytes of the plain-text block get copied into the second column of the state array, and so on.

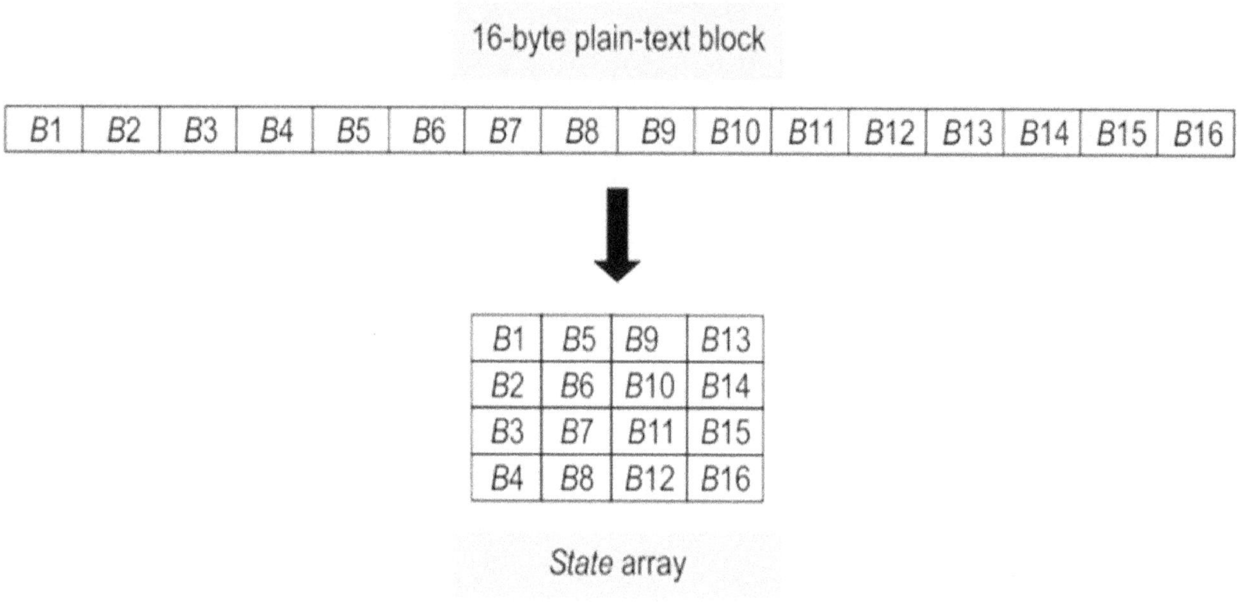

Figure 4.18: 16-Byte Plain-Text Block and Sate Array

XOR the state with the key block

- First 16 bytes (i.e. four words W [0], W [1], W [2], and W [3]) of the expanded key are XORed into the 16-byte state array (B1 to B16).
- Every byte in the state array is replaced by the XOR of itself and the corresponding byte in the expanded key.

AES: PROCESS IN EACH ROUND :-
Apply S-box to each of the plain-text bytes

- Contents of the state array are looked up into the S-box
- Byte-by-byte substitution is done to replace the contents of the state array with the respective entries in the S-box
- Only one S-box is used, unlike DES, which has multiple S-boxes.

Rotate row k of the plain-text block (i.e. state) by k bytes

- Each of the four rows of the state array are rotated to the left
- Row 0 is rotated 0 bytes (i.e. not rotated at all), row 1 is rotated by 1 byte, row 2 is rotated 2 bytes, and row 2 is rotated 3 bytes
- This helps in diffusion of data.

Original array	Modified array
1 5 9 13	1 5 9 13
2 6 10 14	6 10 14 2
3 7 11 15	11 15 3 7
4 8 12 16	16 4 8 12

Figure 4.19: Data Diffusion

Perform a mix-columns operation, Each column is mixed independent of the other. Matrix multiplication is used. Output of this step is the matrix multiplication of the old values and a constant matrix. Two aspects of this step

- The first explains which parts of the state are multiplied against which parts of the matrix.
- The second explains how this multiplication is implemented over what's called a Galois field.

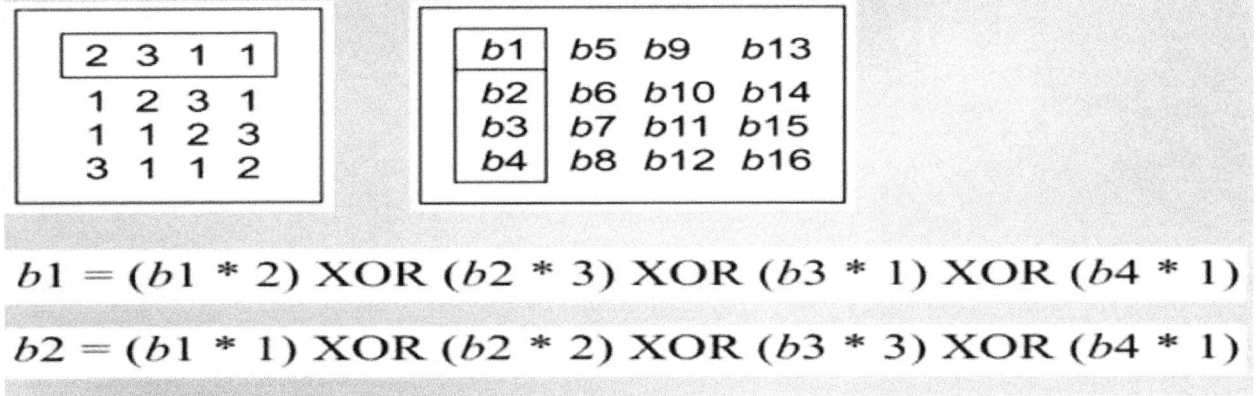

$b1 = (b1 * 2)$ XOR $(b2 * 3)$ XOR $(b3 * 1)$ XOR $(b4 * 1)$

$b2 = (b1 * 1)$ XOR $(b2 * 2)$ XOR $(b3 * 3)$ XOR $(b4 * 1)$

$b1 = (b1 * 2)$ XOR $(b2*3)$ XOR $(b3*1)$ XOR $(b4*1)$

$b2 = (b1 * 1)$ XOR $(b2*2)$ XOR $(b3*3)$ XOR $(b4*1)$

$b3 = (b1 * 1)$ XOR $(b2*1)$ XOR $(b3*2)$ XOR $(b4*3)$

$b4 = (b1 * 3)$ XOR $(b2*1)$ XOR $(b3*1)$ XOR $(b4*2)$

$b5 = (b5 * 2)$ XOR $(b6*3)$ XOR $(b7*1)$ XOR $(b8*$

$b6 = (b5 * 1)$ XOR $(b6*2)$ XOR $(b7*3)$ XOR $(b8*$

$b7 = (b5 * 1)$ XOR $(b6*1)$ XOR $(b7*2)$ XOR $(b8*$

$b8 = (b5 * 3)$ XOR $(b6*1)$ XOR $(b7*1)$ XOR $(b8*$

Figure 4.20: Matrix Multiplication

Galois Field Multiplication

- Result of the multiplication is the output of a look-up of the L-table, followed by the addition of the results, followed by a look-up of the E-table
- Numbers being multiplied using the Mix Column function converted to HEX will form a maximum of a 2-digit hex number
- First digit in the number on the vertical index and the second number on the horizontal index.
- If the value being multiplied is composed of only one digit, we use 0 on the vertical index.

	0	1	2	3	4	5	6	7	8	9	A	B	C	D	E	F
0	01	03	05	0F	11	33	55	FF	1A	2E	72	96	A1	F8	13	35
1	5F	E1	38	48	D8	73	95	A4	F7	02	06	0A	1E	22	66	AA
2	E5	34	5C	E4	37	59	EB	26	6A	BE	D9	70	90	AB	E6	31
3	53	F5	04	0C	14	3C	44	CC	4F	D1	68	B8	D3	6E	B2	CD
4	4C	D4	67	A9	E0	3B	4D	D7	62	A6	F1	08	18	28	78	88
5	83	9E	B9	D0	6B	BD	DC	7F	81	98	B3	CE	49	DB	76	9A
6	B5	C4	57	F9	10	30	50	F0	0B	1D	27	69	BB	D6	61	A3
7	FE	19	2B	7D	87	92	AD	EC	2F	71	93	AE	E9	20	60	A0
8	FB	16	3A	4E	D2	6D	B7	C2	5D	E7	32	56	FA	15	3F	41
9	C3	5E	E2	3D	47	C9	40	C0	5B	ED	2C	74	9C	BF	DA	75
A	9F	BA	D5	64	AC	EF	2A	7E	82	9D	BC	DF	7A	8E	89	80
B	9B	B6	C1	58	E8	23	65	AF	EA	25	6F	B1	C8	43	C5	54
C	FC	1F	21	63	A5	F4	07	09	1B	2D	77	99	B0	CB	46	CA
D	45	CF	4A	DE	79	8B	86	91	A8	E3	3E	42	C6	51	F3	0E
E	12	36	5A	EE	29	7B	8D	8C	8F	8A	85	94	A7	F2	0D	17

	0	1	2	3	4	5	6	7	8	9	A	B	C	D	E	F
0		00	19	01	32	02	1A	C6	4B	C7	1B	68	33	EE	DF	03
1	64	04	E0	0E	34	8D	81	EF	4C	71	08	C8	F8	69	1C	C1
2	7D	C2	1D	B5	F9	B9	27	6A	4D	E4	A6	72	9A	C9	09	78
3	65	2F	8A	05	21	0F	E1	24	12	F0	82	45	35	93	DA	8E
4	96	8F	DB	BD	36	D0	CE	94	13	5C	D2	F1	40	46	83	38
5	66	DD	FD	30	BF	06	8B	62	B3	25	E2	98	22	88	91	10
6	7E	6E	48	C3	A3	B6	1E	42	3A	6B	28	54	FA	85	3D	BA
7	2B	79	0A	15	9B	9F	5E	CA	4E	D4	AC	E5	F3	73	A7	57
8	AF	58	A8	50	F4	EA	D6	74	4F	AE	E9	D5	E7	E6	AD	E8
9	2C	D7	75	7A	EB	16	0B	F5	59	CB	5F	B0	9C	A9	51	A0
A	7F	0C	F6	6F	17	C4	49	EC	D8	43	1F	2D	A4	76	7B	B7
B	CC	BB	3E	5A	FB	60	B1	86	3B	52	A1	6C	AA	55	29	9D
C	97	B2	87	90	61	BE	DC	FC	BC	95	CF	CD	37	3F	5B	D1
D	53	39	84	3C	41	A2	6D	47	14	2A	9E	5D	56	F2	D3	AB
E	44	11	92	D9	23	20	2E	89	B4	7C	B8	26	77	99	E3	A5
F	67	AA	ED	DE	C5	31	FE	18	0D	63	8C	80	C0	F7	70	07

Figure 4.21: Galois Field Multiplication

If the two hex values being multiplied are AF * 8 we first look up L (AF) index which returns B7 and then lookup L (08) which returns 4B.

Once the L-table look-up is complete, we can then simply add the numbers together. If the addition result is greater than FF, we subtract FF from the addition result. For example B7 + 4B = 102. Because 102 > FF, we perform: 102 – FF which gives us 03. The last step is to look up the addition result on the E-table. Again, we take the first digit to look up the vertical index and the second digit to look up the horizontal index. For example, E(03) = 0F. Therefore, the result of multiplying AF * 8 over a Galois field is 0F.

XOR the state with the key block :

- For decryption, the process can be executed in the reverse order.
- The same encryption process, run with some different table values, can also perform decryption.

4.4 ASYMMETRIC-KEY CRYPTOGRAPHY

In any symmetric-key cryptographic scheme, the main issue is :-

How can the sender and the receiver of a message decide upon the key to be used for encryption and decryption?

In computer-based cryptographic algorithms, this problem is even more serious, because the sender and the receiver may be in different countries In the mid-1970s, Whitfield Diffie, a student at the Stanford University met with Martin Hellman, his professor, and the two began to think about the problem of key exchange. After some research and complicated mathematical analysis, idea of asymmetric-key cryptography.

James Ellis of the British Communications Electronic Security Group (CSEG) proposed the idea of asymmetric-key cryptography in the 1960s. Paper written at the Bell Labs during the Second World War , Ellis could not devise a practical algorithm based on his ideas. He then met with Clifford Cocks, who joined the CSEG in 1973. After a short discussion between Ellis and Cocks, Cocks came up with a practical algorithm that could work. Malcolm Williamson, another employee at the CSEG, developed an asymmetric-key cryptographic algorithm CSEG was a secret agency.

US National Security Agency (NSA) was also working on asymmetric-key cryptography. NSA system based on the asymmetric-key cryptography was operational in the mid-1970s. Based on the theoretical framework of Diffie and Hellman, in 1977, Ron Rivest, Adi Shamir and Len Adleman at MIT developed the first major asymmetric-key cryptography system, and published their results in 1978. This method is called RSA algorithm Rivest was working as a professor at the MIT. He had recruited Shamir and Adleman to work on the concept of asymmetric-key cryptography.

RSA is the most widely accepted public-key solution. It solves the problem of key agreements and distribution.

Each communicating party possesses a key pair, made up of one public key and one private key. To communicate securely over any network, all one needs to do is to publish one's public key. All these public keys can then be stored in a database that anyone can consult However, the private key only remains with the respective individuals.

In asymmetric-key cryptography, also called public key cryptography, two different keys (which form a key pair) are used One key is used for encryption and only the other corresponding key must be used for decryption. No other key can decrypt the message—not even the original (i.e. the first) key used for encryption. Simple mathematical basis for this scheme. An extremely large number that has only two factors, which are prime numbers, you can generate a pair of keys.

The number 10 has only two factors, 5 and 2. Apply 5 as an encryption factor, only 2. can be used as the decryption factor , Nothing else—not even 5 itself—can do the decryption.

Key details	A should know	B should know
A's private key	Yes	No
A's public key	Yes	Yes
B's private key	No	Yes
B's public key	Yes	Yes

Figure 4.22: Public Key Cryptography - Who Knows What

When A wants to send a message to B, A encrypts the message using B's public key

- A sends this message (which was encrypted with B's public key) to B
- B decrypts A's message using B's private key

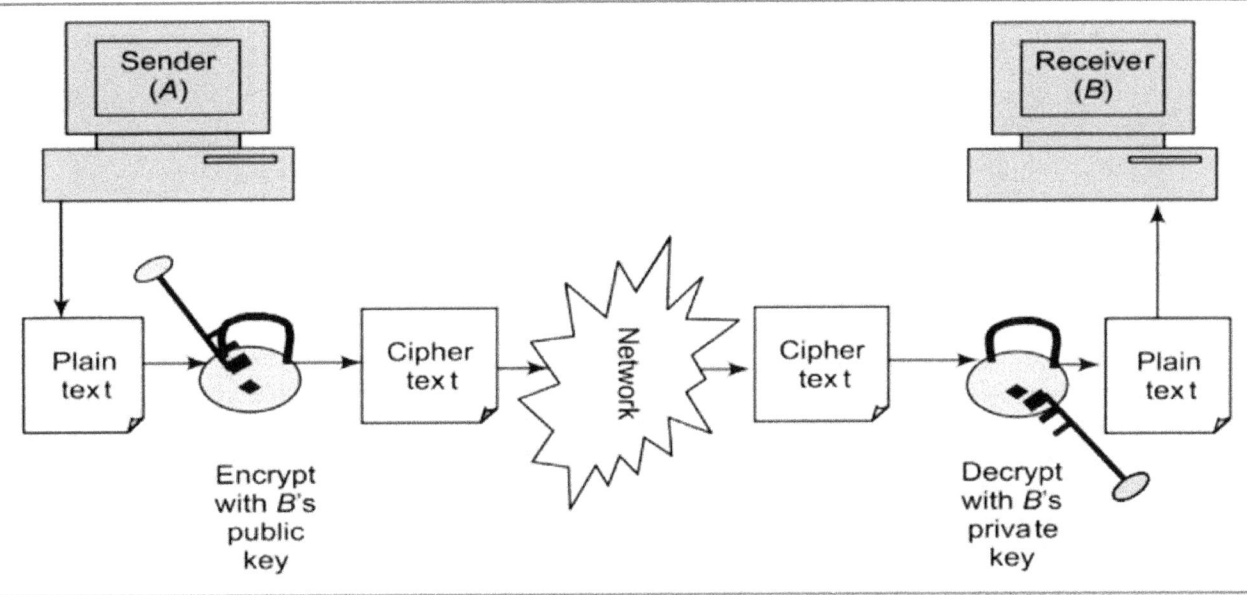

Figure 4.23: Public Key Cryptography/ Assymetric Key Cryptography

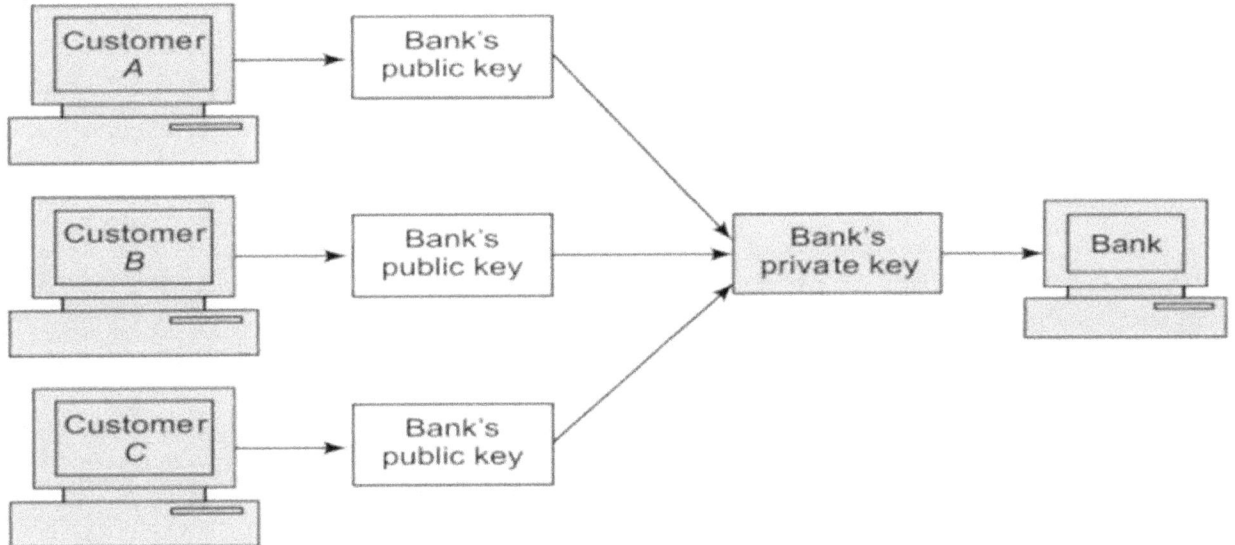

Figure 4.24: Public Key Cryptography Example

4.5 DES and AES Comparison

AES

- AES stands for **Advanced Encryption Standard**
- The date of creation is 2001
- Byte-Oriented
- Key length can be 128-bits, 192-bits, and 256-bits

- Number of rounds depends on key length: 10(128-bits), 12(192-bits), or 14(256-bits)
- The structure is based on a substitution-permutation network
- The design rationale for AES is open
- The selection process for this is secret but accepted for open public comment
- AES is more secure than the DES cipher and is the de facto world standard
- The rounds in AES are: Byte Substitution, Shift Row, Mix Column and Key Addition
- AES can encrypt 128 bits of plaintext
- It can generate Ciphertext of 128, 192, 256 bits

DES

- DES stands for Data Encryption Standard
- The date of creation is 1977
- Bit-Oriented
- The key length is 56 bits in DES
- DES involves 16 rounds of identical operations
- The structure is based on a Feistel network.
- The design rationale for DES is closed
- The selection process for this is secret.
- DES can be broken easily as it has known vulnerabilities. 3DES(Triple DES) is a variation of DES which is secure than the usual DES
- The rounds in DES are: Expansion, XOR operation with round key, Substitution and Permutation
- DES can encrypt 64 bits of plaintext
- It generates Ciphertext of 64 bits

4.6 RSA Technique

1. Choose two large prime numbers P and Q.
2. Calculate $N = P \times Q$.
3. Select the public key (i.e. the encryption key) E such that it is not a factor of $(P - 1)$ and $(Q - 1)$.
4. Select the private key (i.e. the decryption key) D such that the following equation is true:
   $(D \times E) \bmod (P - 1) \times (Q - 1) = 1$
5. For encryption, calculate the cipher text CT from the plain text PT as follows:
   $CT = PT^E \bmod N$
6. Send CT as the cipher text to the receiver.
7. For decryption, calculate the plain text PT from the cipher text CT as follows:
   $PT = CT^D \bmod N$

RSA Algorithm

1. Choose two large prime numbers P and Q.

   Let P = 47, Q = 17.

2. Calculate N = P x Q.

   We have, N = 7 x 17 = 119.

3. Select the public key (i.e. the encryption key) E such that it is not a factor of (P - 1) x (Q - 1).

   - Let us find (7 - 1) x (17 - 1) = 6 x 16 = 96.
   - The factors of 96 are 2, 2, 2, 2, 2, and 3 (because 96 = 2 x 2 x 2 x 2 x 2 x 3).
   - Thus, we have to choose E such that none of the factors of E is 2 and 3. As a few examples, we cannot choose E as 4 (because it has 2 as a factor), 15 (because it has 3 as a factor), 6 (because it has 2 and 3 both as factors).
   - Let us choose E as 5 (it could have been any other number that does not its factors as 2 and 3).

4. Select the private key (i.e. the decryption key) D such that the following equation is true:
   (D x E) mod (P - 1) x (Q - 1) = 1

   - Let us substitute the values of E, P and Q in the equation.
   - We have: (D x 5) mod (7 - 1) x (17 - 1) = 1
   - That is, (D x 5) mod (6) x (16) = 1
   - That is, (D x 5) mod (96) = 1
   - After some calculations, let us take D = 77. Then the following is true: (77 x 5) mod (96) = 385 mod 96 = 1, which is what we wanted.

5. For encryption, calculate the cipher text CT from the plain text PT as follows:
   CT = PT^E mod N

   Let us assume that we want to encrypt plain text 10. Then we have,
   CT = 10^5 mod 119 = 100000 mod 119 = 40

6. Send CT as the cipher text to the receiver.

Send 40 as the cipher text to the receiver.

7. For decryption, calculate the plain text PT from the cipher text CT as follows:
PT = CT^D mod N

- We perform the following:
- PT = CT^D mod N
- That is, PT = 40^{77} mod 119 = 10, which was the original plain text of step 5.

RSA Example

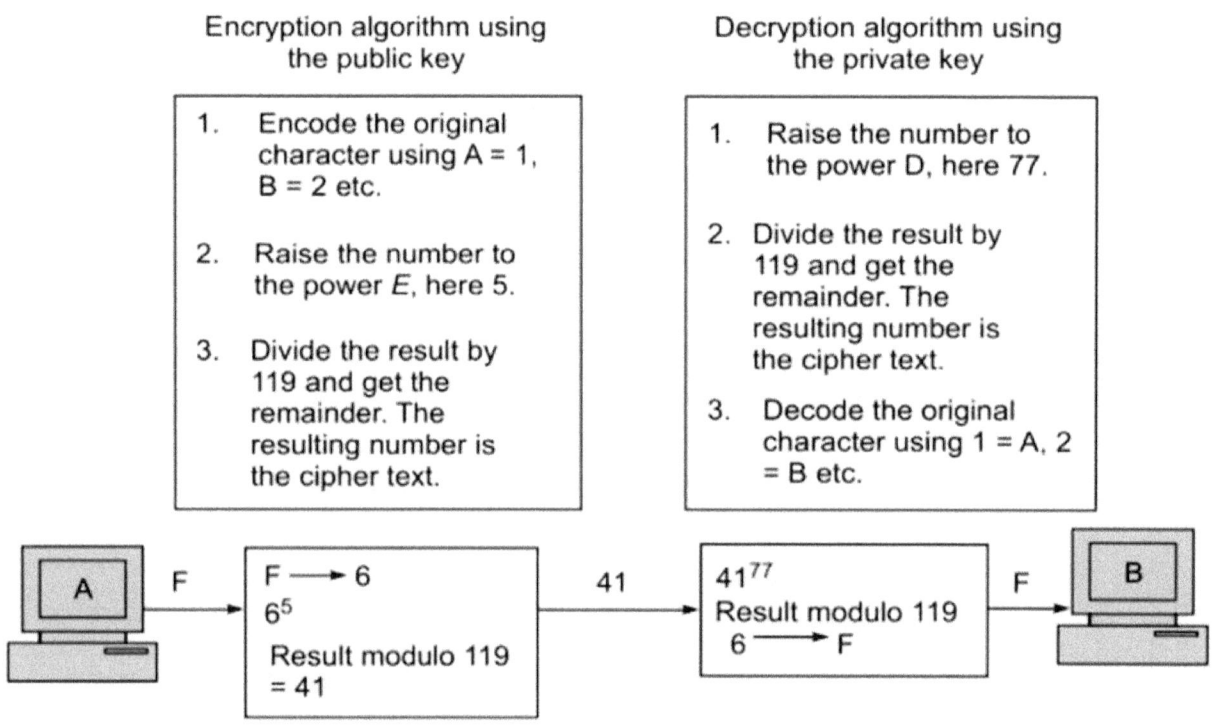

Figure 4.25: RSA Encryption and Decryption Process

SECURITY OF RSA:-

- Plain-text Attacks
  - Short-message Attack

- Cycling Attack
   - Unconcealed Message Attack

- Chosen-cipher text attack (extended Euclidean algorithm)
- Factorization Attack
- Attacks on the Encryption Key
- Attacks on the Decryption Key

   - Revealed Decryption Exponent Attack
   - Low Decryption Exponent Attack.

4.7 Digital Signature

In public key cryptography, If A is the sender of a message and B is the receiver, A encrypts the message with B's public key and sends the encrypted message to B.

In Digital Signature, If A is the sender of a message and B is the receiver, A encrypts the message with A's private key and sends the encrypted message to B.

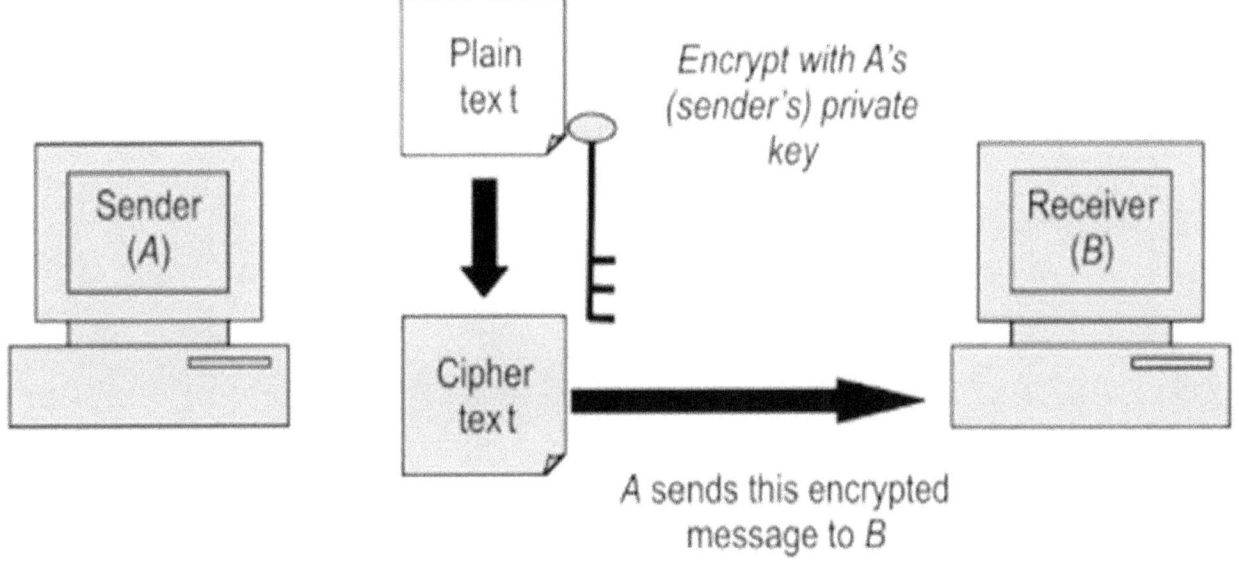

Figure 4.26: Digital Signature - Encryption Process

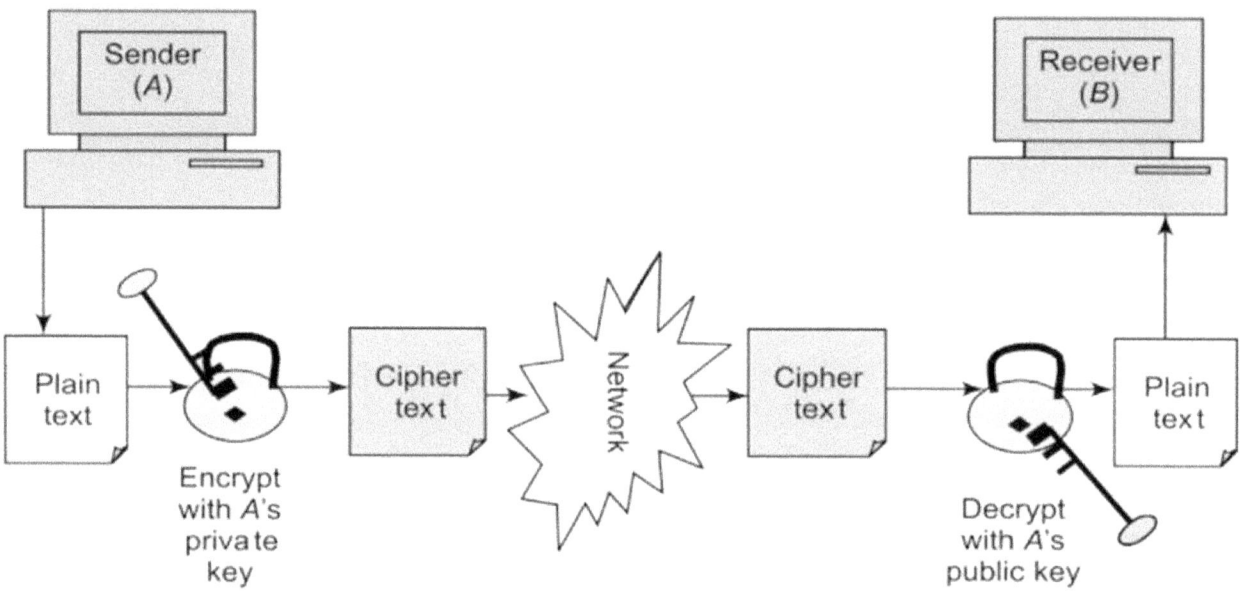

Figure 4.27: Digital Signature - Encryption and Decryption

Hash, Message digest is a fingerprint or the summary of a message. It is similar to the concepts of Longitudinal Redundancy Check (LRC) or Cyclic Redundancy Check (CRC).

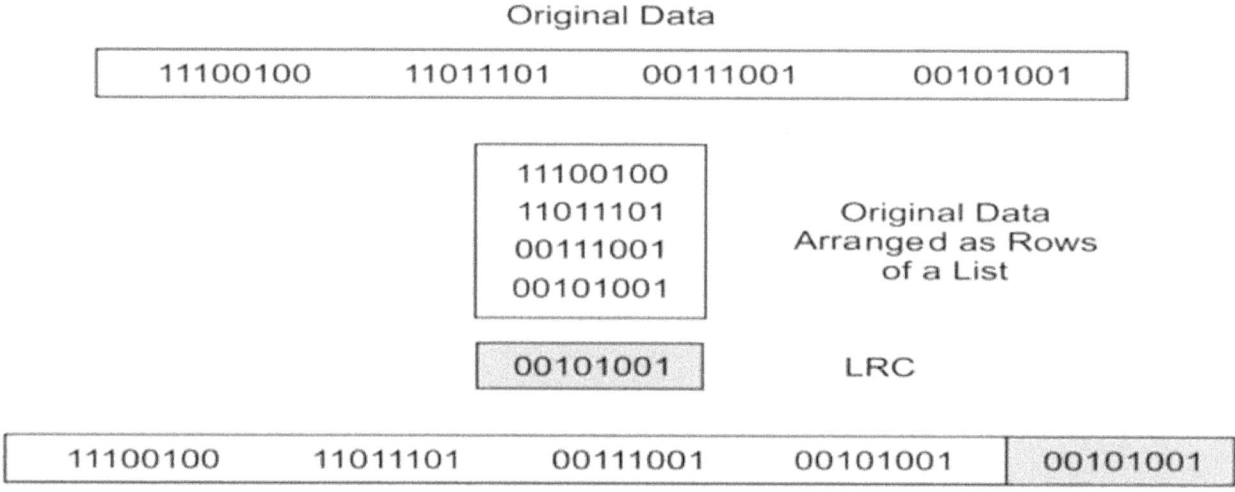

Figure 4.28: Computing LRC for Available Data

Original number is 7391743

Operation	Result
Multiply 7 by 3	21
Discard first digit	1
Multiply 1 by 9	9
Multiply 9 by 1	9
Multiply 9 by 7	63
Discard first digit	3
Multiply 3 by 4	12
Discard first digit	2
Multiply 2 by 3	6

- **Message digest is 6**

Figure 4.29: Computing Message Digest using Simple Multiplication

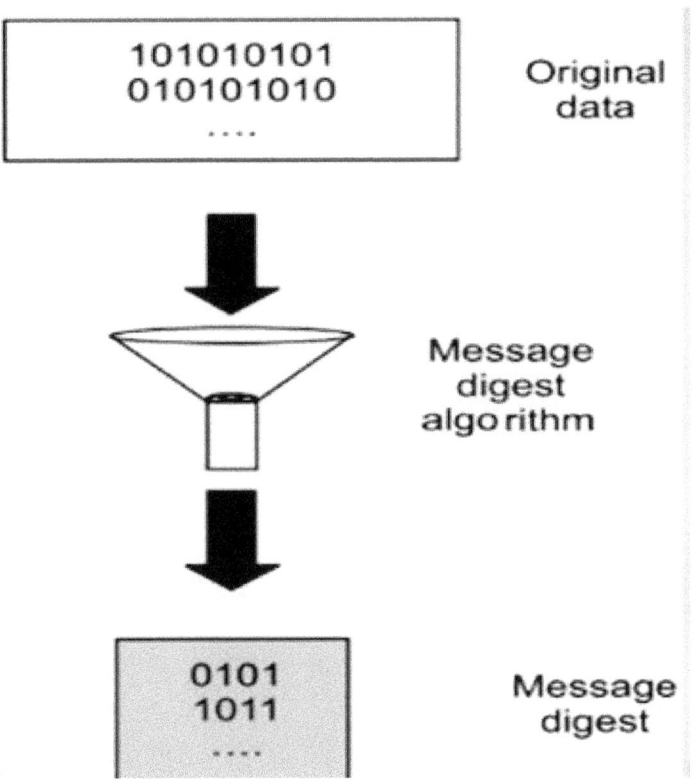

Figure 4.30: Using Message Digest as Digital Signature

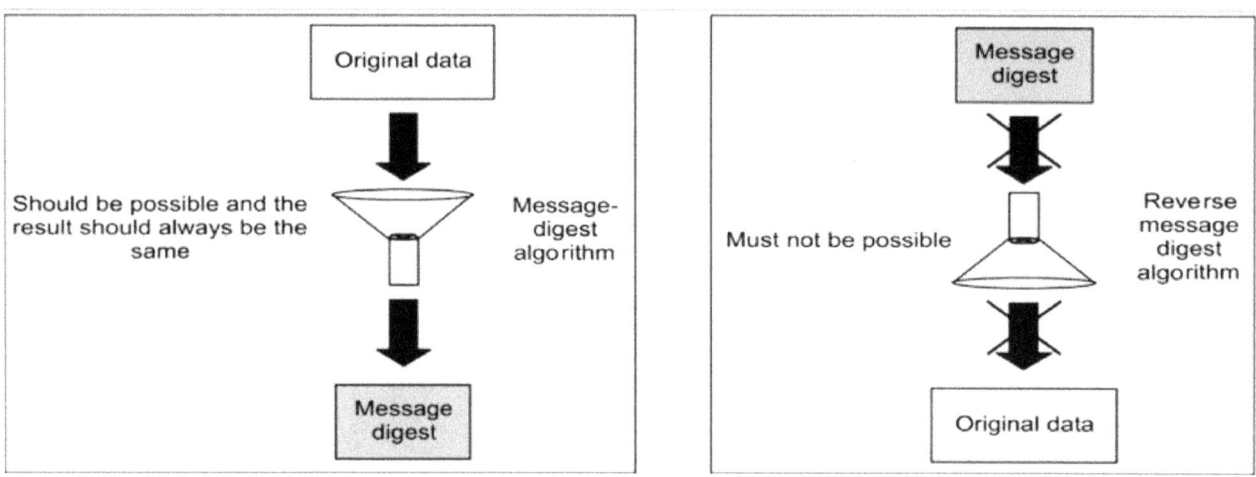

Figure 4.31: Message Digest is Irreversible Process. Used only for Verifying Data Integrity (Data is in Original form. It is not modified)

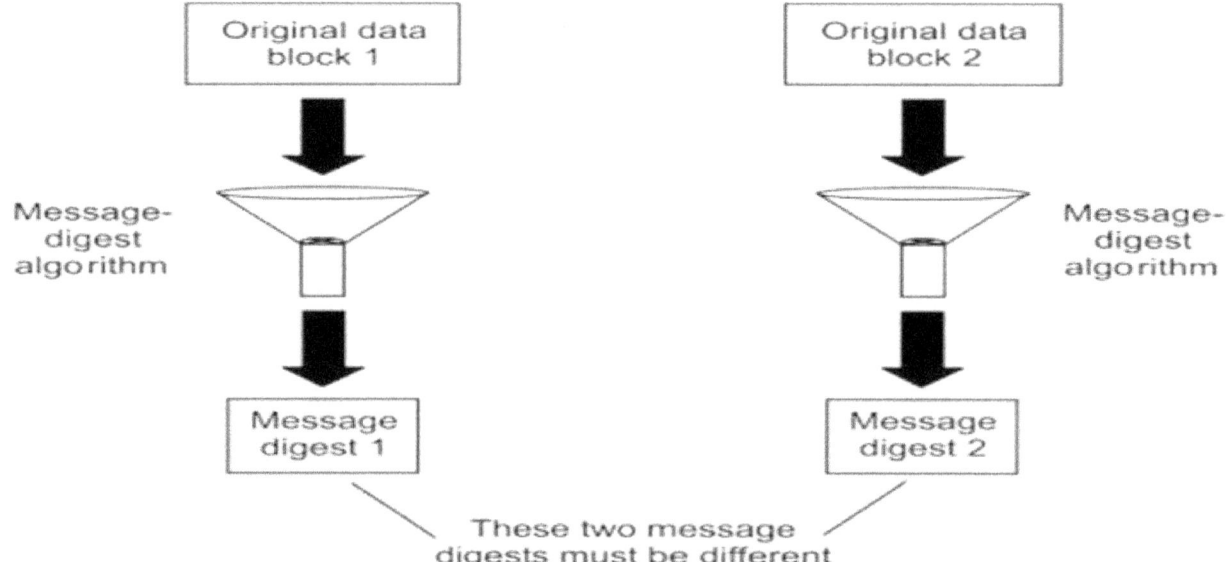

Figure 4.32: Message Digest if Different for Different Data Blocks

CHAPTER FIVE

IP Security: IP Sec

5.1 Overview of IP Security (IP Sec)

IP packets contain data in plain text form. Anyone watching the IP packets pass by can actually access them, read their contents and even change them. Higher-level security mechanisms such as SSL, SHTTP, PGP, PEM, S/MIME, and SET. Higher-level protocols enhance the protection mechanisms. There was a general feeling for a long time that why not secure IP packets. Higher-level security mechanisms can then serve as additional security Measures.

Two levels of security :-

- First offer security at the IP packet level itself
- Continue implementing higher-level security mechanisms, depending on the Requirements

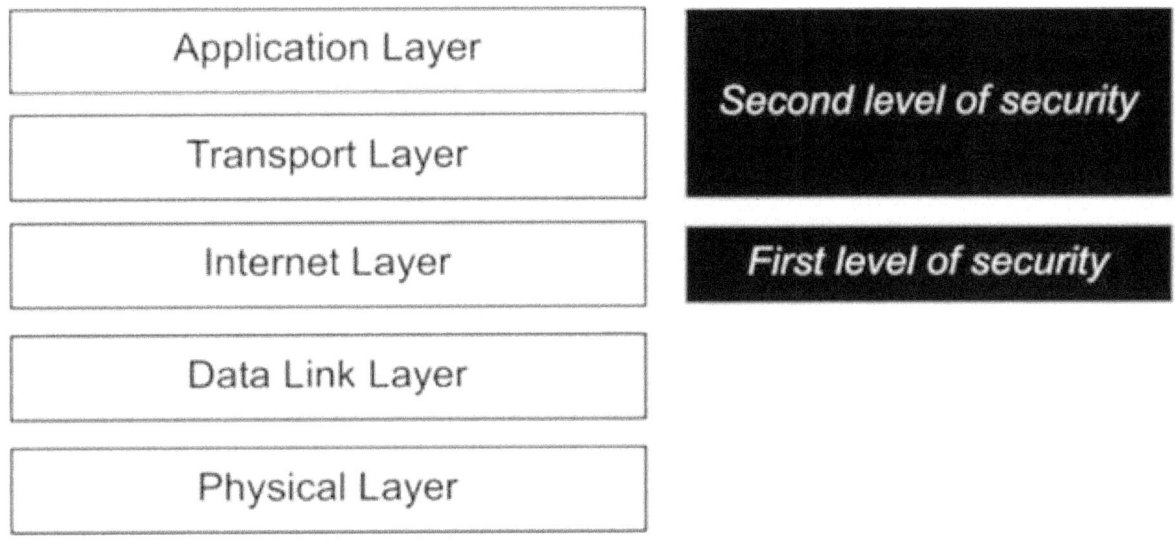

Figure 5.1: Two Levels of Security

In 1994, the Internet Architecture Board (IAB) prepared a report, called Security in the Internet Architecture (RFC 1636). Internet was a very open network, which was unprotected from hostile attacks. Internet needs better security measures, in terms of authentication, integrity and confidentiality 1997, about 150,000 Web sites were attacked in various ways, proving that the Internet was quite an unsafe place at times. IAB decided that authentication, integrity and encryption must be a part of the next version of the IP protocol, called as IP version 6 (Ipv6) or IP new generation (IPng).

Since the new version of IP was to take some years to be released and implemented, the designers devised ways to incorporate these security measures in the current version of IP, called as IP version 4 (IPv4) as well Outcome of the study and IAB's report is the protocol for providing security at the IP level, called as IP Security (IPSec). 1995, the Internet Engineering Task Force (IETF) published five security based standards related to IPSec.

IPv4 may support these features, but IPv6 must support them. Overall idea of IPSec is to encrypt and seal the transport and application-layer data during transmission Offers integrity protection for the Internet layer.

Internet header itself is not encrypted, because of which the intermediate routers can deliver encrypted IPSec messages to the intended recipient. Sender and the receiver look at IPSec as another layer in the TCP/IP protocol stack. This layer sits in-between the transport and the Internet layers of the conventional TCP/ IP protocol stack.

RFC Number	Description
1825	An overview of the security architecture
1826	Description of a packet authentication extension to IP
1827	Description of a packet encryption extension to IP
1828	A specific authentication mechanism
1829	A specific encryption mechanism

Figure 5.2: Progress in IP Security Measures

5.2 IP Security Architecture

IPSec (IP Security) architecture uses two protocols to secure the traffic or data flow. These protocols are ESP (Encapsulation Security Payload) and AH (Authentication Header). IPSec Architecture includes protocols, algorithms, DOI, and Key Management. All these components are very important in order to provide the three main services:

- Confidentiality
- Authentication
- Integrity

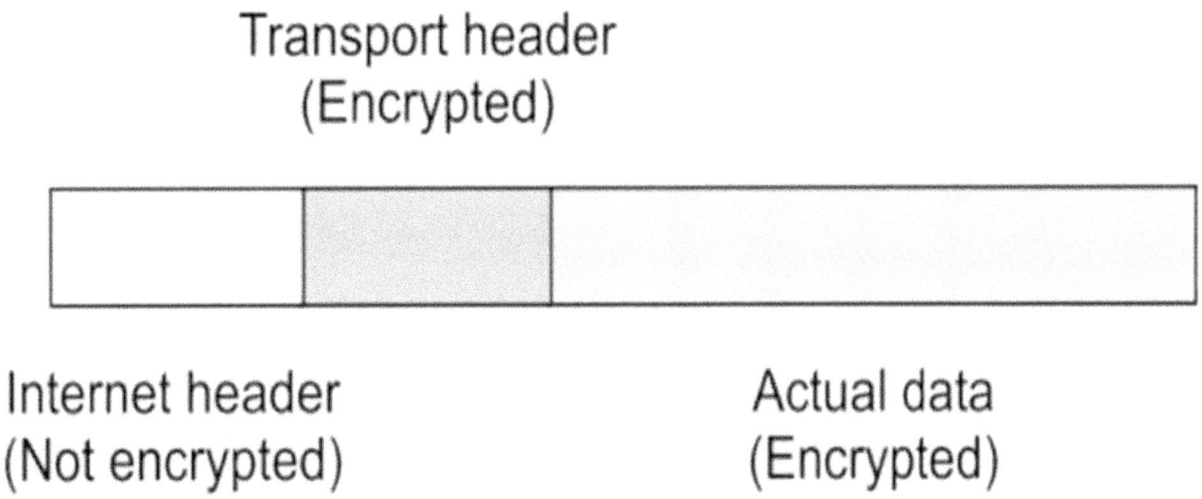

Figure 5.3: IP Security Mechanism

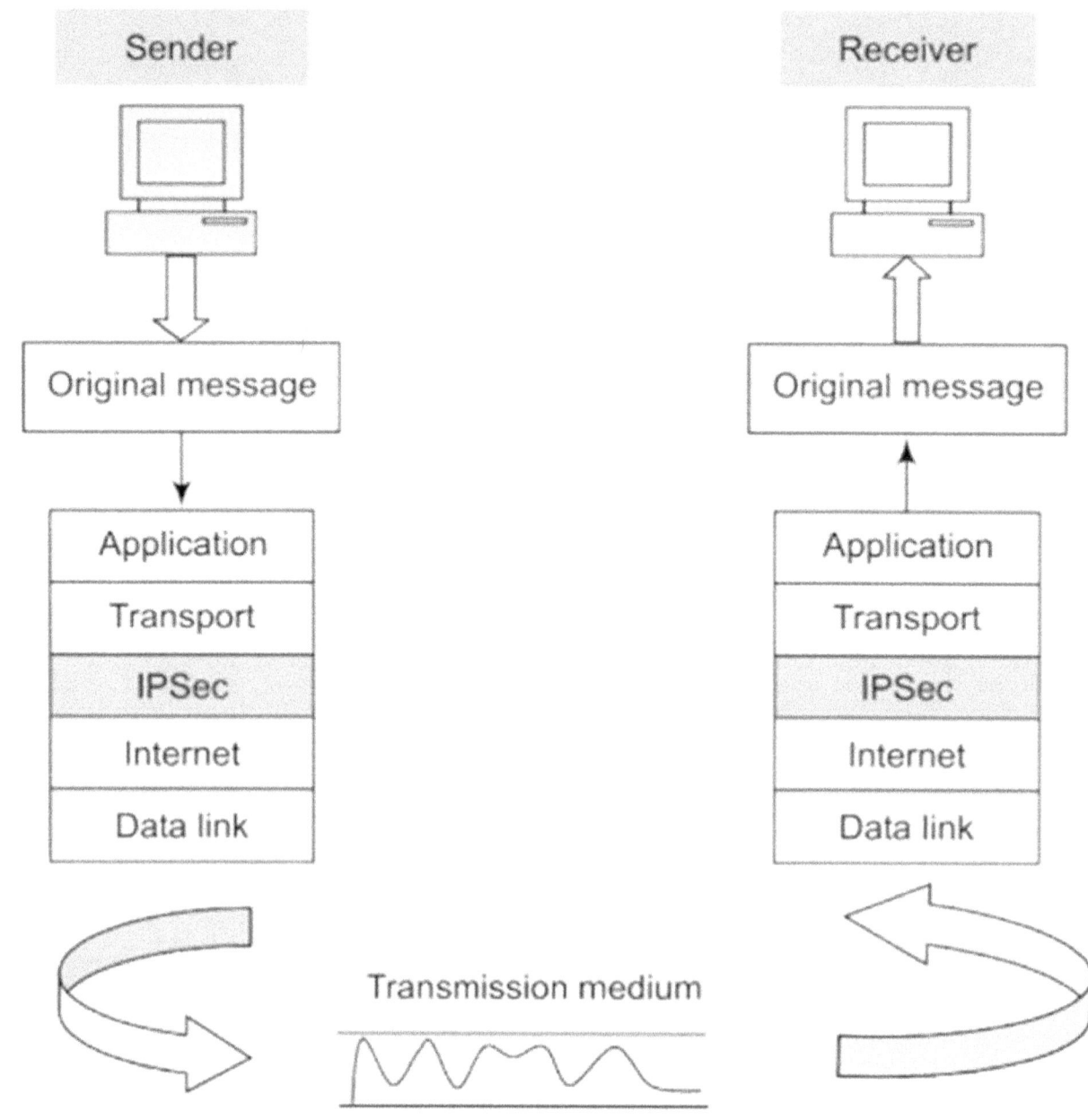

Figure 5.4: IP Security Architecture

5.2.1 APPLICATIONS AND ADVANTAGES

Secure Remote Internet Access

- Make a local call to our Internet Service Provider (ISP) so as to connect to our organization's network in a secure fashion from our home or hotel. From there, we can access the corporate network facilities or access remote desktops/servers

Secure Branch Office Connectivity

- Subscribing to an expensive leased line for connecting its branches across cities/countries, an organization can set up an IPSec-enabled network to securely connect all its branches over the Internet

Set Up Communication with Other Organizations

- Used to connect the networks of different organizations together in a secure and inexpensive fashion
- Transparent to the end users. There is no need for an user training, key issuance or revocation
- Configured to work with a firewall, it becomes the only entry-exit point for all traffic; making it extra secure
- Works at the network layer. Hence, no changes are needed to the upper layers
- Implemented in a firewall or a router, all the outgoing and incoming traffic gets protected. However, the internal traffic does not have to use IPSec. Thus, it does not add any overheads for the internal traffic
- Allow traveling staff to have secure access to the corporate network
- Allows interconnectivity between branches/offices in a very inexpensive manner

5.3 IPSec OVERVIEW: IPSec PROTOCOLS

IP packet consists of two portions: IP header and the actual data. IPSec features are implemented in the form of additional IP headers (called extension headers) to the standard, default IP headers. Extension IP headers follow the standard IP headers. IPSec offers two main services: authentication and confidentiality. To support these two main services, IPSec defines two IP extension headers: one for authentication and another for confidentiality.

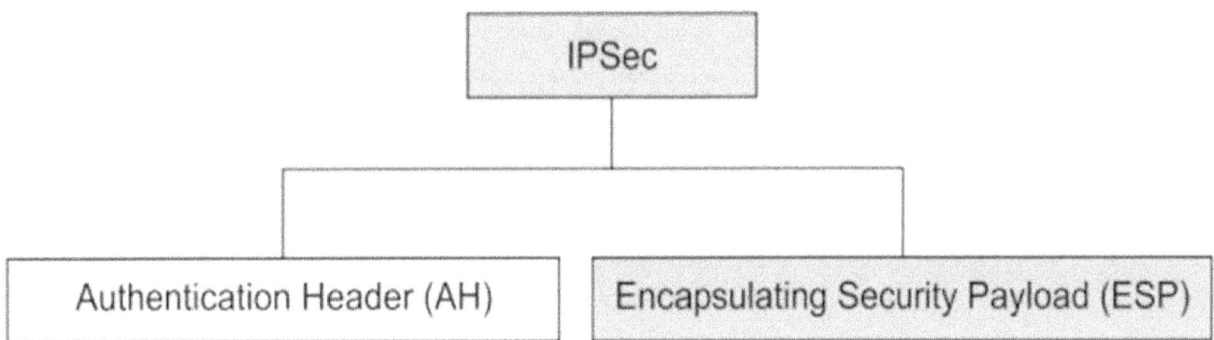

Figure 5.5: IPSec Protocols

AH protocol provides authentication, integrity, and an optional anti-replay service. IPSec AH is a header in an IP packet, which contains a cryptographic checksum (similar to a message digest or hash) for the contents of the packet. Inserted between the IP header and any subsequent packet contents. No changes are required to the data contents of the packet. Security resides completely in the contents of the AH.

Encapsulating Security Payload (ESP) protocol provides data confidentiality. ESP protocol also defines a new header to be inserted into the IP packet. ESP processing also includes the transformation of the protected data into an unreadable, encrypted format. Under normal circumstances, the ESP will be inside the AH. Encryption happens first and then authentication. On receipt of an IP packet that was processed by IPSec, the receiver processes the AH first, if present. The outcome of this tells the receiver if the contents of the packet are all right or whether they have been tampered with, while in transit. If the receiver finds the contents acceptable, it extracts the key and algorithms associated with the ESP and decrypt the contents.

5.4 Modes of Operation

IPSec protects the entire IP datagram. It takes an IP datagram (including the IP header), adds the IPSec header and trailer and encrypts the whole thing. It then adds new IP header to this encrypted datagram.

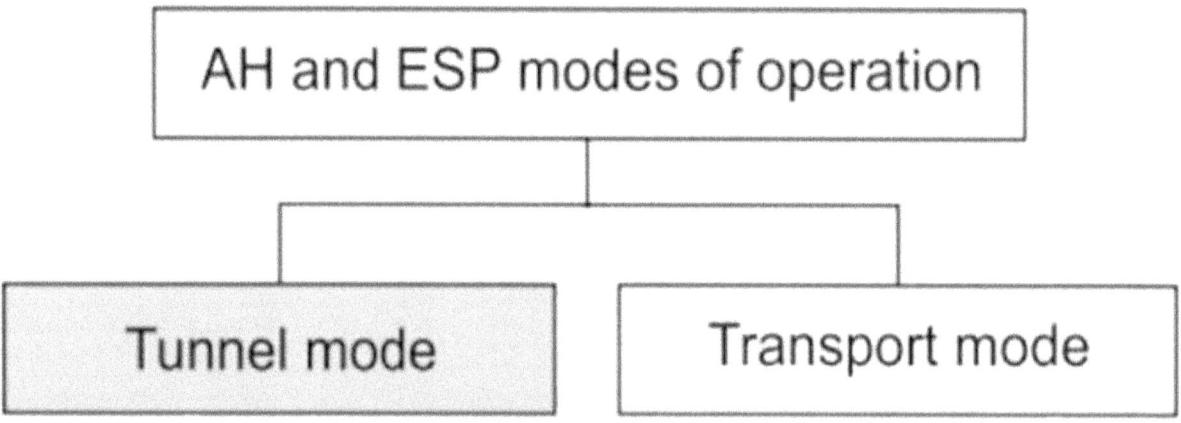

Figure 5.6: AH and ESP Modes of Operation

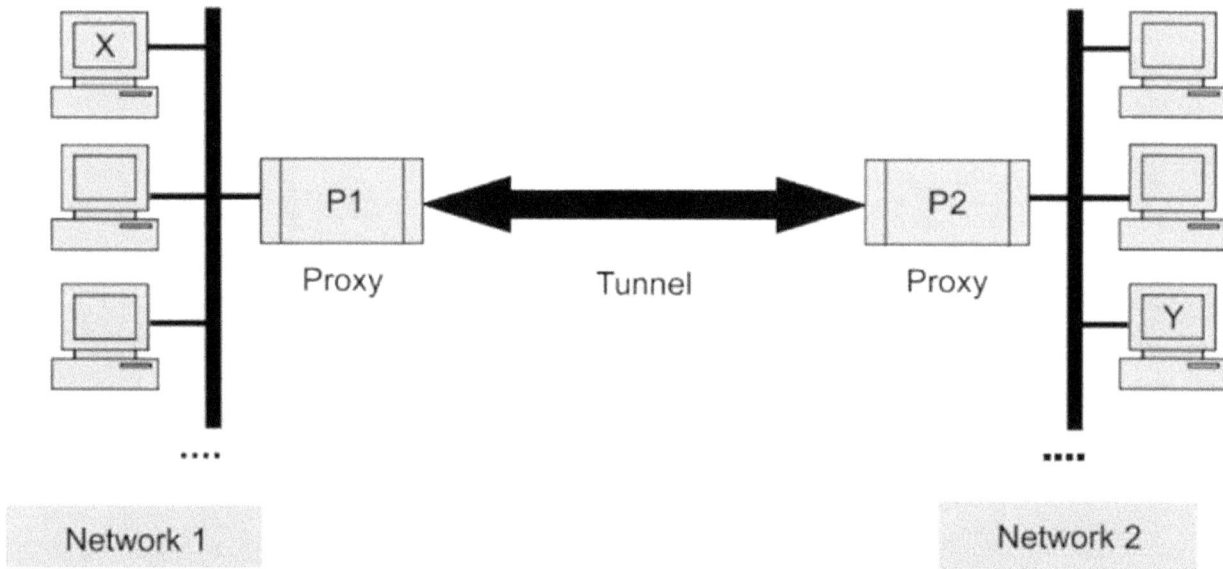

Figure 5.7: Tunnel Mode of Operation

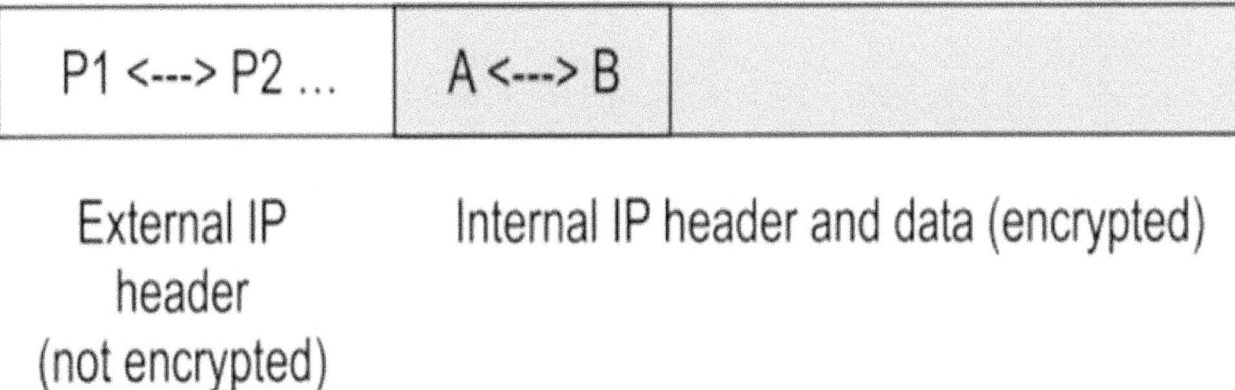

Figure 5.8: Protecting IP Datagram in Tunnel Mode

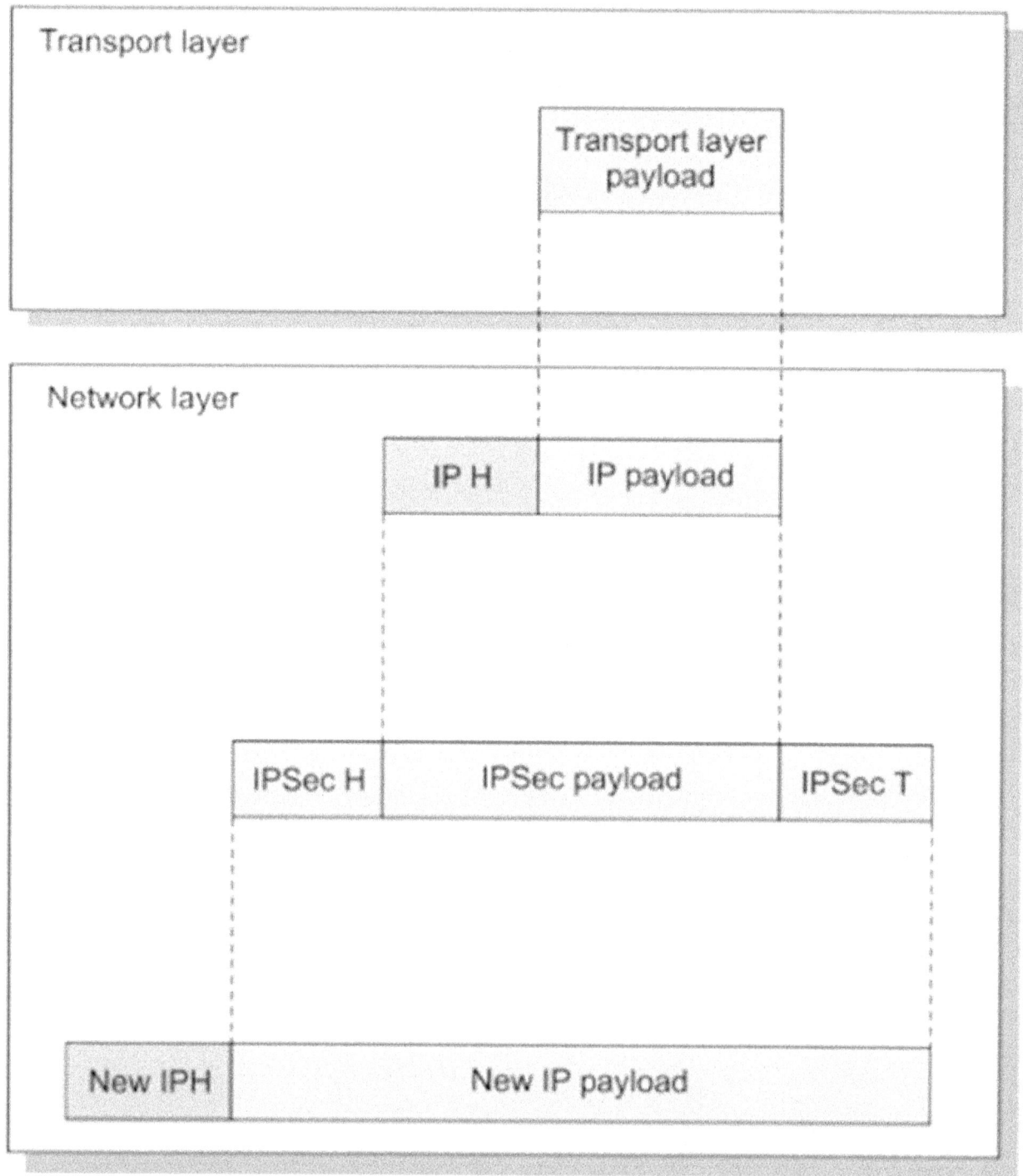

Figure 5.9: Tunnel Mode Operation Overview

Transport mode does not hide the actual source and destination addresses. They are visible in plain text, while in transit. IPSec takes the transport-layer payload, adds IPSec header and trailer, encrypts the whole thing and then adds the IP header. IP header is not encrypted.

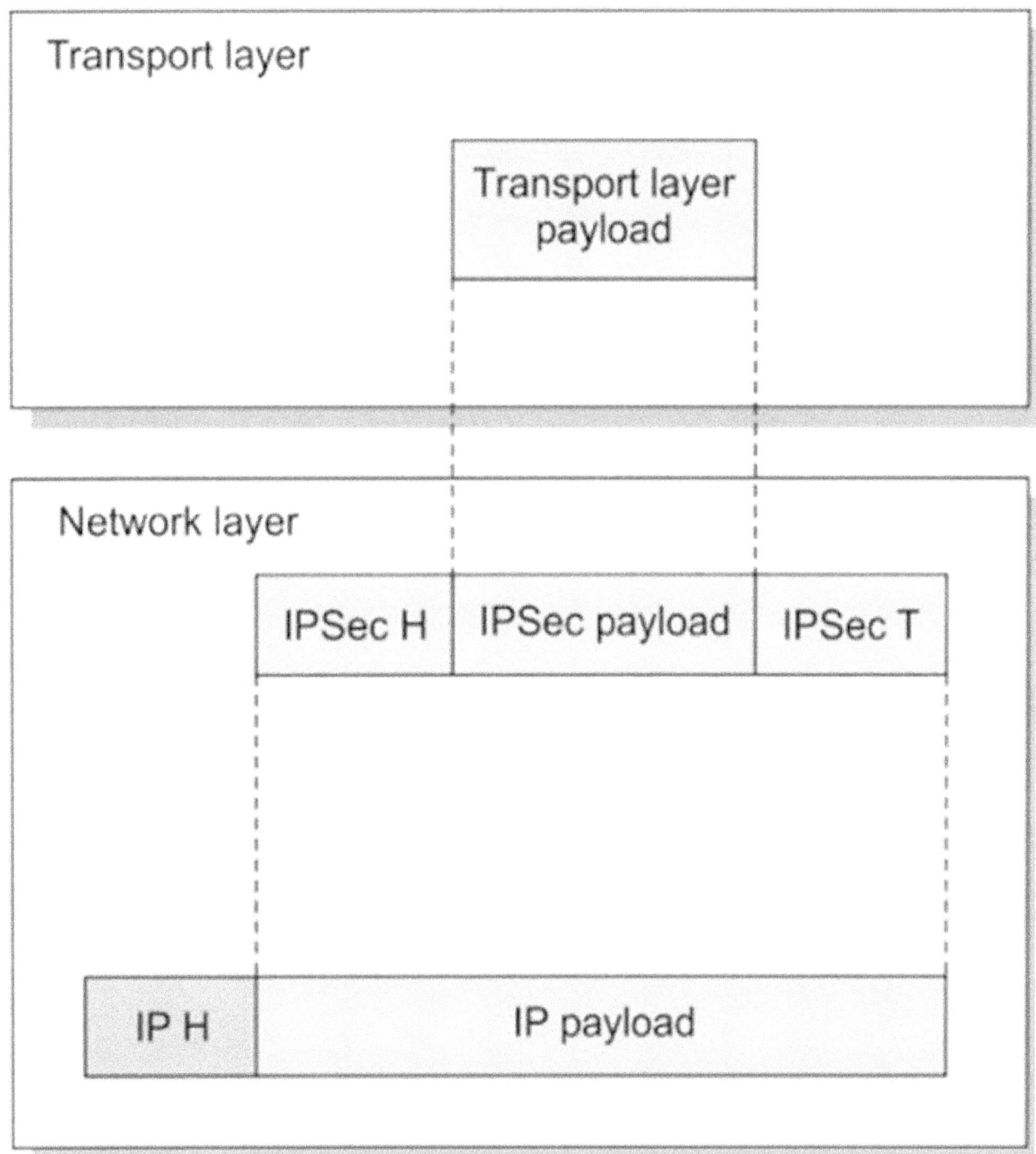

Figure 5.10: Tranport Mode Operation Overview

New IP header has information different from that is there in the original IP header. The tunnel mode is normally used between two routers, a host and a router or a router and a host. It is generally not used between two hosts, since the idea is to protect the original packet, including its IP header. It is as if the whole packet goes through an imaginary tunnel. Host-to-host (i.e. end-to-end) encryption. Sending host uses IPSec to authenticate and/or encrypt the transport layer payload and only the receiver verifies it. Used for the key management procedures. Used to negotiate the cryptographic algorithms to be later used by AH and ESP in the actual cryptographic operations.

IPSec protocols are designed to be independent of the actual lower-level cryptographic algorithms. Internet Key Exchange (IKE) is the initial phase of IPSec, where the algorithms and keys are decided. After the IKE phase, the AH and ESP protocols take over.

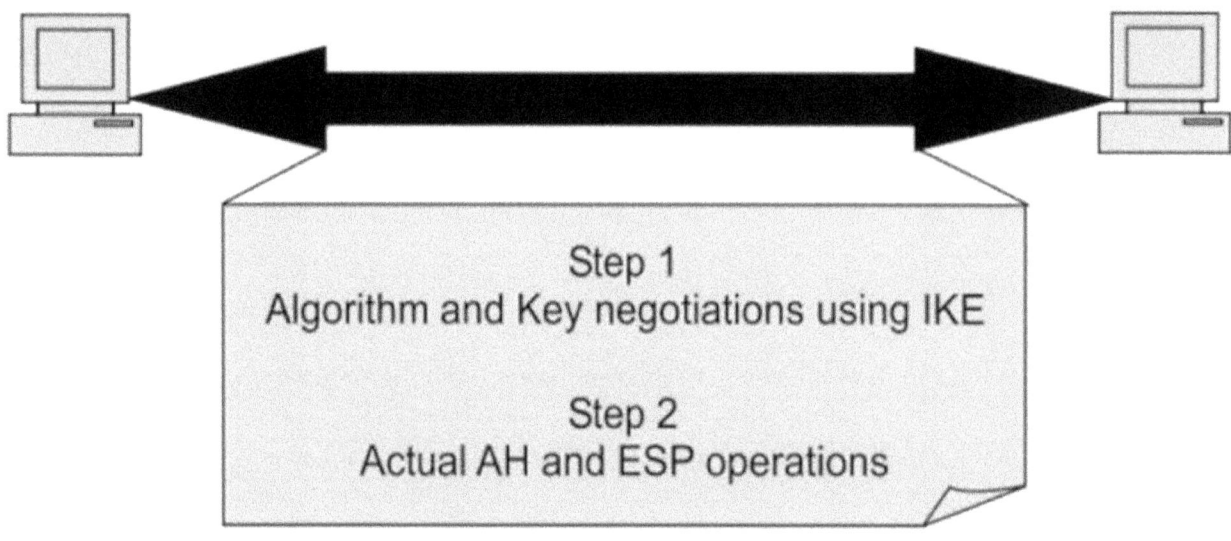

Figure 5.11: IKE and Protocol Operations

5.4 Security Associations Management

The output of the IKE phase is a Security Association (SA). SA is an agreement between the communicating parties about factors such as the IPSec protocol version in use, mode of operation (transport mode or tunnel mode), cryptographic algorithms, cryptographic keys, lifetime of keys, etc.

Principal objective of the IKE protocol is to establish an SA between the communicating parties. Once this is done, both major protocols of IPSec (i.e. AH and ESP) make use of SA for their actual operation. If both AH and ESP are used, each communicating party requires two sets of SA: one for AH and one for ESP.

SA is simplex, i.e. unidirectional. At a second level, two sets of SA per communicating party: one for incoming transmission and another for outgoing transmission. If the two communicating parties use both AH and ESP, each of them would require four sets of SA.

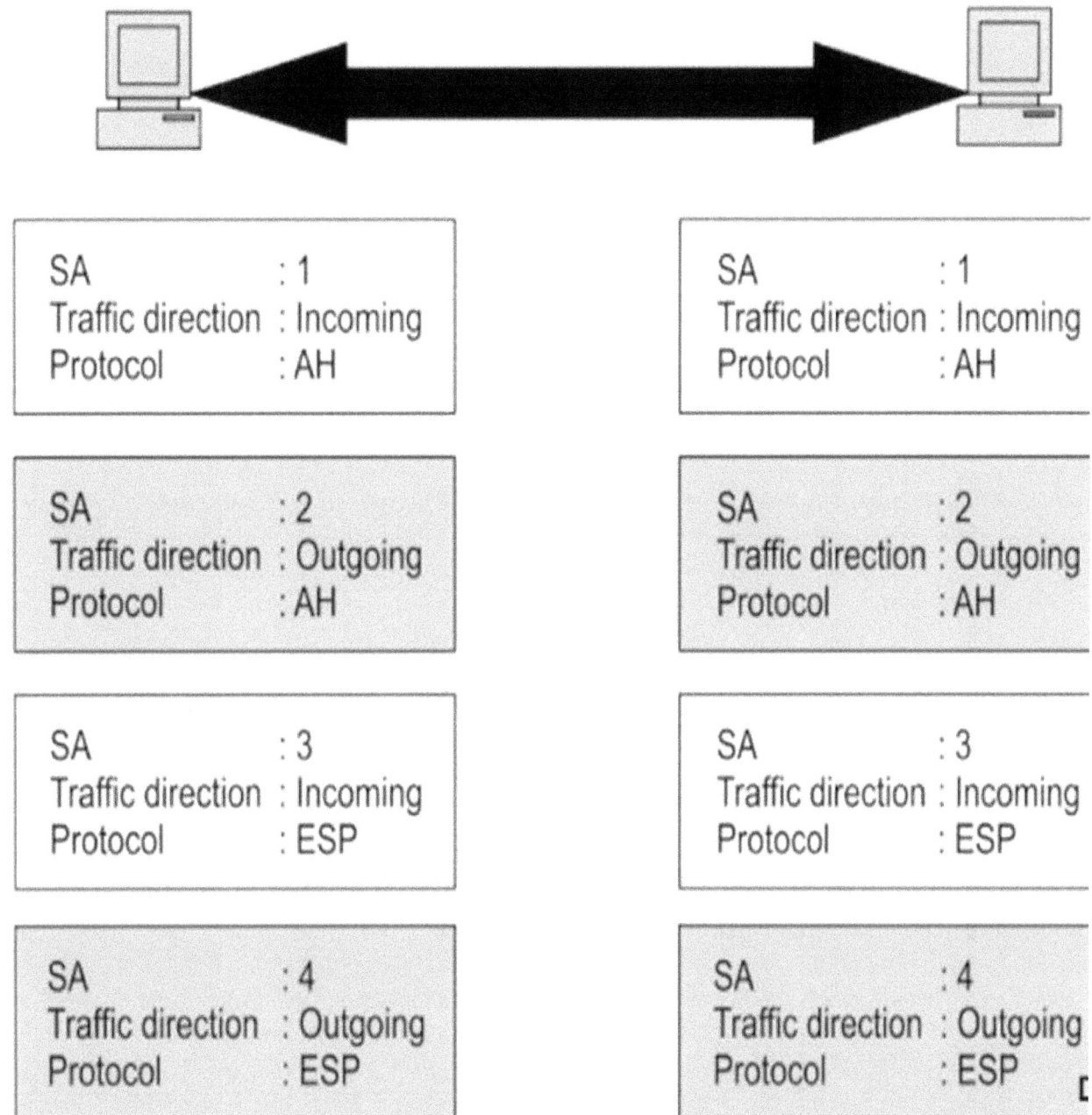

Figure 5.12: Security Associations

Both the communicating parties must allocate some storage area for storing the SA information at their end. A standard storage area called Security Association Database (SAD) is pre-defined and used by IPSec. Each communicating party requires maintaining its own SAD. SAD contains active SA entries.

CHAPTER SIX

IP Security Policy

In 1994, the Internet Architecture Board (IAB) released a report titled "Security in the Internet Architecture" (RFC 1636), which identified key areas for security mechanisms. These included the importance of securing the network infrastructure from unauthorized monitoring and control of network traffic, as well as the need to secure end-user-to-end-user traffic using authentication and encryption mechanisms.

To address these concerns, the IAB included authentication and encryption as necessary security features in the next-generation IP, which was released as IPv6. Fortunately, these security capabilities were designed to be usable with both the current IPv4 and the future IPv6, allowing vendors to offer these features now. As a result, many vendors currently have some IPsec capability in their products.

6.1 IP Security Policy

The operation of IPsec relies on the application of a security policy to each IP packet that travels from a source to a destination. The security policy is primarily determined by two databases: the security association database (SAD) and the security policy database (SPD). This section provides an overview of these two databases and summarizes their use during IPsec operation. Relevant relationships are illustrated in Figure 6.1.

A key concept in both the authentication and confidentiality mechanisms for IP is the security association (SA). An association is a one-way logical connection between a sender and a receiver that provides security services to the traffic carried on it. If a peer relationship is needed for two-way secure exchange, then two security associations are required.

A security association is uniquely identified by three parameters.

- **Security Parameters Index (SPI):** It is a 32-bit unsigned integer assigned to this SA and has local significance only. The SPI is carried in AH and ESP headers to enable the receiving system to select the SA under which a received packet will be processed.
- **IP Destination Address:** Which is the address of the destination endpoint of the SA. The destination endpoint may be an end-user system or a network system such as a firewall or router.
- **Security Protocol Identifier:** Which is a field from the outer IP header that indicates whether the association is an AH or ESP security association.

Therefore, in any IP packet, the security association is uniquely identified by the Destination Address in the IPv4 or IPv6 header and the SPI in the enclosed extension header (AH or ESP).

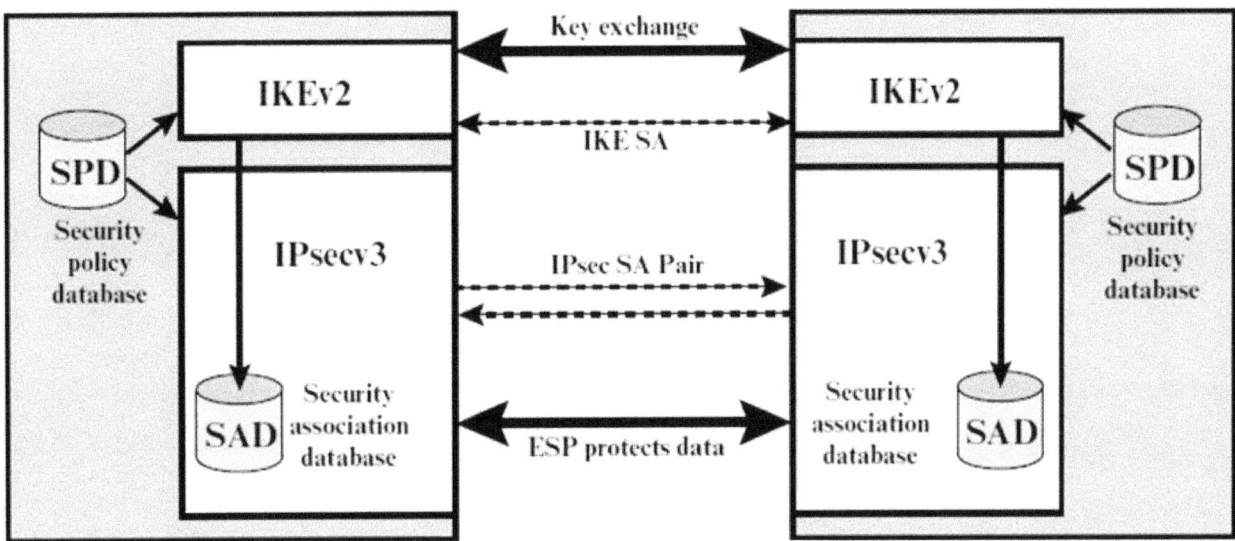

Figure 6.1: IPsec Architecture

6.1.1 Security Association Database

Every IPsec implementation has a nominal Security Association Database (SAD) that specifies the parameters associated with each Security Association (SA). An SA is typically defined by the following parameters in an SAD entry.

- **Security Parameter Index (SPI):** A 32-bit value chosen by the receiving end of an SA to identify the SA uniquely. In an SAD entry for an outbound SA, the SPI is used to create the AH or ESP header of the packet. In an SAD entry for an inbound SA, the SPI is used to map traffic to the appropriate SA.
- **Sequence Number Counter:** A 32-bit value used to generate the Sequence Number field in AH or ESP headers, as described in fig 6.3. This is required for all implementations.
- **Sequence Counter Overflow**: A flag indicating whether an overflow of the Sequence Number Counter should trigger an auditable event and prevent the further transmission of packets on this SA. This is required for all implementations.
- **Anti-Replay Window**: Used to determine whether an inbound AH or ESP packet is a replay, as described in fig 6.1 This is required for all implementations.
- **AH Information:** Authentication algorithm, keys, key lifetimes, and related parameters being used with AH. This is required for AH implementations.
- **ESP Information:** Encryption and authentication algorithm, keys, initialization values, key lifetimes, and related parameters being used with ESP. This is required for ESP implementations.
- **Lifetime of this Security Association**: A time interval or byte count after which an SA must be replaced with a new SA (and new SPI) or terminated, plus an indication of which of these actions should occur.
- **The IPsec protocol mode:** It can be set to either Tunnel, Transport, or Wildcard
- **Path maximum transmission (PMTU):** Which are required for all implementations. The key management mechanism used to distribute keys is connected to authentication and privacy mechanisms through the Security Parameters Index (SPI) only.

Thus, authentication and privacy are specified independently of any specific key management mechanism. IPsec offers users flexibility in applying IPsec services to IP traffic. SAs can be combined in various ways to achieve the desired user configuration.

Additionally, IPsec provides fine granularity in distinguishing between traffic that is protected by IPsec and traffic that can bypass IPsec, such as in the former case, where IP traffic is related to specific SAs.

6.1.2 The Security Policy Database (SPD)

It is responsible for relating IP traffic to specific Security Associations (SAs). It contains entries that define a subset of IP traffic and point to an SA for that traffic. In complex environments, there may be multiple entries that relate to a single SA or multiple SAs associated with a single SPD entry. The selectors in each SPD entry are IP and upper-layer protocol field values that filter outgoing traffic to map it into a particular SA. Outbound processing follows a general sequence for each IP packet.

Firstly, the selector fields in the packet are compared against the SPD to find a matching SPD entry, which will point to zero or more SAs.

Secondly, the SA is determined for this packet and its associated Security Parameter Index (SPI).

Finally, the required IPsec processing (AH or ESP processing) is done. The selectors involved in determining an SPD entry are Remote IP Address, Local IP Address, and Next Layer Protocol.

- **Remote IP Address:** This may be a single IP address, an enumerated list or range of addresses, or a wildcard (mask) address.
- **Local IP Address:** It may be a single IP address, an enumerated list or range of addresses, or a wildcard (mask) address.
- **Next Layer Protocol:** It is the protocol operating over IP and can be an individual protocol number, ANY, or for IPv6 only, OPAQUE. If AH or ESP is used, then this IP protocol header immediately precedes the AH or ESP header in the packet. More information can be found in the relevant IPsec documents.

Protocol	Local IP	Port	Remote IP	Port	Action	Comment
UDP	1.2.3.101	500	*	500	BYPASS	IKE
ICMP	1.2.3.101	*	*	*	BYPASS	Error messages
*	1.2.3.101	*	1.2.3.0/24	*	PROTECT: ESP intransport-mode	Encrypt intranet traffic
TCP	1.2.3.101	*	1.2.4.10	80	PROTECT: ESP intransport-mode	Encrypt to server
TCP	1.2.3.101	*	1.2.4.10	443	BYPASS	TLS: avoid double encryption
*	1.2.3.101	*	1.2.4.0/24	*	DISCARD	Others in DMZ
*	1.2.3.101	*	*	*	BYPASS	Internet

Figure 6.2: Host SPD Example

The following information pertains to the fields available in an SPD (Security Policy Database) on a host system. The user identifier is a

- **Name:** It identifies the user on the operating system and is not found in the IP or upper-layer headers. However, if IPsec is running on the same operating system as the user, this identifier is available.

- **Local and remote ports:** This may be individual TCP or UDP port values, an enumerated list of ports, or a wildcard port.

Figure 6.2 provides an example of an SPD on a host system, as opposed to a network system such as a firewall or router. In this example, the local network configuration consists of two networks: the basic corporate network configuration with the IP network number 1. . . /24 and a secure LAN, also known as a DMZ, identified as 1. . . /24. The DMZ is protected by firewalls from both the outside world and the rest of the corporate LAN. The host in this example has the IP address 1. . . 0 and is authorized to connect to the server 1. . . 0 in the DMZ.

The entries in the SPD are self-explanatory. For example, UDP port 500 is the designated port for IKE. Any traffic from the local host to a remote host for purposes of an IKE exchange bypasses the IPsec processing.

IPsec processes packets on a packet-by-packet basis. When IPsec is implemented, each outbound IP packet is processed by the IPsec logic before transmission, and each inbound packet is processed by the IPsec logic after reception and before passing the packet contents on to the next higher layer (TCP or UDP). The logic of these two situations is discussed in the following sections.

6.1.3 IP Traffic Processing

IPsec is implemented on each IP packet individually. When IPsec is enabled, the IPsec logic handles each outbound IP packet before transmission, and each inbound packet after reception but before passing its contents to the next higher layer, such as TCP or UDP. We will examine the logic of these two scenarios in detail.

OUTBOUND PACKETS:

Figure 6.3 illustrates the primary elements of IPsec processing for outbound traffic. A higher layer, such as TCP, sends a data block down to the IP layer, which creates an IP packet containing an IP header and an IP body. The following steps then occur:

1. IPsec examines the SPD to find a match for the current packet.
2. If no match is found, the packet is discarded, and an error message is generated.
3. Matching entry in the SPD determines the further processing of the packet. If the policy for the packet is DISCARD, the packet is discarded. If the policy is BYPASS, there is no further IPsec processing, and the packet is forwarded to the network for transmission.
4. If policy PROTECT, search is conducted in the SAD for a matching entry. If no entry is found, IKE is invoked to create an SA with the appropriate keys, and an entry is made in the SA.
5. The processing for the packet is determined by the matching entry in the SAD, which can involve encryption, authentication, or both, and either transport or tunnel mode can be used. Once the processing is complete, the packet is forwarded to the network for transmission.

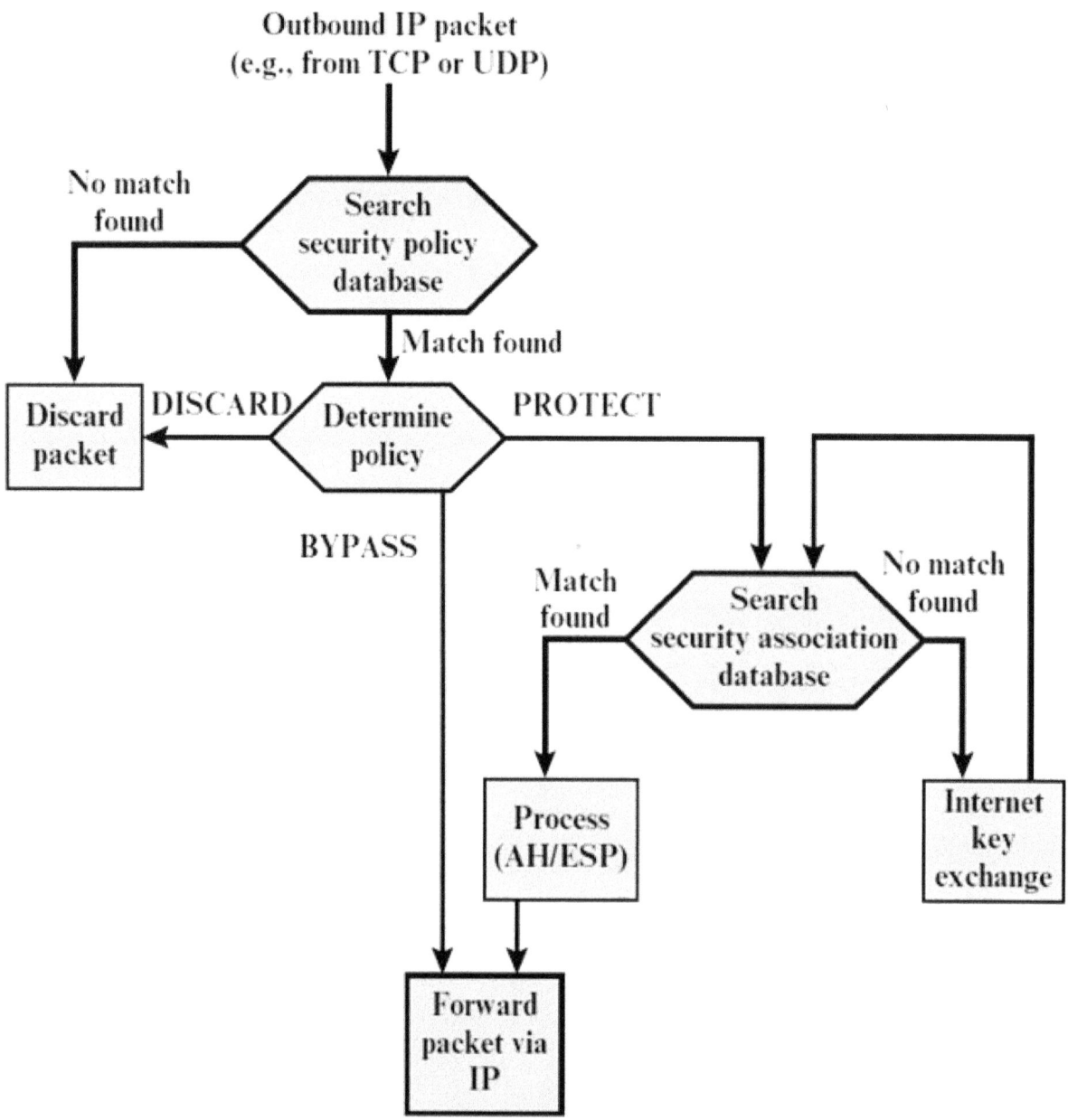

Figure 6.3: Processing Model for Outbound Packets

INBOUND TRAFFIC:

Figure 6.4 illustrates the main elements of IPsec processing for inbound traffic and incoming IP packets triggers the IPsec processing.

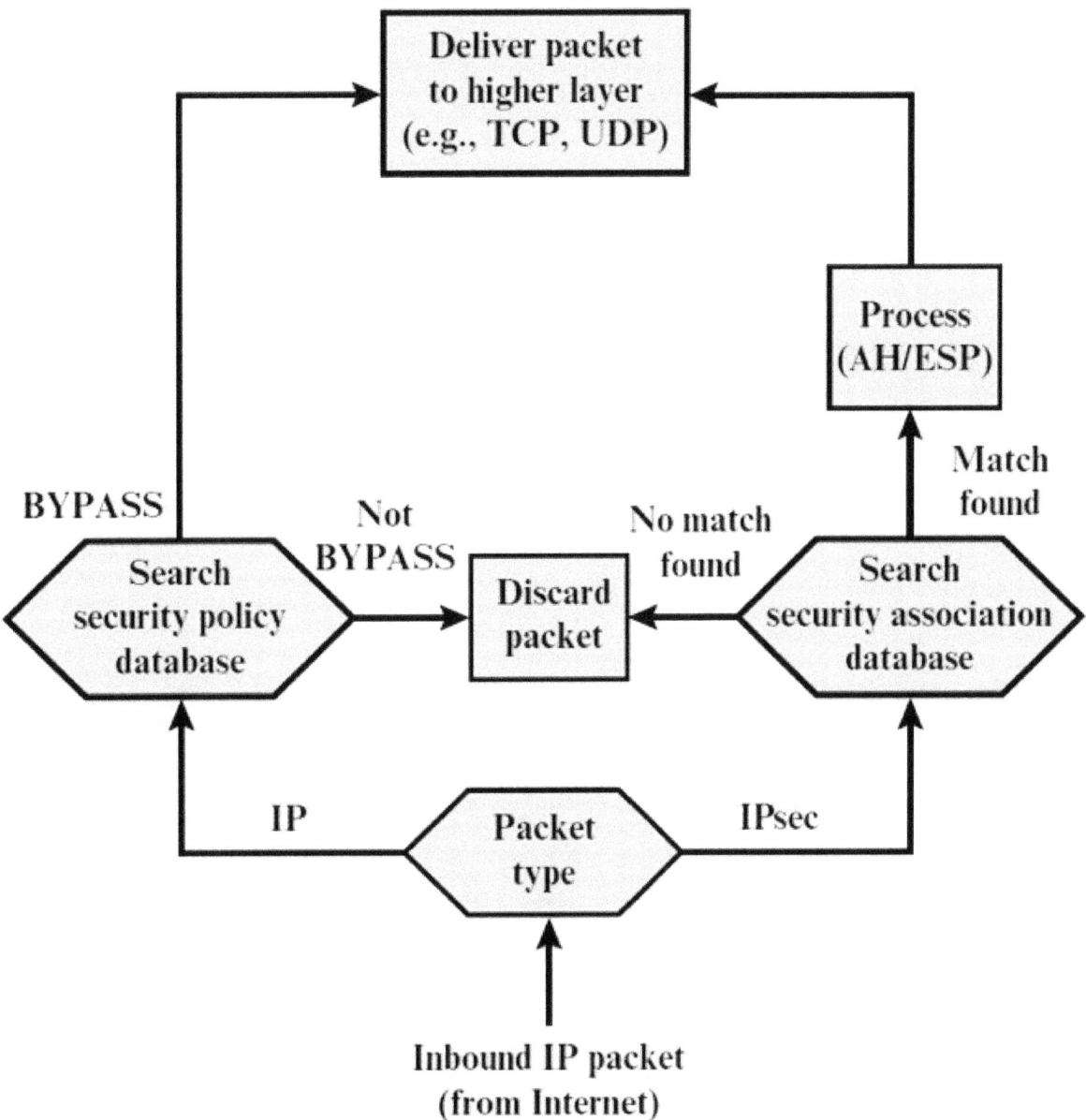

Figure 6.4: Processing Model for Inbound Packets

1. The IPsec protocol examines the IP Protocol field (IPv4) or Next Header field (IPv6) to determine whether an IP packet is unsecured or has ESP or AH headers/trailers.
2. If the packet is unsecured, IPsec looks for a match in the Security Policy Database (SPD). If the first matching entry in the SPD has a policy of BYPASS, the IP header is processed and removed, and the packet body is delivered to the next higher layer, such as TCP. However, if the first matching entry has a policy of PROTECT or DISCARD, or if there is no matching entry, the packet is discarded.
3. On the other hand, for a secured packet, IPsec searches the Security Association Database (SAD). If no match is found in the SAD, the packet is discarded. If a match is found, IPsec applies the appropriate ESP or AH processing. Subsequently, the IP header is processed and removed, and the packet body is delivered to the next higher layer, such as TCP.

6.1.4 IPsec Protocols

A group of technologies known as IPsec (Internet Protocol Security) secure network communication across IP networks. It offers security services for IP network traffic such data confidentiality, authentication, and encryption of critical information.

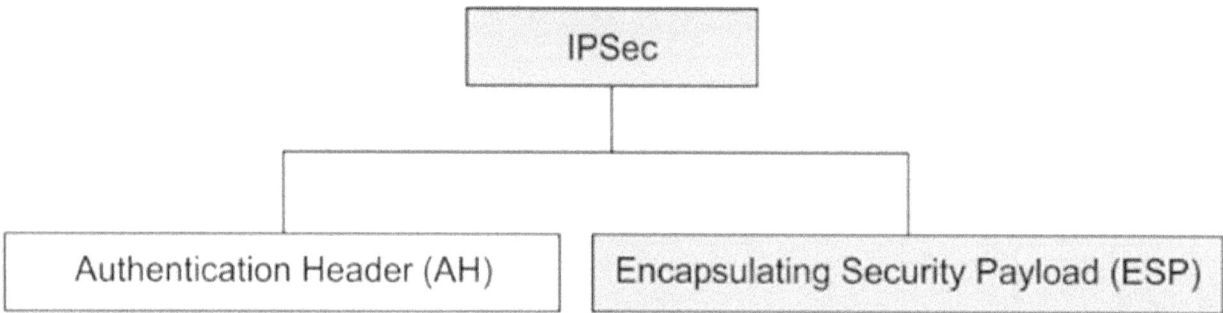

Figure 6.5: IPSec Protocols

6.2 Authentication Header (AH)

Data origin authentication, data integrity, and replay prevention are all provided by the Authentication Header (AH) protocol. Your data is sent in full view because AH does not offer data confidentiality.

With the checksum that a message authentication code, such MD5, creates, AH assures data integrity. The authentication mechanism used by AH contains a secret shared key that ensures data origin authentication. AH makes use of a sequence number field in the AH header to provide replay prevention. It is important to note that these three independent tasks are frequently grouped together and called "authentication" in this context. Simply said, AH makes sure that your data hasn't been altered with while travelling to its destination.

Although AH authenticates as much of the IP datagram as it can, the receiver cannot predict the contents of several fields in the IP header. These so-called changeable fields are not shielded by AH. However, AH always secures the IP packet's payload.

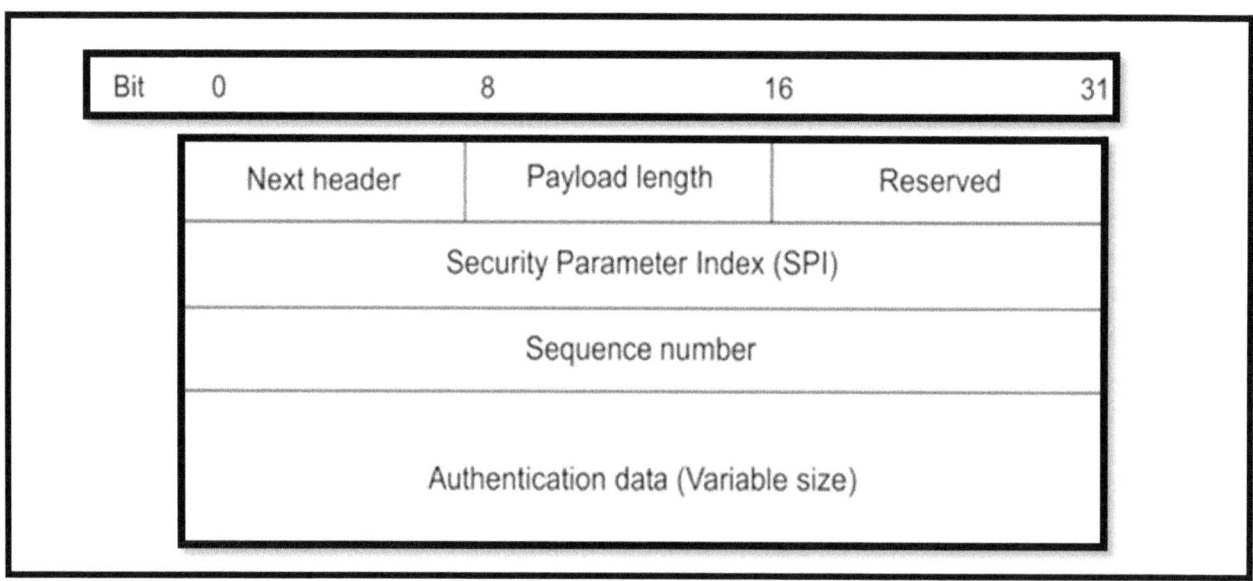

Figure 6.6: AH Format

Field	Description
Next header	This 8-bit field identifies the type of header that immediately follows the AH. For example, if an ESP header follows the AH, this field contains a value 50, whereas if another AH follows this AH, this field contains a value 51.
Payload length	This 8-bit field contains the length of the AH in 32-bit words minus 2. Suppose that the length of the authentication data field is 96 bits (or three 32-bit words). With a three-word fixed header, we have a total of 6 words in the header. Therefore, this field will contain a value of 4.
Reserved	This 16-bit field is reserved for future use.
Security Parameter Index (SPI)	This 32-bit field is used in combination with the source and destination addresses as well as the IPSec protocol used (AH or ESP) to uniquely identify the Security Association (SA) for the traffic to which a datagram belongs.
Sequence number	This 32-bit field is used to prevent replay attacks, as discussed later.
Authentication data	This variable-length field contains the authentication data, called as the Integrity Check Value (ICV), for the datagram. This value is the MAC, used for authentication and integrity purposes. For IPv4 datagrams, the value of this field must be an integral multiple of 32. For IPv6 datagrams, the value of this field must be an integral multiple of 64. For this, additional padding bits may be required. The ICV is calculated generating a MAC using the HMAC digest algorithm.

Figure 6.7: AH Format Field Details

6.2.1 AH: Dealing With Replay Attacks

To clarify, a replay attack occurs when an attacker acquires an authenticated packet and later sends it to the intended destination. If the same packet is received twice, the destination may encounter issues.

- Authentication Header (AH) includes a sequence number field, which is initially set to 0. Every time the sender sends a packet to the same recipient over the same Security Association (SA), it increases the value of this field by 1.
- The sender must ensure that this value does not return to 0 after reaching 232 -1. If the number of packets over the same SA exceeds this number, the sender should establish a new SA with the recipient. On the recipient's side, additional processing is required. The recipient maintains a sliding window with a default size of 64.
- The right edge of the window represents the highest sequence number N that has been received for a valid packet so far.

The following are the specifications for the window size (W) and the maximum highest sequence number (N) received for a valid packet.

- The value of N is always at the right edge of the window. For any packet with a sequence number in the range of (N − W + 1) to N that has been successfully authenticated, the corresponding slot in the window is marked. Any

packet within this range that is not successfully authenticated remains unmarked.
- When a packet is received, the receiver takes action based on its sequence number. This technique thwarts replay attacks, as the receiver will conclude that someone posing as the sender is attempting to resend a packet sent earlier if it receives a packet with a sequence number less than (N – W).
- However, this technique can cause the receiver to believe that a transmission is erroneous when it is not the case under extreme conditions. In this scenario, W is 64 and N is 100.
- The sender sends a burst of packets numbered 101 to 500, but due to network congestion and other issues, the receiver receives a packet with sequence number 300 first. The right edge of the window is then moved to 300 (N = 300) as the next packet received by the receiver is packet number 102.

The sequence number of the packet just received (102) is less than (N – W = 236), causing the third condition to trigger and the receiver to reject the v alid packet and raise an alarm. While such situations are rare, they can be avoided by optimizing the value of W.

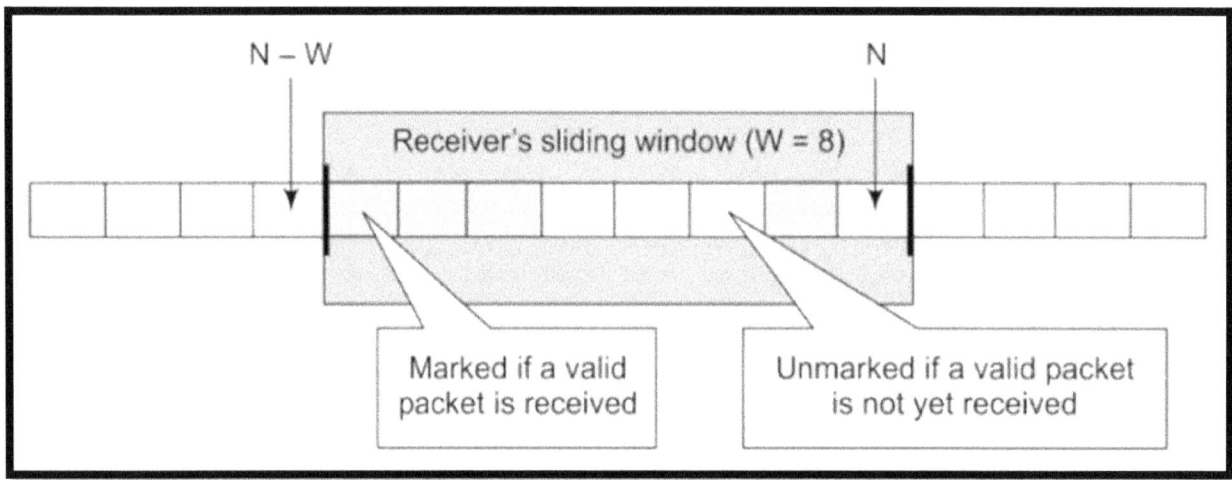

Figure 6.8: AH: Dealing with Replay Attack

6.2.2 Modes Of Operations

AH Transport Mode:

Transport mode is used when the security endpoints are the same as the data endpoints. In this mode, the AH or ESP header is inserted after the original IP header, and before the TCP header. This means that the entire IP packet, including the original IP header, is protected.

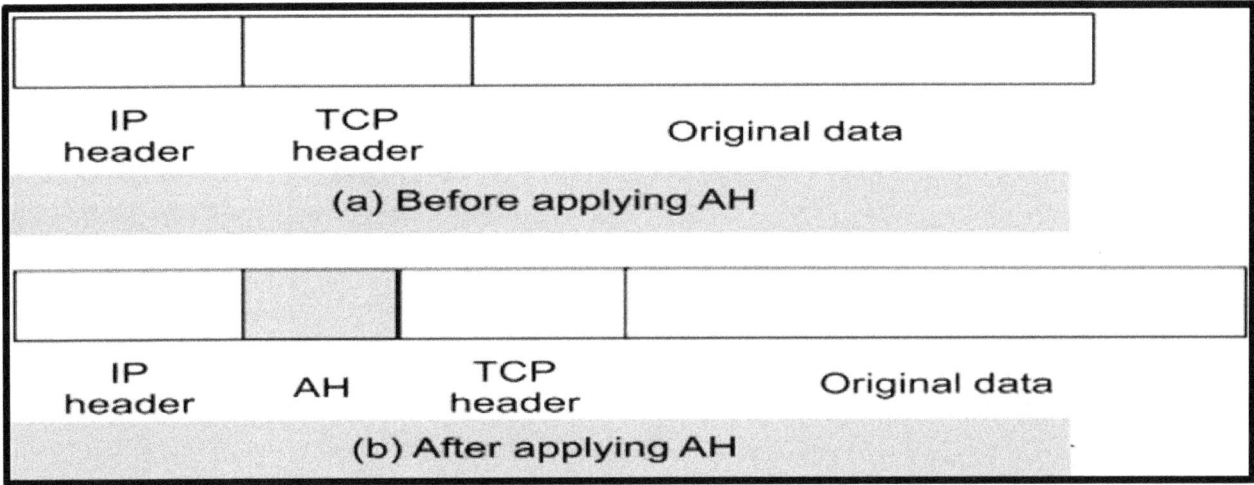

Figure 6.9: AH Transport Mode

The position of the AH header is between the original IP header and the original TCP header of the IP packet. This is because the AH header needs to be able to authenticate the entire IP packet, including the IP header. If the AH header was placed after the TCP header, then it would not be able to authenticate the IP header.

AH Tunnel Mode:

Tunnel mode is used when the security endpoints are different from the data endpoints. In this mode, a new IP header is created that contains the source and destination addresses of the security endpoints. The AH or ESP header is then inserted after the new IP header, and before the original IP header. This means that only the data portion of the IP packet is protected.

- In tunnel mode, the entire original IP packet is authenticated, including the original IP header. This is done by inserting a new outer IP header before the original IP header, and then inserting the AH header between the two IP headers.
- The AH header then authenticates the entire original IP packet, including the new outer IP header. This ensures that the original IP packet has not been tampered with in transit.

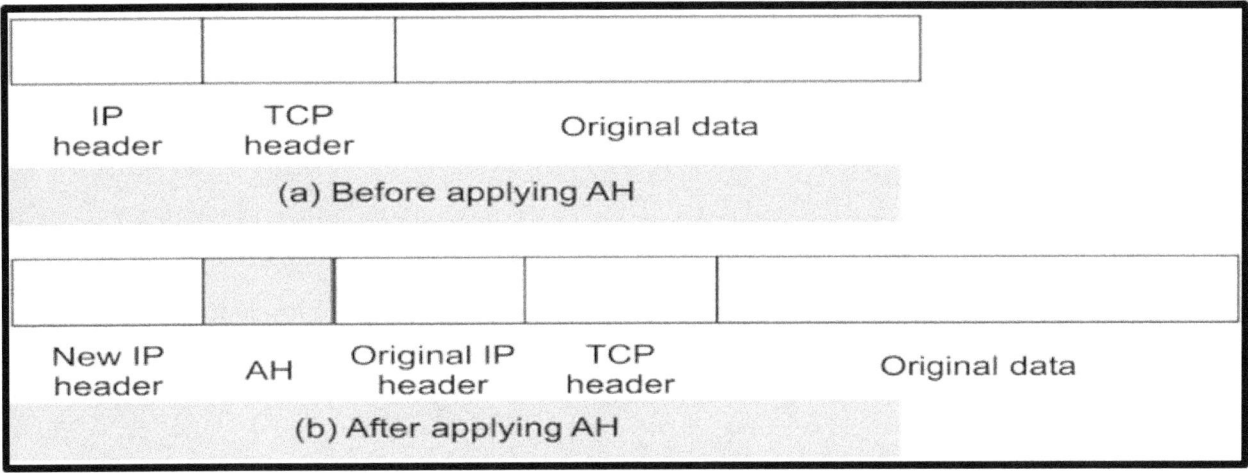

Figure 6.10: AH Tunnel Mode

6.3 Encapsulating Security Payload (ESP)

ESP provides confidentiality, data origin authentication, and connection lessness. integrity, anti-replay service (a form of partial sequence integrity) and (limited) Confidentiality of traffic flow. The range of services offered depends on the option selected at the time of Security Association (SA) formation and location Implementation in network topology.

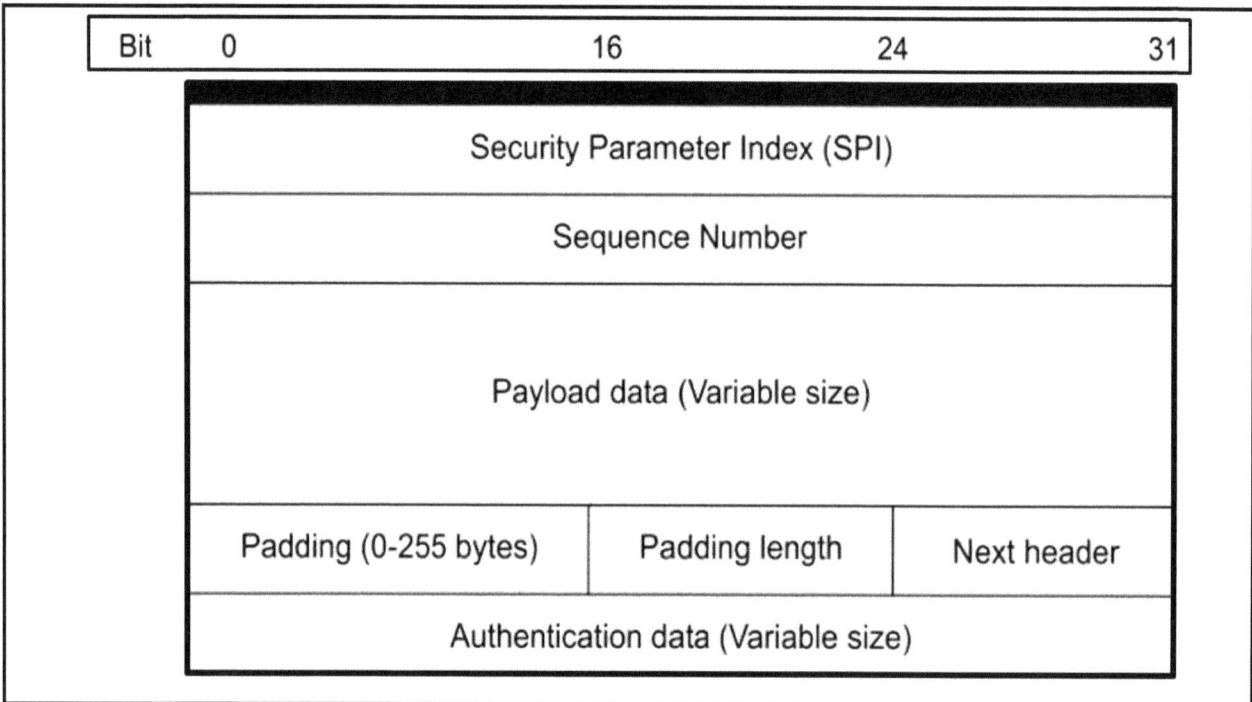

Figure 6.11: ESP Format

Field	Description
Security Parameter Index (SPI)	This 32-bit field is used in combination with the source and destination addresses as well as the IPSec protocol used (AH or ESP) to uniquely identify the Security Association (SA) for the traffic to which a datagram belongs.
Sequence number	This 32-bit field is used to prevent replay attacks, as discussed earlier.
Payload data	This variable-length field contains the transport layer segment (transport mode) or IP packet (tunnel mode), which is protected by encryption.
Padding	This field contains the padding bits, if any. These are used by the encryption algorithm or for aligning the padding length field, so that it begins at the third byte within the 4-byte word.
Padding length	This 8-bit field specifies the number of padding bytes in the immediately preceding field.
Next header	This 8-bit field identifies the type of encapsulated data in the payload. For example, a value 6 in this field indicates that the payload contains TCP data.
Authentication data	This variable-length field contains the authentication data, called as the Integrity Check Value (ICV), for the datagram. This is calculated over the length of the ESP packet minus the Authentication Data

Figure 6.12: Details of ESP Fields

ESP can work with a variety of encryption and authentication algorithms, including certified encryption algorithm such as GCM.

6.3.1 Modes Of Operations

ESP Transport Mode

Transport Mode is a security protocol that is used to encrypt and optionally authenticate the data carried by IP packets. It is inserted into the IP packet immediately before the transport layer header, such as TCP or UDP. This means that the entire transport layer segment, including the data and the transport layer header, is encrypted.

An ESP trailer is then added after the IP packet. The ESP trailer contains three fields:

- **Padding:** This field is used to pad the encrypted data to a multiple of the encryption block size.
- **Padding length:** This field indicates the length of the padding field.
- **Next header:** This field indicates the type of the next header in the IP packet. If authentication is also used, the ESP Authentication Data field is added after the ESP trailer. The ESP Authentication Data field is used to authenticate the entire cipher text, along with the ESP header. This ensures that the data has not been tampered with in transit.

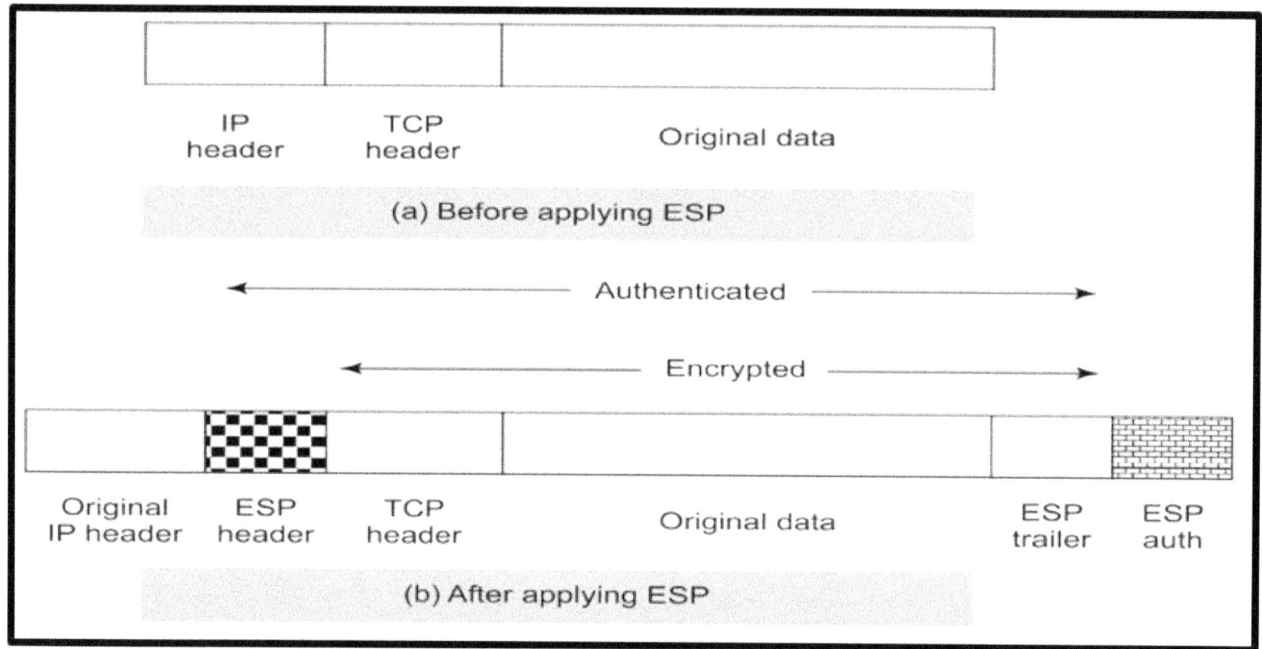

Figure 6.13: ESP Transport Mode

- At the sender's end, the block of data containing the ESP trailer and the entire transport layer segment is encrypted and the plain text of this block is replaced with its corresponding cipher text to form the IP packet. Authentication is appended, if selected. This packet is now ready for transmission
- The packet is routed to the destination. The intermediate routers need to take a look at the IP header as well as any IP extension headers, but not at the cipher text
- At the receiver's end, the IP header plus any plain text IP extension headers is examined. The remaining portion of the packet is then decrypted to retrieve the original plain text transport layer segment

ESP Tunnel Mode

Tunnel Mode is a security protocol that is used to encrypt an entire IP packet. It is inserted into the IP packet before the original IP header, and then the packet along with the ESP trailer is encrypted.

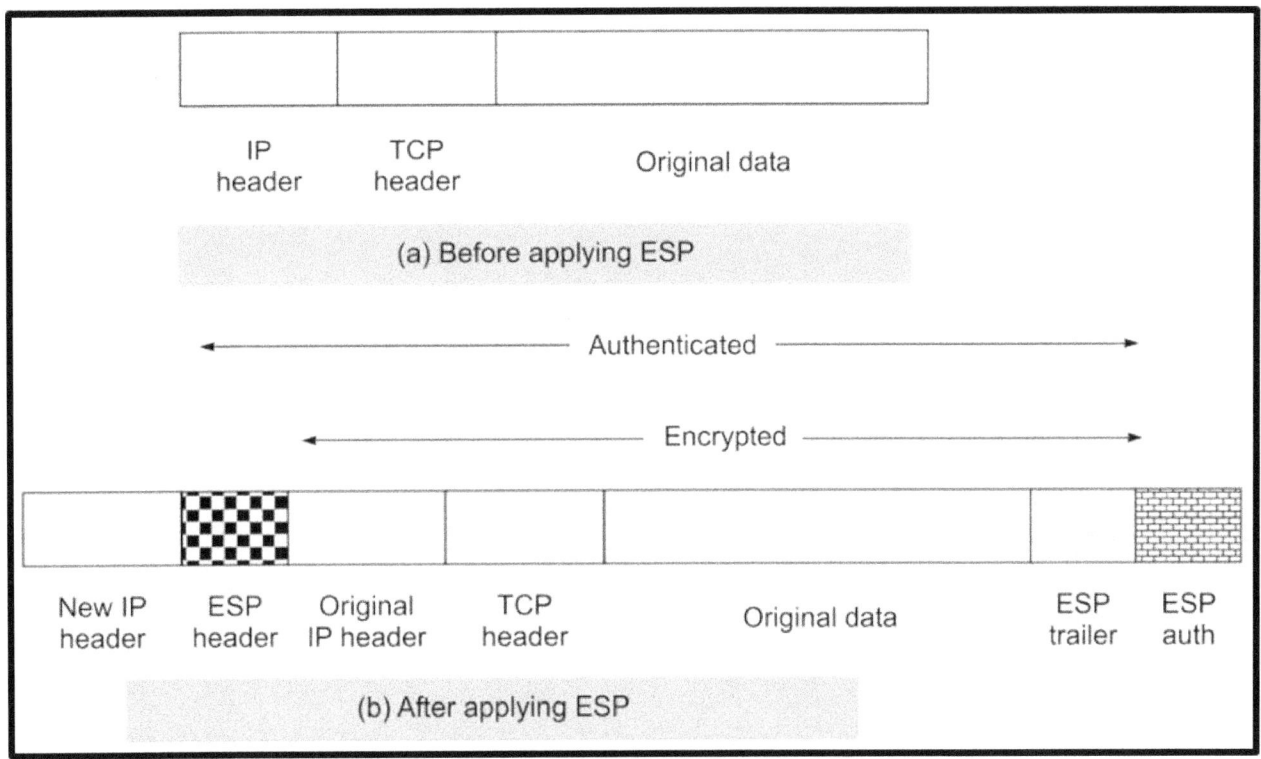

Figure 6.14: ESP Tunnel Mode

The ESP header contains several fields, including:

- **SPI:** Security Parameter Index. This field is used to identify the security association between the two endpoints.
- **Sequence number:** This field is used to track the sequence of packets that are sent.
- **Encryption algorithm:** This field indicates the type of encryption algorithm that is used to encrypt the packet.
- **Authentication algorithm:** This field indicates the type of authentication algorithm that is used to authenticate the packet.

The ESP trailer contains three fields:

- **Padding:** This field is used to pad the encrypted data to a multiple of the encryption block size.
- **Padding length:** This field indicates the length of the padding field.
- **Next header:** This field indicates the type of the next header in the IP packet.

The original IP header contains the destination address as well as intermediate routing information. This information is needed to route the packet to its destination. However, if the original IP header is encrypted, then the routing information would be lost. This would make it impossible to deliver the packet to its destination.

To address this issue, a new IP header is added to the encrypted packet. The new IP header contains only the destination address, and it is used to route the packet to the next hop. The intermediate routing information is not included in the new IP header, because it is not needed for routing.

6.4 Internet Key Exchange

IKE stands for Internet Key Exchange. It is a protocol that is used to establish and manage security associations (SAs) between two hosts. SAs are used to encrypt and decrypt traffic between the two hosts.

IKE is used to negotiate the following:

- The cryptographic algorithms that will be used to protect the traffic
- The keys that will be used to encrypt and decrypt the traffic
- The authentication methods that will be used to verify the identity of the two hosts

IKE is divided into two phases:

- **Phase 1**: In this phase, the two hosts authenticate each other and agree on the cryptographic algorithms that will be used.
- **Phase 2**: In this phase, the two hosts exchange keys and create SAs.

Once the IKE phases are complete, the AH and ESP protocols can be used to encrypt and decrypt traffic between the two hosts. The AH and ESP protocols are independent of the cryptographic algorithms that are used in IKE. This means that the same AH and ESP protocols can be used with different cryptographic algorithms.

In summary, IKE is used to negotiate the cryptographic algorithms and keys that will be used by the AH and ESP protocols to protect traffic between two hosts

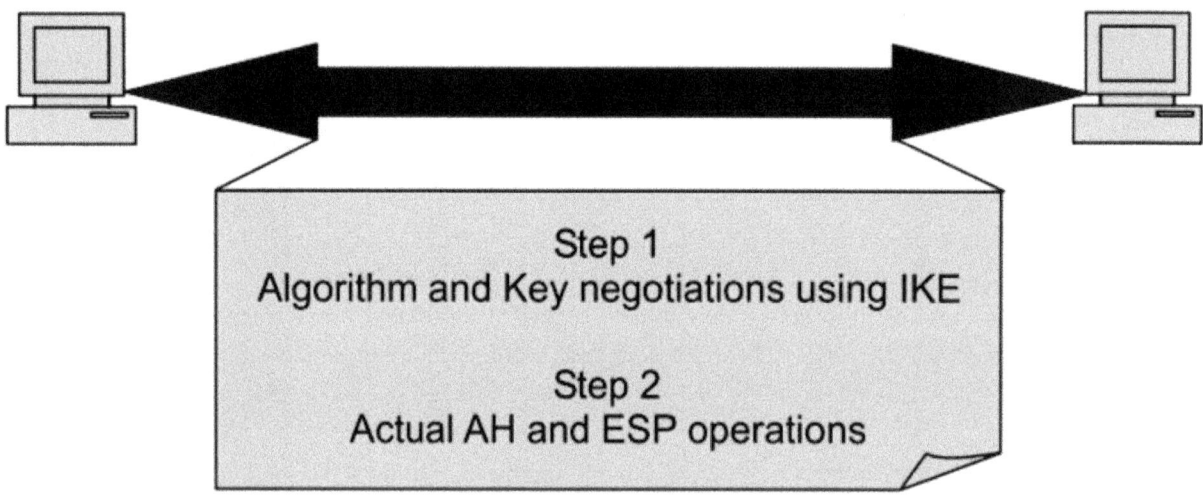

Figure 6.15: Key Exchange

6.4.1 Key Determination Protocol

The technique for determining IKE keys is an improvement over Diffie-Hellman key exchange. Remember that users A and B communicate in the following way while using Diffie-Hellman. Two global parameters, α, a primitive root of q, and q, a huge prime integer, have previously been agreed upon. A transmits its public key to B and chooses a random integer X_A as its private key. $Y_A = \alpha^{X_A} \bmod q$. Similar to how A receives B's public key, B chooses a random integer X_B as its private key. $\alpha^{X_B} \bmod q = B$. Now, both parties may calculate the secret session key:

$$K = (Y_B)^{X_A} \bmod q = (Y_A)^{X_B} \bmod q = \alpha^{X_A X_B} \bmod q$$

The Diffie-Hellman algorithm offers the following two appealing qualities:

- Secret keys are only generated when necessary. There is no need to keep hidden keys around for a long time because doing so makes them more vulnerable.
- The only prerequisite for the exchange is agreement on the global parameters; no pre-existing infrastructure is needed.

Features Of IKE Key Determination:

There are five fundamental characteristics that define the IKE key determination algorithm:

1. To prevent clogging assaults, it uses a system called as cookies.
2. It facilitates group negotiations between the two sides, which in essence defines the Diffie-Hellman key exchange's general characteristics.
3. To guard against replay assaults, it employs nonces.
4. It makes Diffie-Hellman public key values transferable.
5. In order to prevent man-in-the-middle attacks, it authenticates the Diffie-Hellman exchange.

IKE key determination supports three distinct authentication techniques:

- **Digital signatures:** The transaction is verified by signing a hash that is both parties can access and encrypting it with their respective private keys. Important factors, such as user IDs and nonces, are used to construct the hash.
- **Public-key encryption:** The exchange is verified by using the sender's private key to encrypt parameters like IDs and nonces.
- **Symmetric-key encryption:** The exchange can be authenticated by symmetric encryption of the exchange parameters using a key obtained through an out-of-band technique.

CHAPTER SEVEN

Threats and Malwares in Network

Network security is the deployment and oversight of cyber security solutions to safeguard an organization's IT systems from attacks and breaches. Network security is the integration of various technologies, processes, and devices into a comprehensive strategy that safeguards the integrity, confidentiality, and authenticity of computer networks.

Network security is a set of rules and configurations that use software and hardware technologies to secure the network and its data. It covers policies relating to the handling of sensitive information. Organizations of all sizes, sectors, or types of infrastructure must implement network security to safeguard themselves against an ever-evolving cyber threat landscape. But given that today's complex network topologies have a larger, more open attack surface than the standard perimeter-based network, this approach cannot meet their needs.

Look for security vulnerabilities everywhere—in devices, data, users, locations, and applications. Common network security threats include malicious software (malware), phishing schemes, and Distributed Denial of Service (DDoS). Threat actors are aware of how vulnerable modern networks are and use advanced technologies, such as automation and botnets powered by artificial intelligence (AI), to find vulnerabilities, exploit them, and avoid detection.

7.1 Threats in Networks

Effort to access a network or its resources without authorization or to prevent a network from functioning normally is considered as a network threat. Individuals, groups, or even nation-states may represent a danger to a network.

Malware are malicious software applications that are used to acquire data about victims from tampered with equipment. After successful deployments, hackers can mine devices for sensitive data (such as email addresses, bank account numbers, and passwords) and use it for identity theft, extortion, or other commercially destructive activities.

Malware consists of:

- **Worms** spread to other devices by taking advantage of flaws in computer systems.
- **Rootkits** grant unauthorized access to systems by granting false access privileges without the victim's knowledge.
- **Trojan viruses** slink under a network's radar by hitchhiking on other software.
- **Spyware** collects data on how owners use their devices.
- **phishing attacks** use to access networks and steal personal information, such as credit card numbers, hackers use.

Phishing attacks can take the form of emails, texts, or phone calls. They are similar to rogue security software in that they are created to look legitimate. As a result, victims are persuaded to click on malicious links or download malware. -laden accessories

- A **bot** is a small program that automates web requests with various goals.
- **Bots** carry out activities without the assistance of humans, such as scanning website material and testing credit card information that have been stolen.

- **Bot attacks** were initially used primarily for spam and denial of service, but have developed into complex enterprises with economies and infrastructure that enable waging additional, more damaging attacks.
- A bot attack uses automated web requests to defraud, manipulate, or disrupt applications, websites, end-users, or APIs.

Distributed Denial of Service (DDoS) attack makes use of several hacked computer systems to assault a target and deny users access to the resource. These attacks make it difficult to distinguish between legitimate and compromised traffic. An advanced persistent threat (APT) is a targeted and prolonged attack during which intruders gain unauthorized access to a network, remaining undetected for a long time. Threat actors typically launch APT attacks to steal data rather than cause damage to the target's n. Actors select high-value targets like major businesses and nation-states in order to secure a return on their investment.

Drive-by download attack
It happens when malicious software is unintentionally downloaded to a computer or mobile device, leaving the user vulnerable to a cyberattack. A drive-by cyberattack does not need the user to click on anything, hit download, or open a malicious email attachment, unlike other types of assaults that do. Drive-by downloads take use of operating system, web browser, or application security holes that may exist owing to insufficient or failed upgrades.

DNSAttack
This attack was designed for usability rather than security, so threat actors can use the communication between clients and servers to launch attacks. Threat actors frequently exploit the plaintext communication between clients and DNS servers. Another attack strategy involves accessing a DNS provider's website using stolen credentials and redirecting DNS records.

Internal Security Threats
Human mistake accounts for over 90% of cyberattacks; examples include phishing scams, hasty decisions, weak passwords, and more.

Insider activities that harm your company's network and sensitive data can lead to downtime, lost sales, and irate clients.

Rogue security software
Rogue security software tricks businesses into thinking their IT infrastructure is down due to a virus. Once a device is infected with a rogue programmed, the malware spams the victim with messages, forcing them to pay for a non-existent security solution, which is frequently malware. It typically looks like a warning message sent by a legitimate anti-malware solution. Rogue security software might damage your current cyber security programmers to strengthen their attack.

Ransomware
This is a type of malware that encrypts files on infected computers and holds them for ransom, compelling users to pay for a decryption key to free the data. This can take the form of ransomware-as-a-service (RaaS). RaaS providers create programs that consumers may employ to create custom malware and conduct cyberattacks Examples of RaaS that are often used are **BlackMatter**, **LockBit**, **DarkSide**, and **REvi**.

Computer viruses
Computer Viruses are frequently bundled with files that may be downloaded from emails or websites. Once you open the file, the virus takes advantage of flaws in your software to infect your computer with harmful code that can interrupt network traffic, steal data, and do other things. Viruses and worms are two different types of malwares, but they differ in how they infiltrate computer networks. Worms may infect networks as soon as they penetrate a company's IT infrastructure, whereas computer viruses require the host (the file) to be accessed in order to infect systems.

7.2 Threats in Transit

Before starting the actual attack, the attacker can obtain a lot of information about the victim. Once the attack is planned, the attacker is prepared to start.

The attacker has a variety of techniques to cause harm in a computing environment. When a network involves data in transit, we first consider potential harm between a sender and a receiver.

Loss of confidentiality, integrity, or availability to data, hardware or software, processes, or other assets.

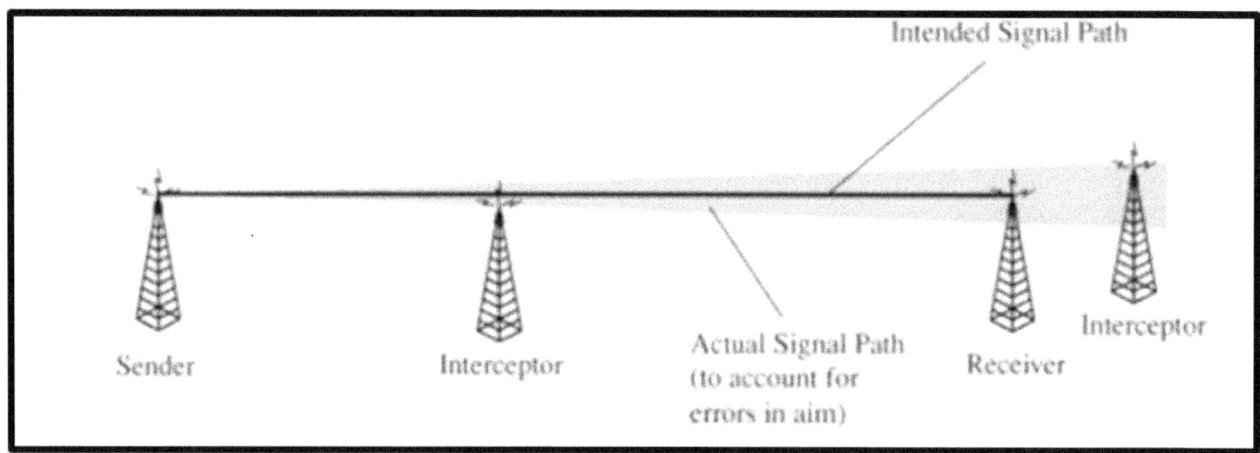

Figure 7.1: Threats in Transit

7.3 Eavesdropping and Wiretapping

Eavesdropping implies overhearing without exerting any additional effort.

- For instance, we might say that an attacker (or a system administrator) is eavesdropping by monitoring all traffic passing through a node.
- Administrators might have a legitimate purpose, such as watching for inappropriate use of resources (for example, visiting non-work-related websites).

Wiretap is a more aggressive phrase that denotes intercepting communications with some effort.

- **Passive wiretapping** is simply "listening," similar to eavesdropping.
  However, **active wiretapping** entails inserting something into the conversation.
- For example, Marvin could substitute Manny's communications with his own or fabricate messages ostensibly from Manny.
- The word wiretapping, which was developed from listening in on telegraph and telephone communications, usually conjures up a physical act in which a gadget harvests information as it runs across a wire. However, no physical interaction is required.
- Wiretapping operates differently depending on the type of communication medium used, and can be done secretly such that neither the sender nor the recipient of a message is aware that the contents have been intercepted.
- **Satellite communication, optical fibre, cable, microwave, and wireless**
- Each LAN connector (such as a computer board) has a unique address; each board and its drivers are programmed to label all packets from its host with its unique address (as a sender's "return address") and to take from the net only those packets addressed to its host.
- At the most local level, all signals in an Ethernet or other LAN are available on the cable for anyone to intercept.

A device called a **packet sniffer** can retrieve all packets on the LAN.

- Alternatively, one of the interface cards can be reprogrammed to have the supposedly unique address of another existing card on the LAN so that two different cards will both fetch **packets** for one address.
- The rogue card will need to re-send copies of the packets it has intercepted to the network in order to avoid detection.
- Fortunately (for now), these attacks don't happen very often because LANs are often exclusively utilised in places that are fairly friendly.

Clever attackers can take advantage of a wire's properties and read packets without any physical manipulation.

- Ordinary wire (and many other electronic components) emit radiation.
- An intruder can tap a wire and read radiated signals without making physical contact with the cable called **inductance**.
- A cable's signals travel only short distances and can be blocked by other conductive materials.
- The simplest method of intercepting a cable is by direct cut.
- If a cable is severed, all service on it stops.
- As part of the repair, an attacker can easily splice in a secondary cable, which then receives a copy of all signals along the primary cable.
- There are methods to be less visible while achieving the same result.
- For example, the attacker could deliberately expose some of the outside conductor and connect to it, followed by carefully exposing some of the inner conductor and connecting to it.
- Both of these activities modify the resistance of the cable, known as its **impedance**.

- In the first case, the repair itself changes the impedance, and the impedance change can be explained (or hidden) as part of the repair.
- Signals on a network are **multiplexed**, which means that more than one signal is transmitted at the same time.
- For example, two analogue (sound) signals can be combined, like two tones in a musical chord, and two digital signals can be combined by interleaving, like playing cards being shuffled.
- A LAN carries distinct packets, but data on a WAN may be heavily multiplexed as it leaves its sending host.
- The fact that **microwave signals** are broadcast through the air rather than along a wire makes them more accessible to outsiders.
- A transmitter's signal is typically focused on the corresponding receiver.
- The signal path is fairly wide to ensure that it reaches the receiver. From a security perspective, the wide swath is an invitation to trouble.
- One can pick up a full broadcast from an antenna that is situated close to but slightly off the direct focal point, in addition to intercepting a microwave transmission by interfering with the line of sight between sender and receiver.
- However, because of the large volume of traffic carried by microwave links, it is unlikely but not impossible that someone will be able to separate an individual transmission from all the others interleaved with it.
- A privately owned microwave link, carrying only communications for one organisation, is not as well protected by volume.

Satellite communication suffers from the same problem of being dispersed over a larger area than the intended point of reception.

- Different satellites have different characteristics, but some signals can be intercepted in an area several hundred miles wide and a thousand miles long.

- However, because satellite communications are often massively multiplexed, the danger of any single transmission being intercepted is low.

Optical fibre has two key security benefits over other transmission media:

- First, the entire optical network must be properly tuned each time a new connection is created; as a result, no one can tap an optical system without being detected; and second, no one can tap an optical system without being detected.
- Clipping only one fibre in a bundle will break the network's equilibrium.
- Second, optical fibre delivers light energy, not electricity. Light does not emit a magnetic field like electricity. As a result, an inductive tap on an optical fibre connection is impossible.
- However, using fibre does not guarantee security any more than using encryption does.
- Repeaters, splices, and taps along a cable are locations where data may be available more easily than in the fibre cable itself.
- Connections from computing equipment to the fibre may also be points for penetration. Fibre is far more secure than cable on its own, but it is not without flaws.

Wireless (commonly known as WIFI) connections allow people to travel freely within an office, house or building while retaining a connection.

- Wireless computer connections share the same frequencies as garage door openers, local radios, some cordless telephones, and other very short distance applications.
- Wireless communications travel by radio.
- Wireless computer connections share the same frequencies as garage door openers, local radios, some cordless telephones, and other very short distance applications.
- However, interference is not the most serious issue; it is interception.
- Consider a typical ten-story office building.
- Assume you set up a wireless base station (receiver) in the corner of the top floor.
- That station could receive signals transmitted from the opposite corner of the ground floor.
- If a similar building was adjacent, the signal could also be received throughout that building Many people could and do take advantage of a network wiretap, whether passive or active.
- A strong signal can be easily picked up.
- A wireless signal can be picked up several miles away with an inexpensive, tuned antenna.
- In other words, someone who wanted to pick up your particular signal could do so from several streets away.
- Parked in a truck or van, the interceptor could monitor your communications for quite some time without arousing suspicion.

7.4 Protocol Flaws

- Each acceptable protocol is identified by its Request for Comment (**RFC**) number.
- Internet protocols are publicly available for review by the whole Internet community Many problems with protocols were identified and corrected by sharp reviewers before the protocol was established as a standard.
- However, protocol definitions are made and reviewed by fallible humans. Protocols are also implemented by fallible humans. For example, TCP connections are established using sequence numbers.
- The client (initiator) sends a sequence number to open a connection, the server responds with that number and its own sequence number, and the client responds with the server's sequence number.

- Suppose (as Morris [MOR85] points out) someone can guess a client's next sequence number.
- That person could impersonate the client in an interchange.
- Sequence numbers are incremented regularly, so it can be easy to predict the next number.
- Protocol flaws are vulnerabilities in the design or implementation of a protocol that can be exploited by attackers to gain unauthorized access to a system or network.

Protocol flaws can be caused by a number of factors, including:

- **Design errors:** These are errors that are made in the original design of the protocol. Design errors can be difficult to identify and fix, as they may not be apparent until the protocol is actually implemented and used.
- **Implementation errors:** These are errors that are made when the protocol is implemented in software. Implementation errors can be more easily identified and fixed than design errors, as they can be seen in the code that implements the protocol.
- **Misconfiguration:** This is the incorrect configuration of a protocol. Misconfiguration can lead to vulnerabilities that can be exploited by attackers.

Protocol flaws can be exploited in a number of ways, including:

- **Man-in-the-middle attacks:** These attacks involve an attacker intercepting communications between two parties and then injecting malicious code into the communications.
- **Replay attacks:** These attacks involve an attacker capturing a legitimate communication and then replaying it at a later time.
- **Forgery attacks:** These attacks involve an attacker creating a fraudulent communication that appears to be legitimate.

There are a number of things that can be done to protect against protocol flaws, including:

- **Using a secure protocol:** There are a number of secure protocols available, such as TLS and SSH. These protocols should be used whenever possible to protect communications from eavesdropping and other attacks.
- **Keeping software up to date:** Software updates often include security patches that can help to protect against protocol flaws. It is important to keep software up to date to ensure that the latest security patches are installed.
- **Using a firewall:** A firewall can help to protect a system or network from unauthorized access. Firewalls can be configured to block traffic that is associated with known protocol flaws.
- **Educating users:** Users should be educated about the risks of protocol flaws and how to protect themselves. Users should be aware of the signs of a protocol flaw attack and what to do if they think they have been attacked.

CHAPTER EIGHT

Network Security Controls

The preventative, investigative, corrective, and compensating methods used to safeguard a network against unauthorised access, usage, disclosure, interruption, alteration, or destruction are known as network security controls.

Network security measures come in three different categories.

- **Technical controls:** Tools like firewalls, intrusion detection systems, and antivirus software are used to apply these controls.
- **Administrative controls:** These controls are put into place through policies, practises, and training, such security awareness classes and password management rules.
- **Physical controls:** These measures, such closed doors and surveillance cameras, are used to safeguard a network's physical infrastructure.

8.1 Network Architecture

When building or modifying computer-based systems, we may think about their general design and plan to "build in" security as one of the main elements, just as it is the strongest control in so many other areas. A network's architecture or design can also have a big impact on how secure it is.

Segmentation may restrict the potential for harm in a network in two crucial ways, much as it was an effective security measure in operating systems:

- **Segmentation** decreases the number of risks and restricts the amount of harm that can be caused by a single vulnerability.
- Suppose a network introduces electronic commerce for Internet users.
- The core components of a network may include:

    ◦ Web server, which manages HTTP sessions for users;
    ◦ Application code, which displays your goods and services for purchase;

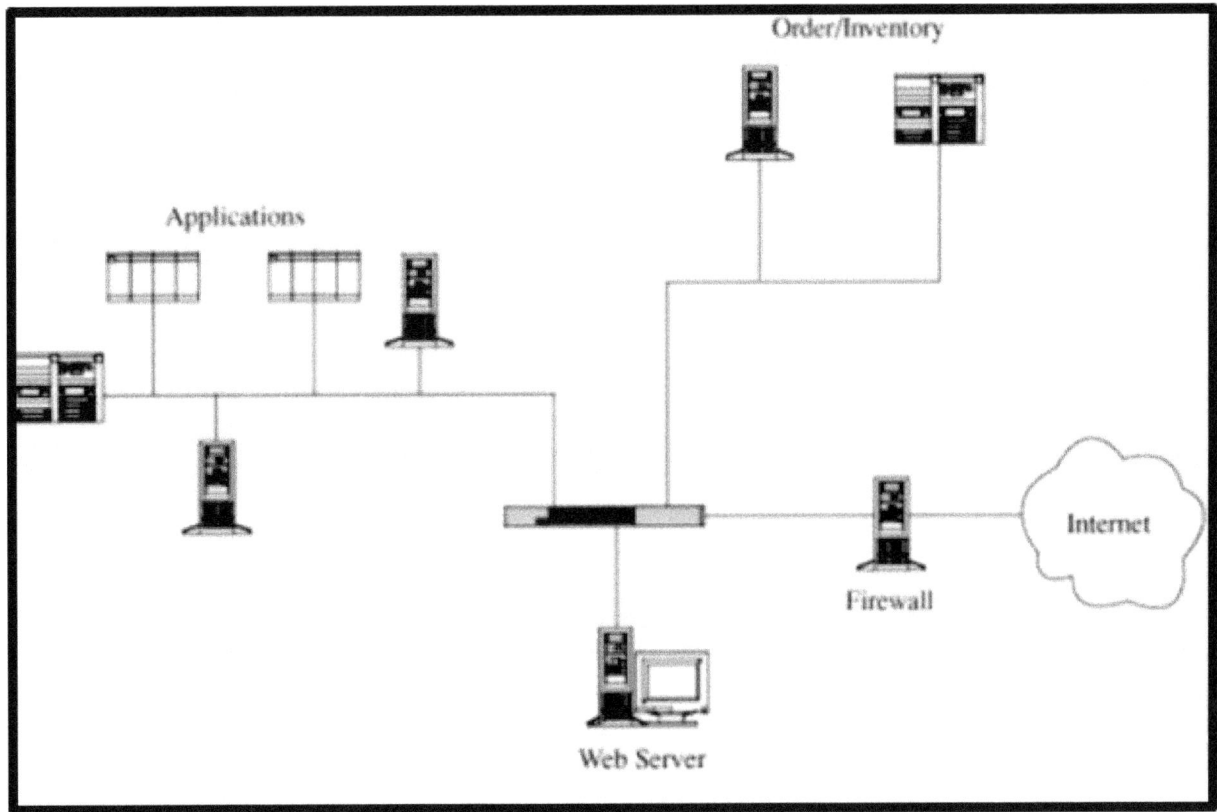

Figure 8.1: Network Architectur

- Database of goods, possibly with an accompanying inventory to track the amount of stock on hand and that is being requested from suppliers;
- Database of orders placed.

• Your network would be in difficulty if all these operations were carried out on a single computer: Your whole capacity for trade would be destroyed by any breach or malfunction of the device.
• A more secure design uses multiple segments.

Assume that one piece of equipment will be a web server box that the public may access. That box shouldn't also have other, more sensitive tasks on it to lessen the chance of an attack from outside the system, including user authentication or access to a repository of sensitive data. If any subsystem is hacked, the potential damage is reduced by using separate segments and servers that follow the concepts of least privilege and encapsulation.

Another kind of network segmentation is separate access. For example, let's say a network is being used for the "live" production system, testing the subsequent production version, and building future systems.

External users should only be able to access the live system, testers should only be able to access the test system, and developers should only be able to access the development system, if the network is properly segmented. Segmentation allows these three populations to coexist without running the risk that, for example, a developer will unintentionally change the production system.

- For example, the design on the previous slide has only one web server; lose it and all connectivity is lost. A better design would have two servers, using what is known as **failover mode**. In failover mode, the servers communicate with each other periodically, each determining if the other is still active. If one fails, the other will take over. **Redundancy** is another key architectural control. It allows a function to be performed on more than one node, to avoid "putting all the eggs in one basket."

- One way to assess the network architecture's tolerance for failure is to look for **single points of failure**. The architecture should make the network immune to failure. The architecture should at least ensure that the system tolerates failure in an acceptable way (such as slowing down but not stopping processing, or recovering and restarting incomplete transactions).
- For example, a single database in one location is vulnerable to all failures that could influence that site. We should consider whether there is a single point in the network that, if it were to fail, could prevent access to all or a sizable portion of the network.
- Distributing the database and placing copies of it on various network segments, possibly even in various physical places, might lessen the danger of major harm from a failure at any one point. Good network architecture minimises **single points of failure**.
- Implementing such a design frequently involves significant overhead; for example, the independent databases must be synchronised. However, in most cases, we can deal with the failure-tolerant features more easily than the damage brought on by a failed single link.
- **Schneider and Zhou [SCH05]** investigate distributed trust through a corps of communicating, state-sharing agents. The concept is simple: Just like with soldiers, you know some agents will be stopped and others will be subverted by the enemy, but some agents can work for good. Good agents might look for unsecured wireless access, software vulnerabilities, or embedded malicious code.
- **Schneider and Zhou** offer a design where no single agent is essential to the overall success but the group as a whole can be trusted.

8.2 Virtual Private Networks

A secure link between two networks across a public network, such the internet, is known as a virtual private network (VPN). Although connecting remote users to a business network via a VPN is a common use for them, they can also be used for other things like viewing geo-restricted content or enhancing online privacy.

By encrypting all of the traffic between the two networks, VPNs function. This implies that even if the traffic is intercepted, no one will be able to read it. Additionally, VPNs use tunnelling techniques to encapsulate the traffic so that it appears to originate from the distant user's network. This makes it less likely that firewalls or other security measures will block the remote user.

Site-to-site VPNs and remote access VPNs are the two main categories of VPNs. Two networks, such as a corporate network and a branch office network, can be connected via site-to-site VPNs. Remote users are linked to a business network via remote access VPNs.

Networks, both public and private, a private network is made up of computers owned by a single organisation that share information with one another. Local Area Networks (LAN), Metropolitan Area Networks (MAN), and Wide Area Networks (WAN) are examples of private networks. The public telephone system and the Internet are large collections of communicators that are generally unrelated to one another.

An effective firewall can divide a private network from a public network. A company wants to connect the networks of two of its branches, but they are quite a distance apart. One branch is in Mumbai, and the other is in Delhi.

Connect the two branches with the aid of a public network, such as the Internet. Connect the two branches using a personal network, such as running cables between the two offices or obtaining a leased line between the two branches.

- First one offers much more security and control. It is also rather complicated. The

- Second method appears to be simpler to adopt because no specific infrastructure has to be put up, but it also appears to be vulnerable to potential attacks. Laying cables between two cities is difficult and typically not permitted.

In order to use a public network (like the Internet) as if it were a private network (like a physical network created and controlled by you), we could combine the two solutions. **Virtual Private Networks (VPN)** provides such a solution. VPN offers high levels of security while requiring no special cabling on the part of the organisation that wants to use it.

In order to connect distant organisational networks or to enable remote access to a private network (such as the organization's intranet) securely over the Internet, a VPN is a tool that simulates a private network over a public network. VPNs combine the benefits of a public network (cheap and easily accessible) with those of a private network (secure and reliable). The use of virtual connections, which are transient and do not have any physical presence, is indicated by the term "virtual," and these connections are made up of packets.

8.2.1 VPN Architecture

A company has two networks, Network 1 and Network 2, that are physically separate from one another, and we wish to use a VPN to connect them.

- Install two firewalls, Firewall 1 and Firewall 2.
- The firewalls handle encryption and decryption.

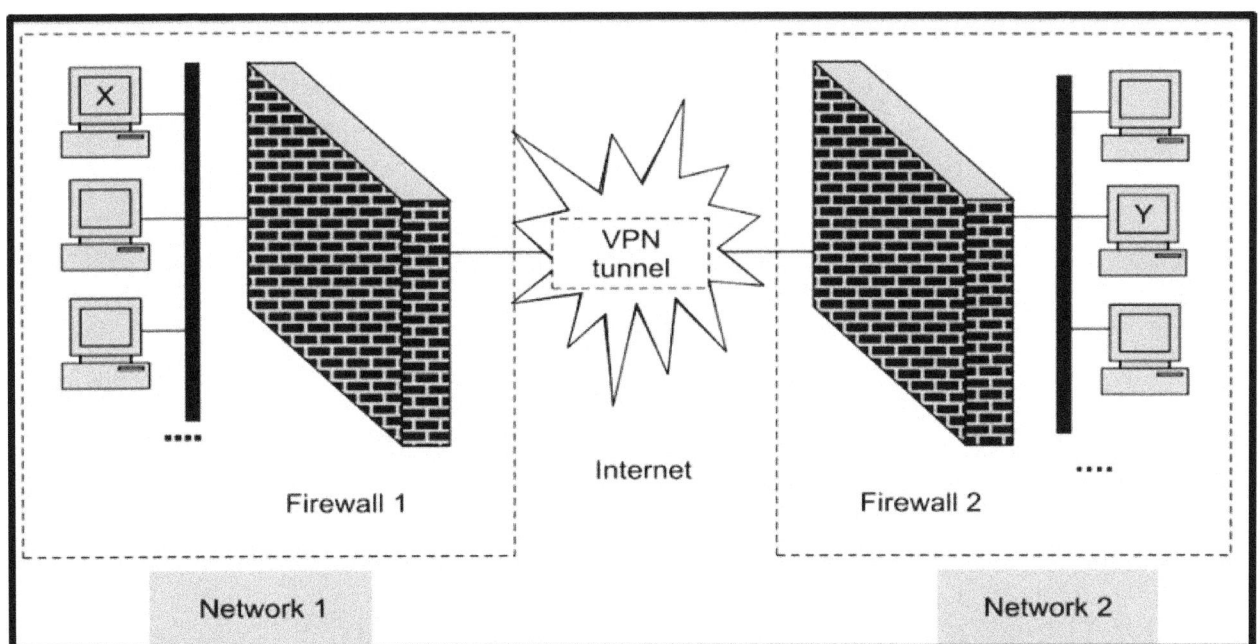

Figure 8.2: VPN Architecture

Consider a scenario in which host X on Network 1 wishes to transmit a data packet to host Y on Network 2. Host X produces the packet, inserting its own IP address as the source address and host Y's IP address as the destination address. Host X then delivers the packet using the proper mechanism.

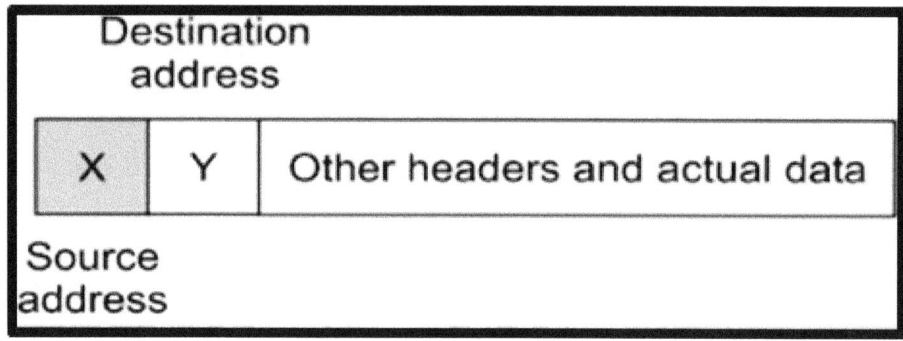

When a packet reaches Firewall 1, Firewall 1 adds new headers to the packet, changes the source IP address from host X to its own address (i.e., Firewall 1's IP address, say F1), and changes the destination IP address from host Y to Firewall 2's IP address, say F2.

Executes packet authentication and encryption, as appropriate, and sends the modified packet over the Internet.

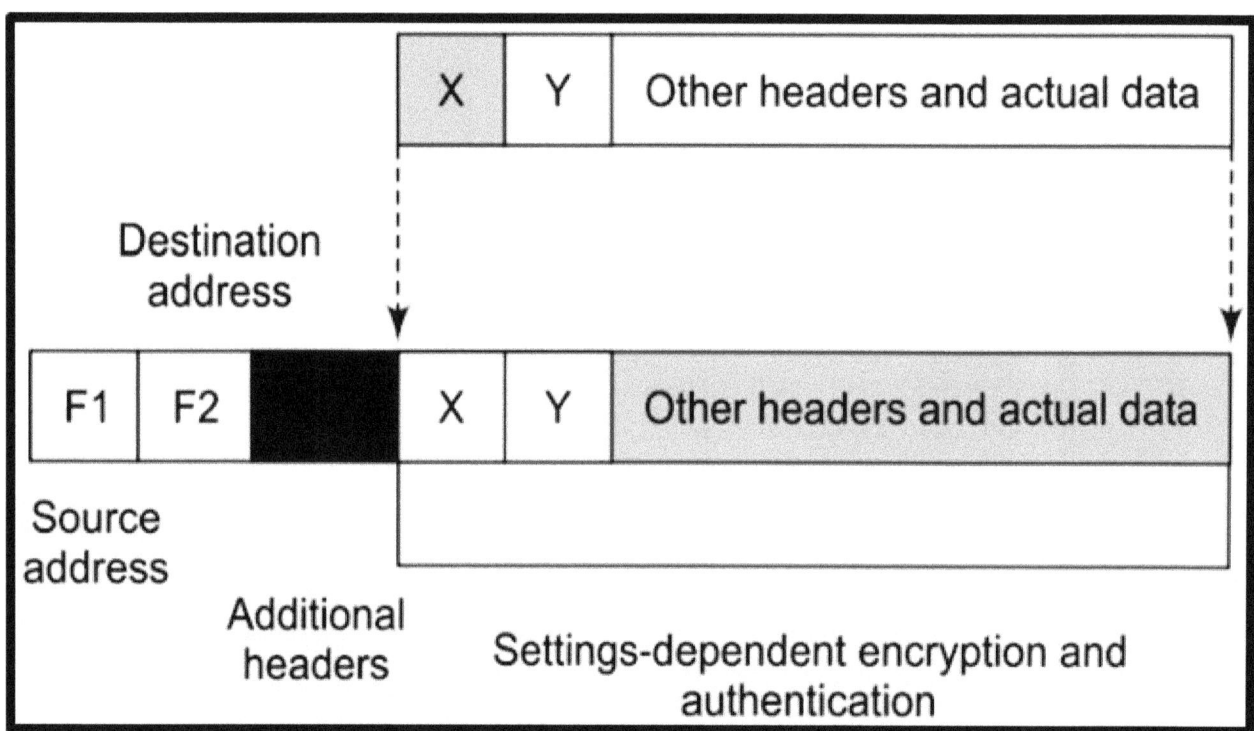

Packet travels through one or more routers to reach Firewall 2 over the Internet.

Firewall 2 discards the outer header and executes the necessary decryption and other cryptographic operations, producing the original packet as it was originally produced by host X. It next examines the packet's plain text contents and determines that host Y is its intended recipient because host Y is listed in the destination address. It then sends the packet to host Y.

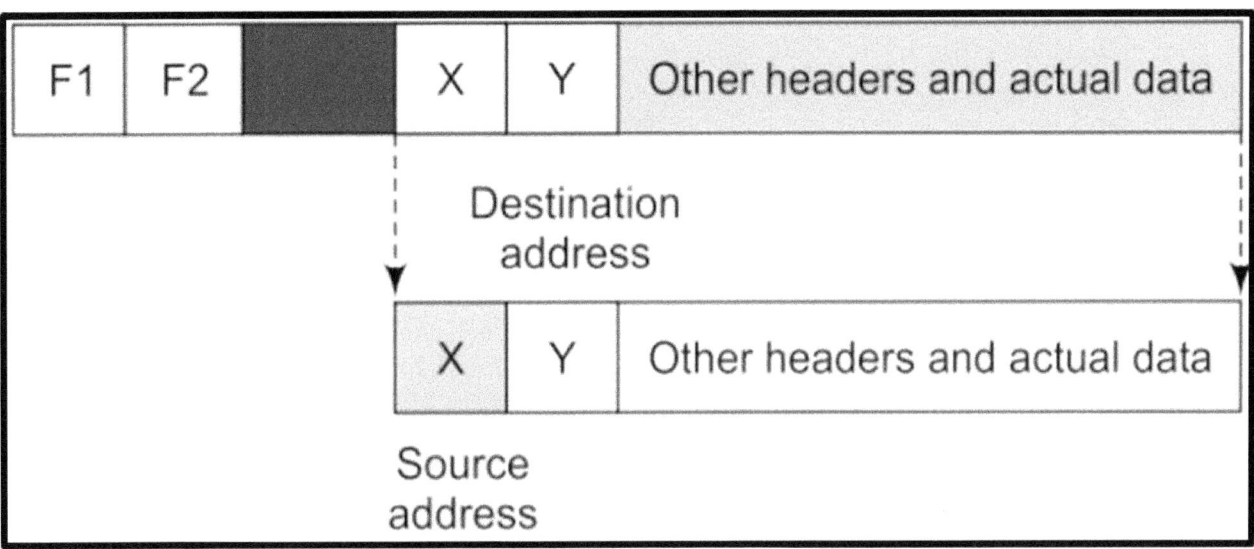

8.2.2 VPN Protocols:

Data packaging and transmission via a VPN tunnel are governed by a set of rules called a VPN protocol. These protocols are used by VPN companies to offer their customers dependable and secure connections.

There are three main VPN protocol:

- **The point-to-Point tunnelling protocol (PPTP)**: It is a straightforward and user-friendly VPN protocol that is widely supported by hardware and VPN service providers. It is not advised for use in high-security environments because it is not as secure as some of the other protocols compared to PPTP.
- **Layer 2 Tunnelling Protocol (L2TP)**: Itis an advancement and is thought to be more secure. L2TP includes the IPSec protocol for encryption and can be used for both user-to-LAN and LAN-to-LAN communications.
- **Internet Protocol Security (IPSec)**: VPN traffic can be encrypted using the security protocol known as Internet Protocol Security (IPSec). L2TP and other protocols, such as IPSec, may be used together or separately.

8.3 Public Key Infrastructure (PKI) and Certificates

A public key and a private key are used together in public key cryptography to encrypt data. The private key is kept a secret, whereas the public key can be shared with everyone. This makes it possible for users to encrypt data that can only be decoded by the owner of the private key. A system called public key cryptography encrypts and decrypts data using two keys: a public key and a private key. While the private key needs to be kept a secret, the public key can be shared with anybody. PKI is a system that controls users' public keys. It enables safe data encryption and decryption as well as user identity verification.

PKI provides consumers with the following services:

- **Making Certificates:** A certificate is a legal document that connects a user's identity to a public key. Users' identities can be confirmed via certificates, which can also be used to encrypt and decode data.
- **Certificate Issuance:** Users may receive certificates from a PKI. This indicates that the user's public key is legitimate and that the PKI can vouch for the user's identity.

- **Signing Certificates:** A PKI can sign certificates. This means that the PKI can add its credibility to the authenticity of the certificate.
- **Validate Certificate:** A PKI has the ability to validate certificates. As a result, the PKI is able to confirm the legitimacy of a certificate and the matching of a user's public key to their intended identity.
- **Invalidate Certificates:** A PKI has the ability to invalidate certificates. This implies that a certificate can be revoked by the PKI and declared invalid.

Housley and Polk [HOU01b] describe both the technical aspects and the procedural issues in developing a PKI. Policies define the rules under which the cryptographic systems should operate. Policies specify how to handle keys and valuable information and how to match level of control to level of risk.

The general idea is that a certificate authority is trusted, so users can delegate the creation, issuance, acceptance, and revocation of certificates to the authority, much like one would use a trusted bouncer to permit only certain people to enter a restricted nightclub. PKI creates entities, called certificate authorities, that implement the PKI policy on certificates.

A certificate authority's specific actions consist of the following.

- The management of public key certificates throughout their entire life cycle.
- The binding of a user's or system's identity to a public key with a digital signature.
- The planning of certificate expiration dates, and the publication of certificate revocation lists ensure that certificates are revoked as needed.

The functions of a certificate authority can be performed internally, by a commercial service, or by a trusted third party. PKI also involves a registration authority that serves as an interface between a user and a certificate authority. The registration authority captures and authenticates the identity of a user before sending a certificate request to the proper certificate authority. Before issuing a certificate to a user, a **registration authority (RA)** must confirm their identity. The degree of trust that can be placed in the issued certificates depends on how well the RA's identity verification procedure works. The certificates that are issued, for instance, won't be as reliable as certificates that are granted after the RA has confirmed the user's identification using more stringent techniques, like a **government-issued ID**, because the RA merely checks the user's name and email address.

Each certificate in a PKI is signed by a certificate at a higher level since PKIs are hierarchical systems. Because of this hierarchy, it is possible to trace the origin of a certificate's trust back to a root certificate, which is normally issued by a reputable third party. PKI is thus a logical fit for hierarchically structured organisations like governmental institutions. PKI standards come in a variety, which can make it challenging for businesses and government organisations to collaborate. To create interoperable PKI standards, however, there are initiatives in place, such as the Government PKI Interoperable Framework (GPIF) in the United States.

For example, a Federal PKI Initiative in the United States will eventually allow any U.S. government agency to send secure communication to any other U.S. government agency, when appropriate.

A national PKI is being developed for the US government as part of the Federal PKI Initiative (FPKI). Even if they employ various PKI systems, government entities will be able to securely communicate with one another thanks to the FPKI. Although the FPKI is currently being developed, it is anticipated to be finished in the upcoming years.

The European Union has a similar project. Major PKI solution providers include Baltimore Technologies, Northern Telecom/Entrust, and Indentures. The programme also specifies how commercial PKI-enabled tools should function, allowing agencies to purchase pre-made PKI products rather than building their own.

CHAPTER NINE

Web and System Security

Web security and system security are two important aspects of cybersecurity that protect organizations from a variety of threats. These two crucial components of cybersecurity that shield organisations from various. Web security describes the precautions used to guard websites and web applications against intrusion. This covers safeguarding against malicious software, phishing, cross-site scripting (XSS), SQL injection, and DoS assaults.

The steps performed to safeguard computer systems from assault are referred to as system security. Defending against viruses, unauthorized access, and data breaches is part of this. Organisations must use both system security and online security to fend off cyberattacks. Their breadth and purpose, however, varies from one another. While system security focuses on defending computer systems, web security is concerned with defending websites and web applications.

9.1 Web and Types of Webs Pages

Web is also referred to as the World Wide Web (WWW) or simply the net, documents and other web resources are identified by Uniform Resource Locators (URLs), which are sent from web servers to client devices via the Hypertext Transfer Protocol (HTTP). **Tim Berners-Lee created the Web in 1989 at CERN, a European research facility.** In 1991, the first website was made, and the Web soon spread throughout the world. Millions of individuals use the Web every day to get information, communicate with others, and conduct business.

A **Web Page** is a hypertext document that is given a specific Uniform Resource Locator (URL) to identify it. A web server sends web pages to the user, who then sees them on a web browser. A website is made up of numerous web pages connected by a common domain name. The term "web page" refers to a collection of paper pages that have been bound into a book.

9.1.1 Types of web Pages in Web Security

- Static Web Pages
- Dynamic Web Pages
- Active Web Pages

Static Web Pages:
Static web pages are those that don't have any interactive features or dynamic material. This indicates that they are sent to users in their raw form after being stored as static files on a web server. Due to the absence of exploitable code, static web pages are often less susceptible to security concerns than dynamic web pages.
Static web pages should be protected against security risks by:

- Use a secure web server: The static web pages' hosting web server ought to be set up with security tools like firewalls and intrusion detection systems.

- Update the static web pages' files: The static web pages' files should be maintained current with the most recent security updates.
- Check for malware on static web sites: Static web pages need to be regularly checked for malware.
- Consider using a content delivery network (CDN): Static web pages can be protected from DDoS assaults with the aid of a CDN.

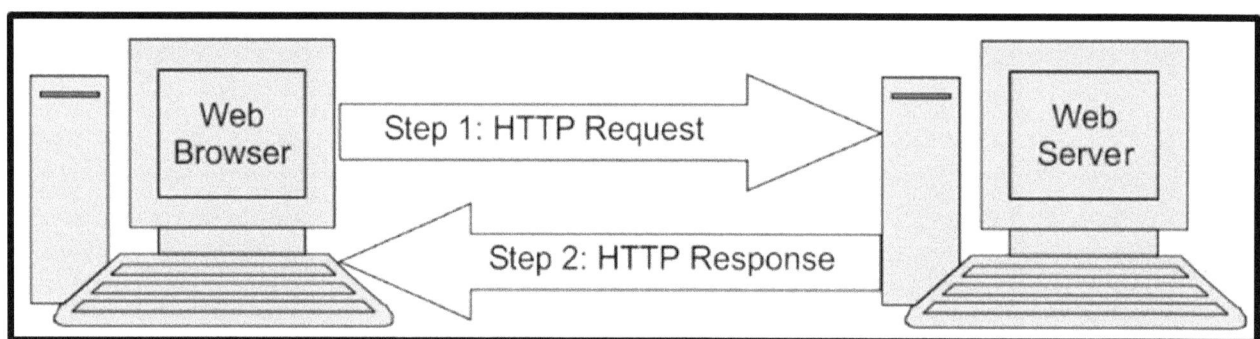

Figure 9.1: Static Web Pages

Dynamic Web Pages:

A dynamic web page is one that a web server creates instantly in response to a user request. This means that based on the user's input or other conditions, the content of the website may change each time it is visited.

For websites that need to be updated often, including news sites, blogs, and e-commerce sites, dynamic web pages are widely employed. They can also be used to give users more customised experiences, for example, by showing them content that is more relevant to their location or interests.

The two primary categories of dynamic web pages are:

1. Web servers use scripting languages like PHP, ASP, or JSP to create **server-side dynamic sites**. The scripting language is used to build the HTML code for the page after gaining access to a database or other data source.
2. A scripting language, such as JavaScript, is used by the user's web browser to create **client-side dynamic sites**. After interacting with the user, the scripting language is utilized to create the HTML code for the page.

Compared to static web pages, dynamic web pages provide a number of benefits, such as:

- The capacity to regularly update content. It is possible to update dynamic web pages without altering the underlying HTML code. This makes it simple to update websites with the most recent information.
- The capability of content personalization. Each user's experience can be customised with the use of dynamic web pages. Depending on the user's location, interests, or other characteristics, various content may be displayed to achieve this.
- The capacity for user interaction. Real-time user interaction is possible with dynamic web sites. JavaScript can be used to accomplish this by reacting to events or user input.

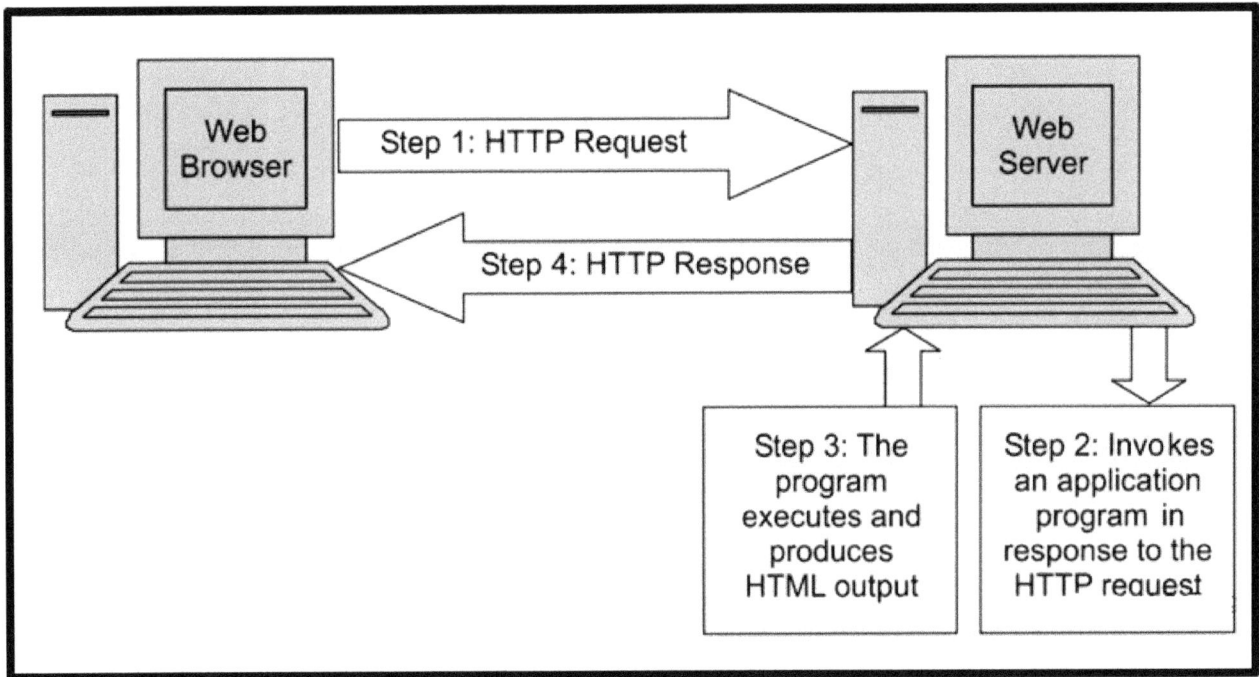

Figure 9.2: Dynamic Web Pages

Active Web Pages:
A website page that performs dynamic activities using client-side scripting is said to be active. This indicates that rather than the server performing the logic, it is the browser. This can be applied to develop compelling and interactive web experiences. For building interactive and interesting web experiences, active web pages can be an effective tool. But it's crucial to use them sensibly. They can impede a web page's performance if utilized excessively.

The following are some advantages of using active web pages:

- Greater interaction. The use of active web pages can produce more **interactive** and captivating web experiences. This may encourage users to stay interested and return for more.
- **Personalization**. Each user's experience can be customised using active web pages.
- Depending on the user's interests or location, different content may be displayed to achieve this a better **usability**. A website's usability can be increased by using active web pages.

Here are some of the drawbacks of using active web pages:

- **Performance**. Active web pages can slow down the performance of a website if they are not used wisely. This is because the browser has to execute the JavaScript code every time the page is loaded.
- **Security**. Active web pages can be vulnerable to security attacks. This is because the JavaScript code can be executed by the browser, which means that it can be used to steal data or to inject malicious code into a website.

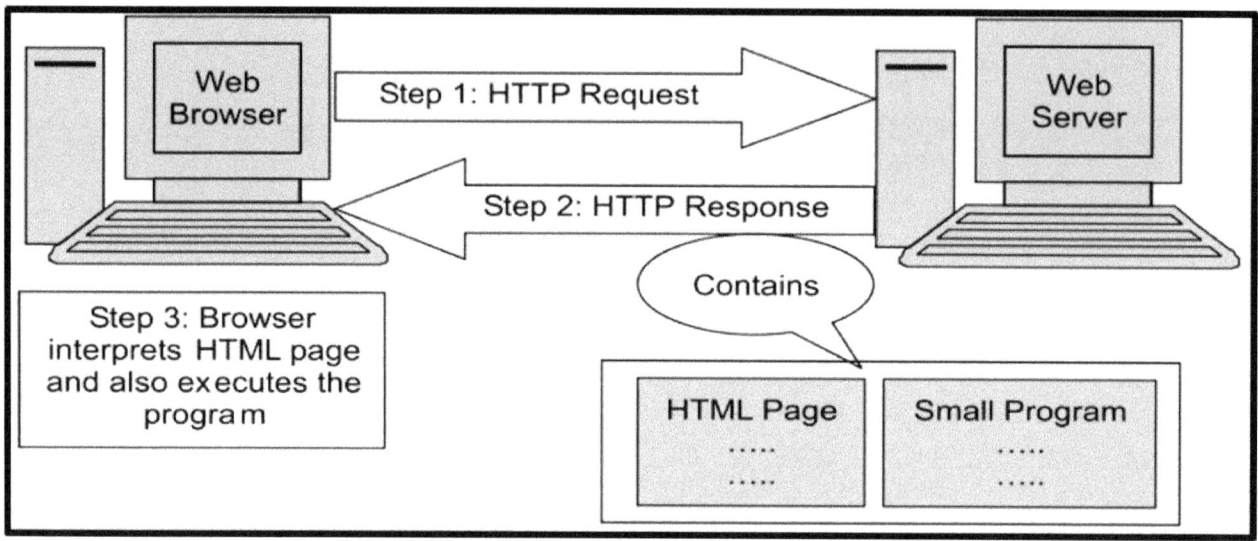

Figure 9.3: Active Web Pages

9.2 Secure socket layer and transport layer security

Secure Socket Layer (SSL):
SSL protocol is an Internet protocol for the secure exchange of information between a Web browser and a Web server also it provides two basic security services: authentication and confidentiality. Logically, it provides a secure pipe between the Web browser and the Web server

Transport Layer Security (TLS):
Transport Layer Security (TLS) is an IETF standardization initiative, whose goal is to come out with an Internet standard version of SSL. Netscape wanted to standardize SSL, and hence handed the protocol over to IETF.

9.2.1 Secure Socket Layer (SSL)

Web browsers and Web servers can communicate information securely using the SSL protocol, which offers two fundamental security services: authentication and secrecy. It makes sense that it would offer a safe conduit between the Web browser and the Web server.

All of the major web browsers support SSL, which was created in 1994 by Netscape Corporation. There are currently three versions of SSL available: versions 2, 3, and 3.1. SSL has grown to become the most widely used web-security method in the world. Version 3, which was launched in 1995, is the most widely used of all.

9.2.2 Position Of SSL In TCP/IP Protocol Suite

As usual, the application layer of the sending computer (X) prepares the data to be sent to the receiving computer (Y). However, unlike the normal case, the application-layer data is now passed to the SSL layer, which performs encryption on the data received from the application layer (which is indicated by a different color) and also adds its own encryption. The data from the SSL layer (L5) is then used as the input for the transport layer. It then passes it on to the Internet layer after adding its own header (H4).

When the data reaches the physical layer, it is sent as voltage pulses across the transmission medium. When the data reaches the receiver's end, the process is very similar to how it is when a normal TCP/IP connection is made, up until it reaches the new SSL layer. The SSL layer at the receiver's end removes the SSL Header (SH), decrypts the encrypted data, and generates it. No encryption is used for the lower-layer headers. It should be evident that SSL must be placed below the data-link layer in order to encrypt all headers; otherwise, it would be useless and cause issues.

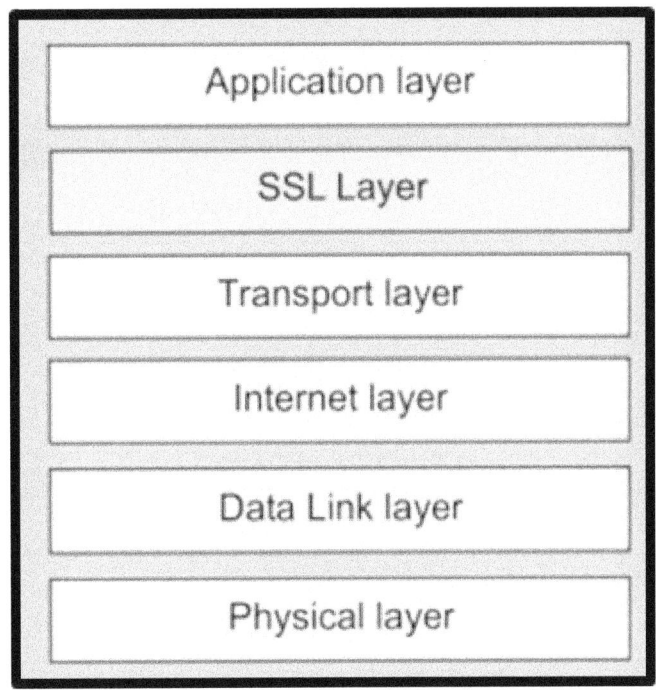

Figure 9.4: Position of SSL in OSI Layers

Even the IP and physical addresses of the computers (sender, receiver, and intermediate nodes) would be encrypted and rendered unreadable if SSL encrypted all lower-layer headers Therefore, a major concern would be where to distribute the packages. To comprehend the issue, consider what would occur if we included both the sender's and recipient's addresses within the envelope of a letter.

A conceptual model that defines how computers communicate with one another over a network is called the Open Systems Interconnection (OSI) paradigm. It separates communication into seven layers, each of which is in charge of a particular duty.

In the OSI paradigm, the application layer is at the top. It is in charge of offering the user services including email sending and receiving, online surfing, and file transfers.

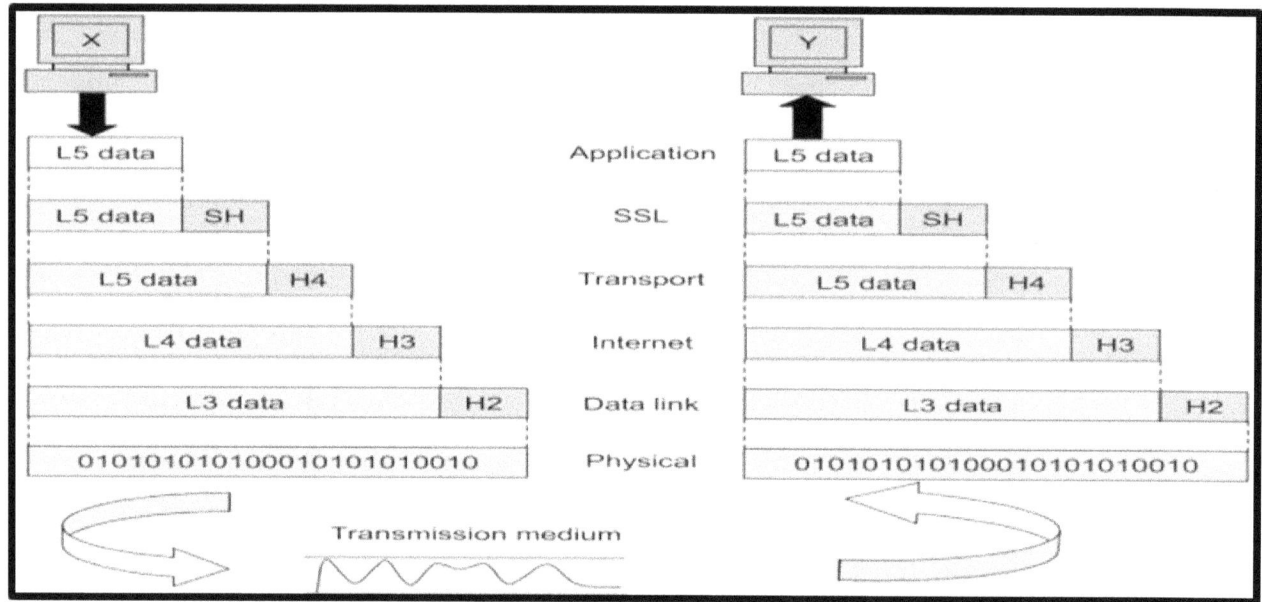

Figure 9.5: Communication between the Various TCP/IP Protocol Layers

The task of establishing a dependable connection between two apps falls on the transport layer. This is accomplished by segmenting the data before transmitting it over the network in smaller pieces. Data flow between two applications is encrypted using the SSL (Secure Sockets Layer) protocol. It offers a secure route to send sensitive data, such passwords and credit card details, and it is located between the application layer and the transport layer. As is customary, the application layer of the sending computer (X) prepares the data to be sent to the receiving computer (Y), but unlike in the normal case, the application-layer data is now passed to the SSL layer rather than directly to the transport layer. In this instance, the SSL layer encrypts the data received from the application layer (which is denoted by a different color) and adds its own encryption information header, known as SSL Header (SH), to the encrypted data. The data from the SSL layer (L5) is then used as the input for the transport layer. It then passes it on to the Internet layer after adding its own header (H4). This process happens exactly the way it happens in the case of a normal TCP/IP data transfer.

Finally, when the data reaches the physical layer, it is sent in the form of voltage pulses across the transmission medium. At the receiver's end, the process happens pretty similar to how it happens in the case of a normal TCP/ IP connection, until it reaches the new SSL layer. SSL layer at the receiver's end removes the SSL Header (SH), decrypts the encrypted data, and gives the plain-text data back to the application layer of the receiving compute. Thus, only the application layer data is encrypted by SSL. The lower-layer headers are not encrypted. This is quite obvious: if SSL has to encrypt all the headers, it must be positioned below the data-link layer.

That would serve no purpose at all. In fact, it would lead to problems. If SSL encrypted all the lower-layer headers, even the IP and physical addresses of the computers (sender, receiver, and intermediate nodes) would be encrypted, and become unreadable. Thus, where to deliver the packets would be a big question. To understand the problem, imagine what would happen if we put the address of the sender and the receiver of a letter inside the envelope!

9.2.3 SSL: Working Of SSL

SSL has three sub-protocols, namely the Handshake Protocol, the Record Protocol, and the Alert Protocol. These three sub-protocols constitute the overall working of SSL. Together, SSL's three sub-protocols enable a secure connection to be established between two devices.

- **Handshake Protocol** its secure connection. The client and server can agree on the encryption settings for the connection and mutually authenticate one another using this protocol.
- **Record Protocol** handled data transmission and reception via the secure connection. Data is encrypted before being transferred via this protocol, and it is then decrypted after being received.
- **Alert Protocol** is used to send error messages and other status information between the client and server. This protocol allows the two devices to communicate about the health of the secure connection.

9.2.3.1 Handshake protocol

Handshake protocol of SSL is the first sub-protocol used by the client and the server to communicate using an SSL-enabled connection. This is similar to how Alice and Bob would first shake hands with each other accompanied with a hello before they start conversing. Handshake protocol consists of a series of messages between the client and the server. Each of these messages has the format as shown

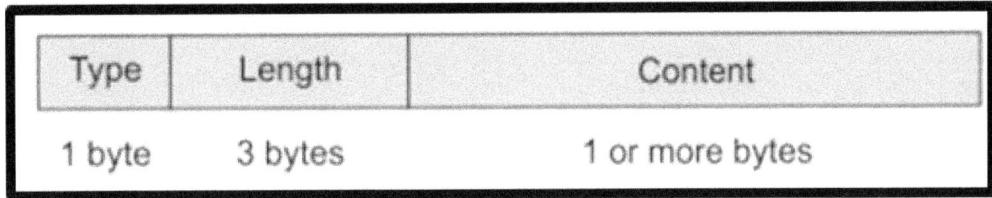

Each handshake message has three fields, as follows:

- **Type (1 byte):** This field indicates one of the ten possible message types.
- **Length (3 bytes):** This field indicates the length of the message in bytes.
- **Content (1 or more bytes):** This field contains the parameters associated with this message, depending on the message type.

Possible messages exchanged by the client and the server in the handshake protocol, along with their corresponding parameters

Message Type	Parameters
Hello request	None
Client hello	Version, Random number, Session id, Cipher suite, Compression method
Server hello	Version, Random number, Session id, Cipher suite, Compression method
Certificate	Chain of X.509V3 certificates
Server-key exchange	Parameters, signature
Certificate request	Type, authorities
Server hello done	None
Certificate verify	Signature
Client-key exchange	Parameters, signature
Finished	Hash value

Figure 9.6: Handshake Message Type & Parameters

The handshake protocol is actually made up of four phases:

1. Establish Security Capabilities
2. Server Authentication and Key Exchange 3.
3. Client Authentication and Key Exchange
4. Finish

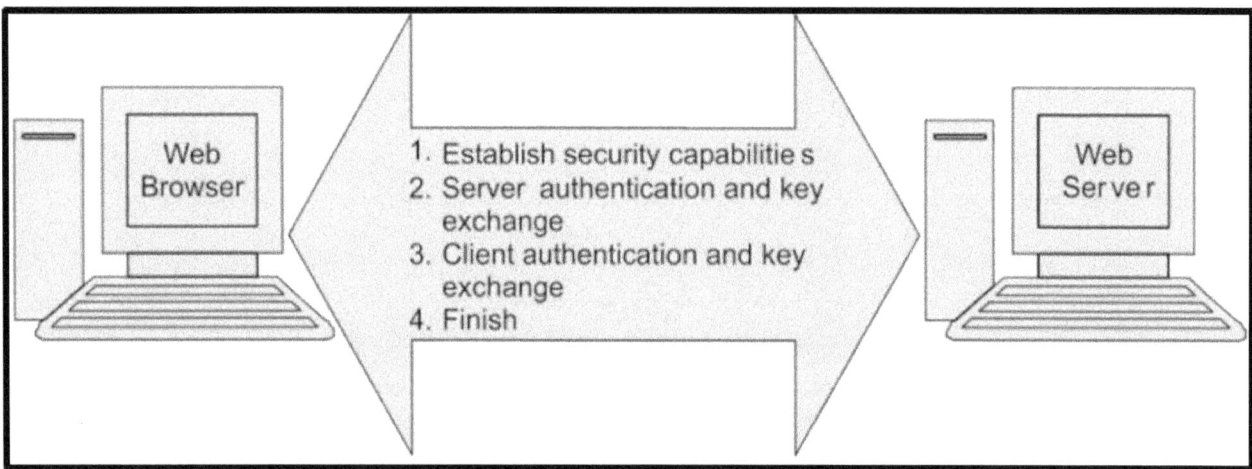

Figure 9.7: Four Phases of Handshake Protocol

Establish Security Capabilities

In this phase, the client and server exchange information about the security capabilities they support. This includes the type of encryption they will use, the size of the keys, and the compression method. This first phase of the SSL handshake is used to initiate a logical connection and establish the security capabilities associated with that connection. This consists of two messages, the client hello and the server hello.

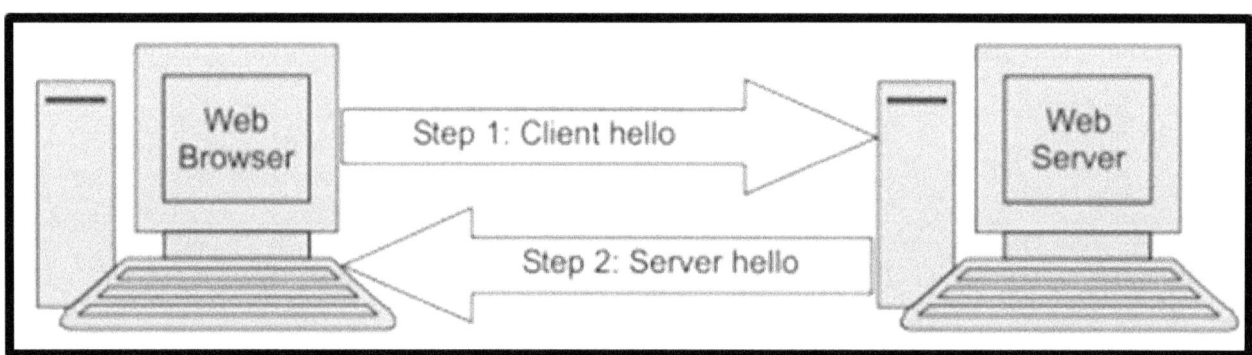

Figure 9.8: Establish Security Capabilities

- **Random**: This field has the same structure as the Random field of the client. However, the Random value generated by the server is completely in dependent of the client's Random value.
- **Session id:** If the session id value sent by the client was non-zero, the server uses the same value. Otherwise, the server creates a new session id and puts it in this field

- **Cipher suite:** Contains a single cipher suite, which the server selects from the list sent earlier by the client.
- **Compression method:** Contains a compression algorithm, which the server selects from the list sent earlier by the client

Server Authentication and Key Exchange

In this phase, the server sends its certificate to the client. The certificate is a digital document that proves the identity of the server. The client then uses the certificate to verify the server's identity.

The server also sends a key exchange message to the client. This message contains a randomly generated key that will be used to encrypt the data that is sent between the client and server. The server initiates this second phase of the SSL handshake, and is the sole sender of all the messages in this phase. The client is the sole recipient of all these messages. This phase contains four steps: **Certificate, Server key exchange, Certificate request, and Server hello done**

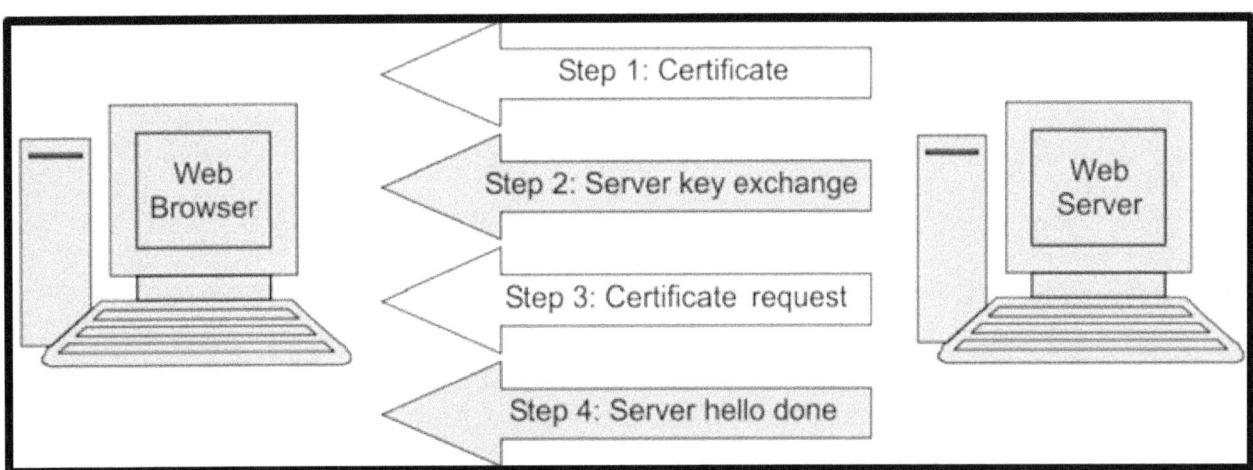

Figure 9.9: Server Authentication and Key Exchange

- **Certificate:** The server sends its digital certificate and the entire chain leading up to root CA to the client. This will help the client to authenticate the server using the server's public key from the server's certificate. The server's certificate is mandatory in all situations, except if the key is being agreed upon by using Diffie-Hellman.
- **Server Key Exchange:** It is optional. It is used only if the server does not send its digital certificate to the client instep 1 above. In this step, the server sends its public key to the client (as the certificate is not available)
- **Certificate Request:** The server can request for the client's digital certificate. The client authentication in SSL is optional, and the server may not always expect the client to be authenticated. Therefore, this step is optional.
- **Server Hello Done:** Message indicates to the client that its portion of the hello message (i.e., the server hello message) is complete. This indicates to the client that the client can now (optionally) verify the certificates sent by the server, and ensure that all the parameters sent by the server are acceptable.

This message does not have any parameters. After sending this message, the server waits for the client's response.

Client Authentication and Key Exchange

In this phase, the client sends its certificate to the server, if it has one. The client may also send a randomly generated key to the server.

If the client does not have a certificate, the server may authenticate the client using a challenge-response mechanism. The client initiates this third phase of the SSL handshake, and is the sole sender of all the messages in this phase. The server is the sole recipient of all these messages. This phase contains three steps: **Certificate, Client** key exchange, and Certificate verify.

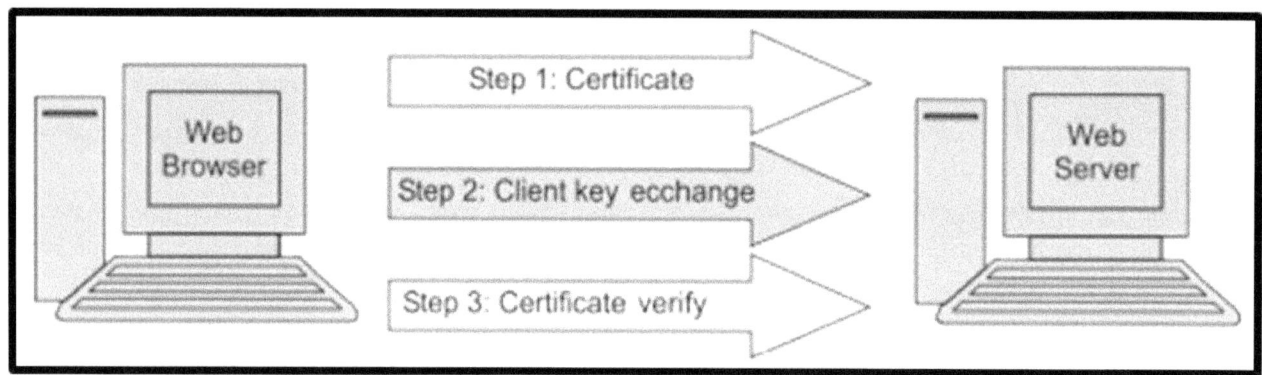

Figure 9.10: Client Authentication and Key Exchange

- **Certificate:** It is optional. This step is performed only if the server had requested for the client's digital certificate. If the server has requested for the client's certificate, and if the client does not have one, the client sends a No certificate message, instead of a Certificate message. It then is up to the server to decide if it wants to still continue or not.
- **Client Key Exchange:** It allows the client to send information to the server, but in the opposite direction. This information is related to the symmetric key that both the parties will use in this session. Client creates a 48-byte pre-master secret, and encrypts it with the server's public key and sends this encrypted pre-master secret to the server.
- **Certificate Verify:** It is necessary only if the server had demanded client authentication. If this is the case, the client has already sent its certificate to the server. Additionally, the client also needs to prove to the server that it is the correct and authorized holder of the private key corresponding to the certificate. For this purpose, in this optional step, the client combines the pre-master secret with the random numbers exchanged by the client and the server earlier

(In Phase 1: Establish security capabilities) after hashing them together using MD5 and SHA-1, and signs the result with its private key

Finish

In this phase, the client and server agree on the encryption parameters that will be used for the session. They also exchange a message that indicates that the handshake is complete.

Once the handshake is complete, the client and server can start sending encrypted data to each other. The handshake protocol is a critical part of secure communication over the internet. It ensures that the client and server are who they say they are, and that the data that is sent between them is encrypted. The client initiates this fourth phase of the SSL handshake, which the server ends. This phase contains four steps. The first two messages are from the client: **Change cipher specs, Finished**. The server responds back with two identical messages: **Change cipher specs, Finished**

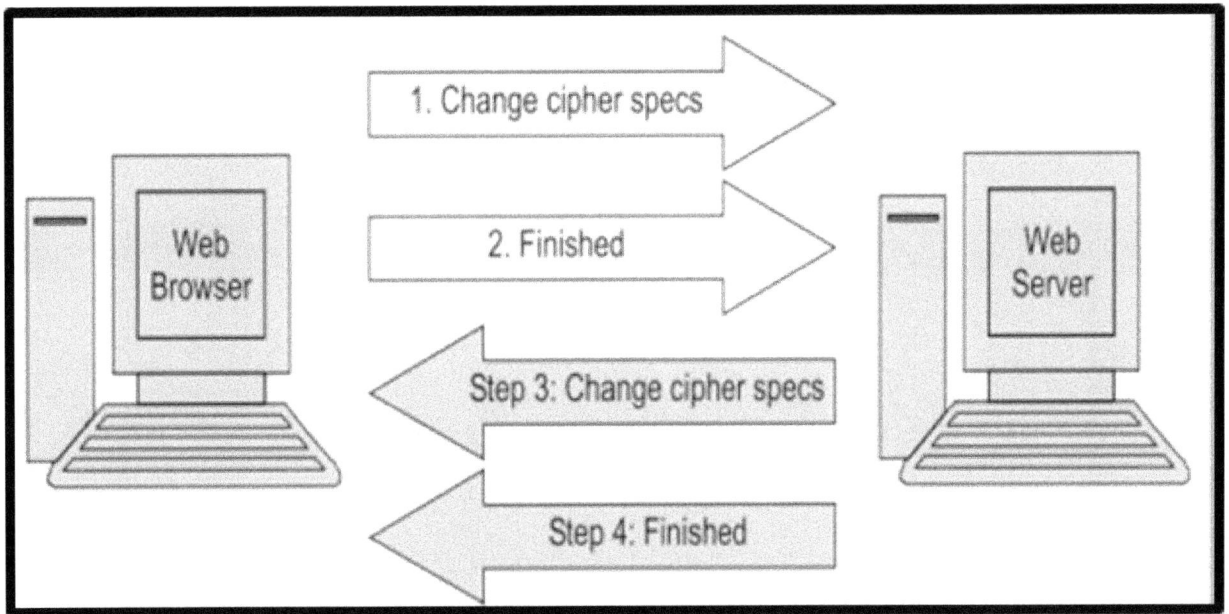

Figure 9.11: Finish

9.2.3.2 Record Protocol

Record Protocol in SSL comes into picture after a successful handshake is completed between the client and the server. That is, after the client and the server have optionally authenticated each other and have decided what algorithms to use for secure information exchange, we enter into the SSL record protocol. This protocol provides two services to an SSL connection.

Confidentiality: This is achieved by using the secret key that is defined by the handshake protocol.

Integrity: The handshake protocol also defines a shared secret key (MAC) that is used for assuring the message integrity. Operation of the record protocol.

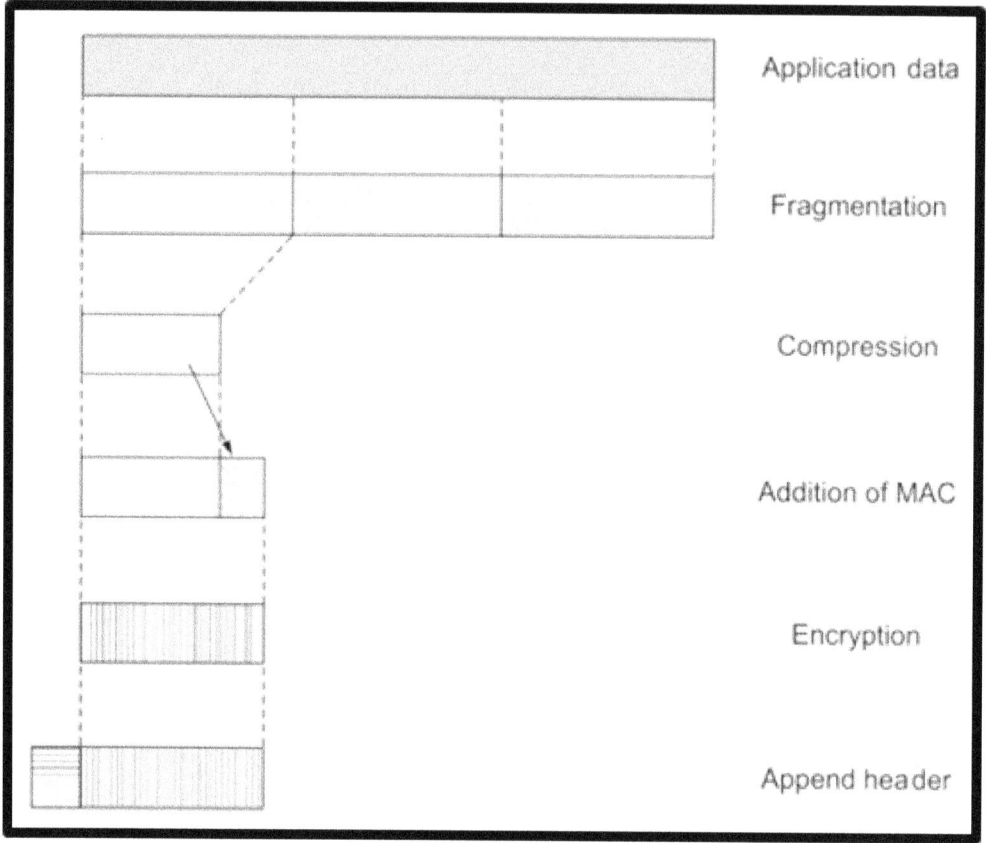

Figure 9.12: Record Protocol

SSL record protocol takes an application message as input. First, it fragments it into smaller blocks, optionally compresses each block, adds MAC, encrypts it, adds a header and gives it to the transport layer, where the TCP protocol processes it like any other TCP block. At the receiver's end, the header of each block is removed; the block is then decrypted, verified, decompressed, and reassembled into application messages.

- **Fragmentation:** The original application message is broken into blocks, so that the size of each block is less than or equal to 214 bytes (16,384 bytes)
- **Compression:** The fragmented blocks are optionally compressed. The compression process must not result into the loss of the original data, which means that this must be a lossless compression mechanism.
- **Addition of MAC:** Using the shared secret key established previously in the handshake protocol, the Message Authentication Code (MAC) for each block is calculated. This operation is similar to the HMAC algorithm.
- **Encryption:** Using the symmetric key established previously in the handshake protocol, the output of the previous step is now encrypted. This encryption may not increase the overall size of the block by more than 1024 bytes

Stream cipher		Block cipher	
Algorithm	Key size	Algorithm	Key size
RC4	40	AES	128, 256
RC4	128	IDEA	128
		RC2	40
		DES	40
		DES	56
		DES-3	168
		Fortezza	80

Figure 9.13: Permitted SSL Algorithm

Append Header: Finally, a header is added to the encrypted block. The header contains the following fields.

- **Content type (8 bits):** Specifies the protocol used for processing the record in the next higher level (e.g., handshake, alert, change cipher).
- **Major version (8 bits):** Specifies the major version of the SSL protocol in use. For instance, if SSL version 3.1 is in use, this field contains 3.

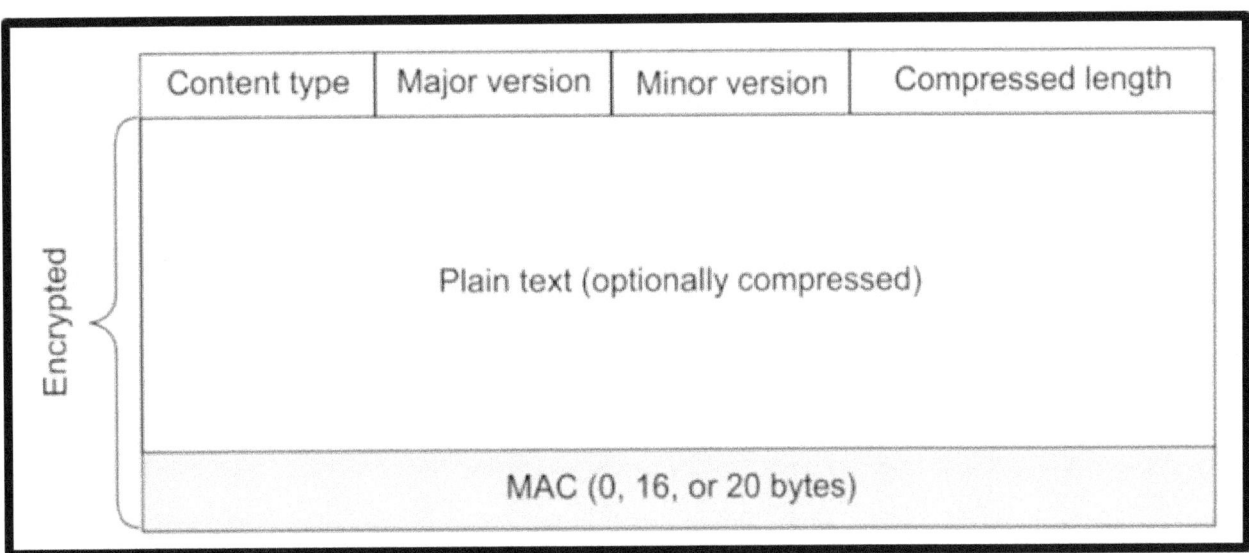

Figure 9.14: Final SSL Message

- **Minor version (8 bits):** Specifies the minor version of the SSL protocol in use. For instance, if SSL version 3.0 is in use, this field contains 0.
- **Compressed length (16 bits):** Specifies the length in bytes of the original plain-text block (or the compressed block, if compression is used)

9.2.3.3 Alert Protocol

When either the client or the server detects an error, the detecting party sends an alert message to the other party. If the error is fatal, both the parties immediately close the SSL connection (which means that the transmission from both the ends is terminated immediately).

Both the parties also destroy the session identifiers, secrets and keys associated with this connection before it is terminated. Other errors, which are not so severe, do not result in the termination of the connection. Instead, the parties handle the error and continue Each alert message consists of two bytes.

- The first byte signifies the type of error. If it is a warning, this byte contains 1. If the error is fatal, this byte contains 2.
- The second byte specifies the actual error

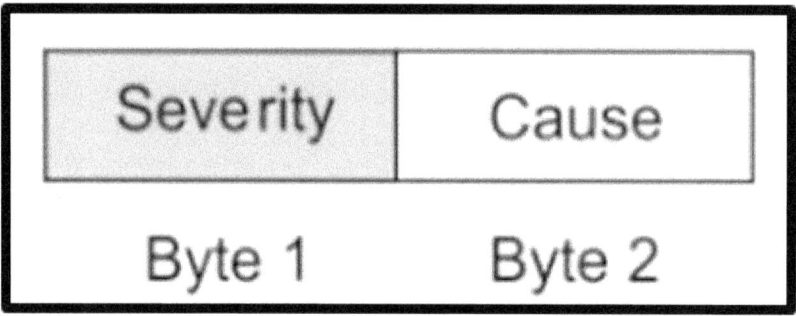

Figure 9.15: Alert Protocol Message Format

Alert	Description
Unexpected message	An inappropriate message was received.
Bad record MAC	A message is received without a correct MAC.
Decompression failure	The decompression function received an improper input.
Handshake failure	Sender was unable to negotiate an acceptable set of security parameters from the available options.
Illegal parameters	A field in the handshake message was out of range or was inconsistent with the other fields.

Fatal Alert

Alert	Description
No certificate	Sent in response to certificate request if an appropriate certificate is not available.
Bad certificate	A certificate was corrupt (its digital signature verification failed).
Unsupported certificate	The type of the received certificate is not supported.
Certificate revoked	The signer of a certificate has revoked it.
Certificate expired	A received certificate has expired.
Certificate unknown	An unspecified error occurred while processing the certificate.
Close notify	Notifies that the sender will not send any more messages in this connection. Each party must send this message before closing its side of the connection.

Non-Fatal Alert

9.2.4 Closing & Resuming SSL Connections

Before ending their communication, the client and the server must inform each other that their side of the connection is ending. Each party sends a Close notify alert to the other party. This ensures a graceful closure of the connection. When a party receives this alert, it must immediately stop whatever it is doing, send its own Close notify alert and end the connection from its side as well. If an SSL connection ends without a Close notify from either party, it cannot be resumed the handshake protocol in SSL is quite complex and time consuming, as it uses asymmetric-key cryptography.

Therefore, if desired, a client and a server can decide to reuse or resume an earlier SSL connection, rather than creating a fresh one with a new handshake. However, for this to be possible, both the parties must agree on the reuse. If either party feels that it is dangerous to reuse the earlier connection, or if the other party's certificate has expired since the last connection, it can force the other party to perform a fresh handshake. As per the SSL specifications, any SSL connection should not be reused after 24 hours in any case.

9.2.5 Buffer Overflow Attacks On SSL

A buffer overflow occurs when a program or process tries to store more data in a buffer (a temporary data storage area) than what it was designed to hold. Because buffers are created to contain a fixed amount of data, the extra information—which has to go somewhere—can overflow into adjacent buffers, corrupting or overwriting the valid data held in them. Although this may happen accidentally through programming error, buffer overflow is an increasingly common type of security attack on data integrity. In buffer overflow attacks, the extra data may contain codes designed to cause specific actions, thus sending new instructions to the attacked computer. This could damage the user's files, change data, or compromise confidential information. OpenSSL is an open-source implementation of the Secure Sockets Layer (SSL) protocol. OpenSSL is subject to four remotely exploitable buffer overflows. The buffer overflow vulnerabilities can allow an attacker to execute arbitrary code on the target (victim) computer with the privilege level of the OpenSSL process, as well as providing opportunities for launching a denial-of-service attack. These have been more in theory than in practice.

Three of the four buffer-overflow vulnerabilities occur in the SSL handshakes. The last one deals with 64-bit operating systems

These have been more in theory than in practice.

- The first vulnerability is found in the key exchange implemented in SSL Version 2. A client can be used to send an oversized master key to an SSL Version 2 server, enabling denial of service or malicious code execution on the server.
- The second buffer overflow is contained in the SSL Version 3 handshake. A malicious server can execute code on an OpenSSL client by sending a malformed session ID during the first phase of the handshake.
- The third buffer overflow exists in OpenSSL servers running SSL Version 3 with Kerberos authentication enabled. A malicious client can send an oversized master key to a Kerberos-enabled SSL server.
- The fourth set of overflows exists only on 64-bit operating systems. Several buffers used to store ASCII representations of integers are smaller than required.

9.2.6 Transport Layer Security (TSL)

A security technology called Transport Layer Security (TLS) offers network communication security. Data in transit between two applications is protected by it.

Netscape Communications Corporation created TLS for the first time in 1994. The Internet Engineering Task Force (IETF) took on the TLS development after Netscape turned it over to it in 1999. The Secure Sockets Layer (SSL) protocol, created by Netscape in 1995, is the foundation of TLS.

TLS, however, has a number of advantages over SSL, including:

- It makes advantage of stronger encryption techniques.
- It is expandable and more flexible.
- It is more resistant to assaults.

RFC 2246, a document that details the protocol's technical specifications, defines TLS. TLS is a secure protocol that is used to protect data in transit between two applications. It is based on the SSL protocol, but it has several improvements that make it more secure. TLS is defined in RFC 2246.

Property	SSL	TLS
Version	3.0	1.0
Cipher suite	Supports an algorithm called Fortezza	Does not support Fortezza
Cryptography secret	Computed as explained earlier in the chapter	Uses a pseudorandom function to create master secret
Alert protocol	As explained earlier in the chapter	The *No certificate* alert message is deleted. The following are newly added: *Decryption failed, Record overflow, Unknown CA, Access denied, Decode error, Export restriction, Protocol version, Insufficient security, Internal error.*
Handshake protocol	As explained earlier in the chapter	Some details are changed
Record protocol	Uses MAC	Uses HMAC

Differences between SSL and TLS

Some additional details about the differences between **SSL** and **TLS**:

- SSL uses the Message Authentication Code (MAC) protocol to authenticate and encrypt data, while TLS uses the Hashed Message Authentication Code (HMAC) protocol.
- SSL supports older encryption algorithms that are no longer considered secure, while TLS only supports newer, more secure encryption algorithms.
- SSL is less flexible and extensible than TLS.

TLS is a more secure and modern protocol than SSL. It is recommended to use TLS whenever possible.

9.2.7 TLS Architecture

TLS is made to utilize. TCP in order to deliver a dependable end-to-end secure service. TLS consists of two layers of protocols rather than one, as seen in figure 9.19. To numerous higher-layer protocols, the TLS Record Protocol offers fundamental security features. TLS can be used on top of the **Hypertext Transfer Protocol (HTTP)**, which offers the transfer service for Web client/server interaction. The Handshake Protocol, Change Cypher Spec Protocol, and Alert Protocol are three higher-layer protocols that are included in TLS. These TLS-specific protocols, which are looked at later in this section, are used to manage TLS exchanges. The Heartbeat Protocol, a fourth protocol, is specified in a different RFC and is also covered further in this section.

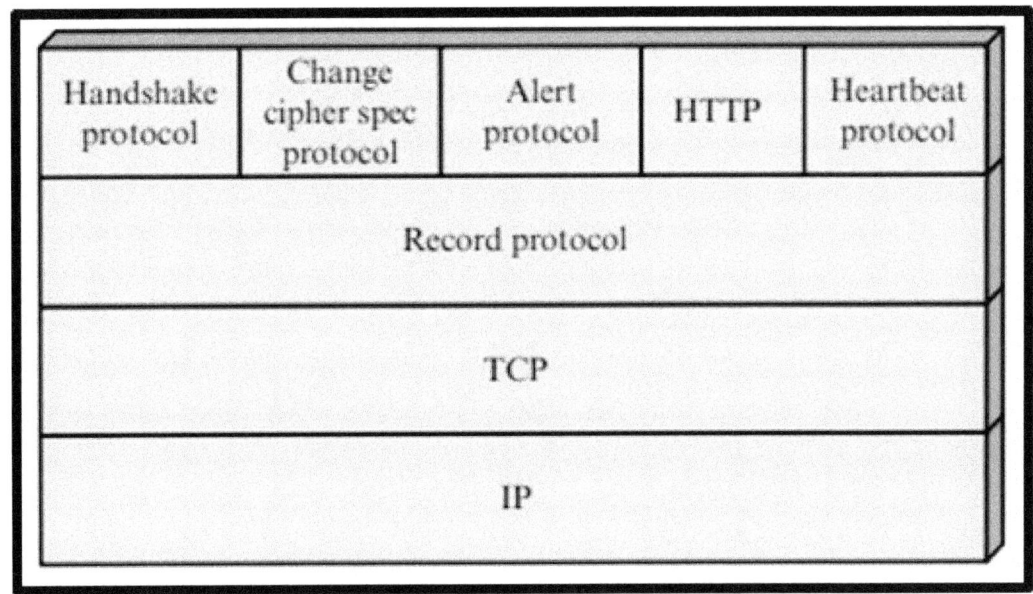

Figure 9.16: TLS Protocol Stack

TLS session and TLS connection are two crucial TLS concepts, and their definitions may be found in the standard as follows:

- **Connection**: According to the OSI layering model, a link is a transport that offers the appropriate kind of service. Such connections are peer-to-peer partnerships in terms of TLS. The relationships are fleeting. One session is connected to each connection.
- **Session**: A client and a server are associated with one another during a TLS session. The Handshake Protocol establishes sessions. A set of cryptographic security settings are defined by sessions and can be shared by many connections. The costly negotiation of new security parameters for each connection is avoided by using sessions.

For TLS connections, the TLS Record Protocol offers two services:

Confidentiality: The Handshake Protocol specifies a shared secret key that is applied to the standard TLS payload encryption.

Message Integrity: The Handshake Protocol also specifies how to create a message authentication code (MAC) using a shared secret key.

The complete functionality of the TLS Record Protocol is shown in figure 9.20. The Record Protocol takes an application message that needs to be sent over the network, breaks it up into smaller, more manageable chunks, optionally applies a MAC, encrypts it, adds a header, and then sends the whole thing over the network in a TCP segment. Before being sent to higher-level users, received data are decrypted, validated, decompressed, and reassembled.

The first step is fragmentation. Each upper-layer message is fragmented into blocks of 214 bytes (16,384 bytes) or less. Next, compression is optionally applied. Compression must be lossless and may not increase the content length by more than 1024 bytes.1 In TLSv2, no compression algorithm is specified, so the default compression algorithm is null. The next step in processing is to compute a message authentication code over the compressed data. TLS makes use of the HMAC algorithm defined in RFC 2104.

$$HMACK(M) = H\,[(K+ \oplus opad)\,`H\,[(K+ \oplus ipad)\,`M]]$$

Where,

H = embedded hash function (for TLS, either MD5 or SHA-1)

M = message input to HMAC

$K+$ = secret key padded with zeros on the left so that the result is equal to the block length of the hash code (for MD5 and SHA-1, block length = 512 bits)

ipad = 00110110 (36 in hexadecimal) repeated 64 times (512 bits)

opad = 01011100 (5C in hexadecimal) repeated 64 times (512 bits)

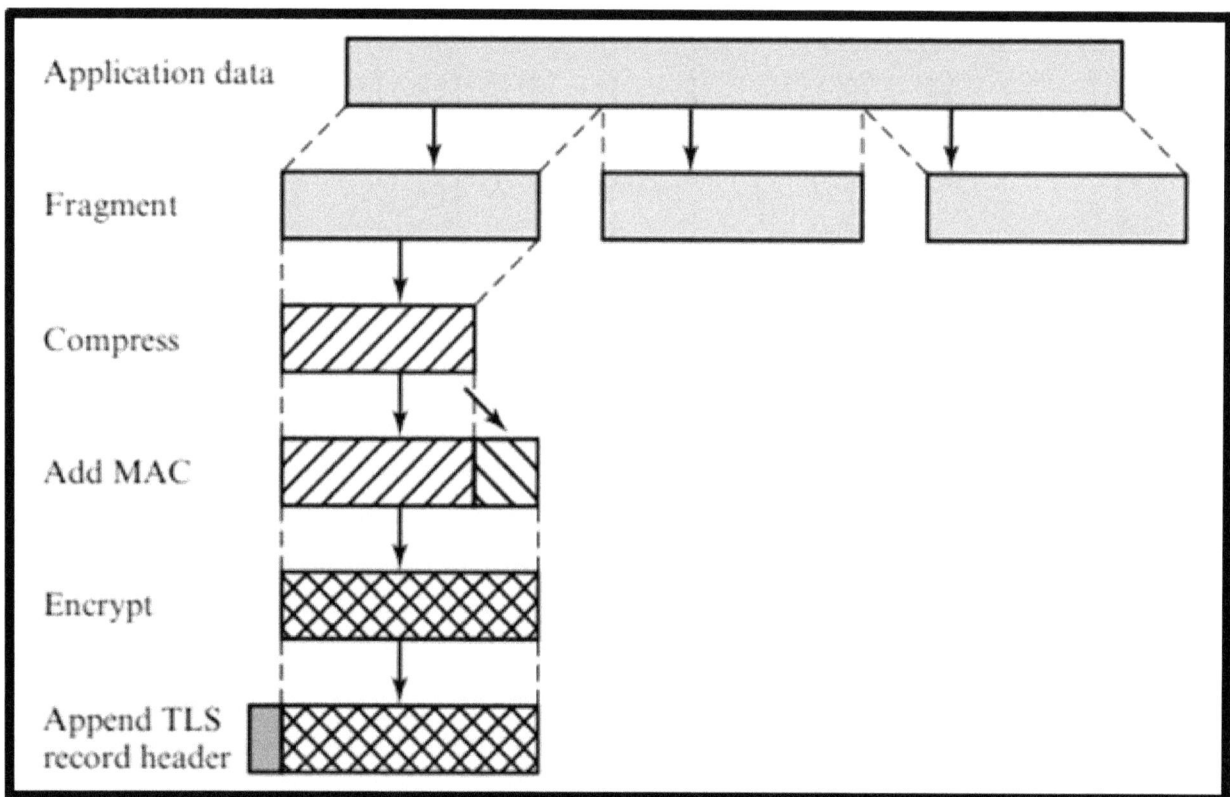

Figure 9.17: TLS Record Protocol Operation

9.3 Secure Electronic Transaction (SET)

The Secure Electronic Transaction (SET) is an open encryption and security specification that is designed for protecting credit-card transactions on the Internet. The pioneering work in this area was done in 1996 by MasterCard and Visa jointly. They were joined by IBM, Microsoft, Netscape, RSA, Terisa, and VeriSign. Starting from that time, there have been many tests of the concept, and by1998 the first generation of SET-compliant products appeared in the market.

The need for SET came from the fact that MasterCard and Visa realized that for e-commerce payment processing, software vendors were coming up with new and conflicting standards Microsoft mainly drove these on one hand, and IBM on the other. To avoid all sorts of future incompatibilities, MasterCard and Visa decided to come up with a standard, ignoring all their competition issues, and in the process, involving all the major software manufacturers. SET is not a payment system. Instead, it is a set of security protocols and formats that enable the users to employ the existing credit-card payment infrastructure on the Internet in a secure manner

SET services can be summarized as follows:

- Provides a secure communication channel among all the parties involved in an ecommerce transaction
- Provides authentication by the use of digital certificates
- Ensures confidentiality, because the information is only available to the parties involved in a transaction, and that too only when and where necessary

SET is a very complex specification. In fact, when released, it took 971 pages to describe SET across three books! (Just for the record, SSL Version 3 needs 63 pages to describe)

9.3.1 SET: Participants

1. Cardholder
2. Merchant
3. Issuer
4. Acquirer
5. Payment Gateway
6. Certification Authority (CA)

1. **Cardholder**: Using the Internet, consumers and corporate purchasers interact with merchants for buying goods and services. A cardholder is an authorized holder of a payment card such as MasterCard or Visa that has been issued by an issuer
2. **Merchant**: A merchant is a person or an organization that wants to sell goods or services to cardholders. A merchant must have a relationship with an acquirer for accepting payments on the Internet
3. **Issuer**: The issuer is a financial institution (such as a bank) that provides a payment card to a cardholder. The most critical point is that the issuer is ultimately responsible for the payment of the cardholder's debt.
4. **Acquirer**: This is a financial institution that has a relationship with merchants for processing payment-card authorizations and payments. The reason for having acquirers is that merchants accept credit cards of more than one brand, but are not interested in dealing with so many bank card organizations or issuers. Instead, an acquirer provides the merchant an assurance (with the help of the issuer) that a particular cardholder account is active and that the purchase amount does not exceed the credit limits, etc. The acquirer also provides electronic funds transfer to the merchant account. Later, the issuer reimburses the acquirer using some payment network
5. **Payment Gateway**: This is a task that can be taken up by the acquirer or it can be taken up by an organization as a dedicated function. The payment gateway processes the payment messages on behalf of the merchant. Specifically

in SET, the payment gateway acts as an interface between SET and the existing card-payment networks for payment authorizations. Merchant exchanges SET messages with the payment gateway over the Internet Payment gateway, in turn, connects to the acquirer's systems using a dedicated network line in most cases

6. **Certification Authority (CA)**: This is an authority that is trusted to provide public key certificates to cardholders, merchants and payment gateways. In fact, CAs are very crucial to the success of SET.

9.3.2 SET: The SET Process

- The Customer Opens an Account
- The Customer Receives a Certificate
- The Merchant Receives a Certificate
- The Customer Places an Order
- The Merchant is Verified
- The Order and Payment Details are Sent
- The Merchant Requests Payment Authorization
- The Payment Gateway Authorizes the Payment
- The Merchant Confirms the Order

The Customer Opens an Account

The customer opens a credit-card account (such as MasterCard or Visa) with a bank(issuer) that supports electronic payment mechanisms and the SET protocol.

The Customer Receives a Certificate

After the customer's identity is verified (with the help of details such as passport, business documents, etc.), the customer receives a digital certificate from a CA. The certificate also contains details such as the customer's public key and its expiration date.

The Merchant Receives a Certificate

A merchant that wants to accept a certain brand of credit cards must possess a digital certificate

The Customer Places an Order

This is a typical shopping-cart process wherein the customer browses the list of items available, searches for specific items, selects one or more of them, and places the order. The merchant, in turn, sends back details such as the list of items selected, their quantities, prices, total bill, etc., back to the customer for his record, with the help of an order form

The Merchant is Verified

The merchant also sends its digital certificate to the customer. This assures the customer that he/she is dealing with a valid merchant.

The Order and Payment Details are Sent

The customer sends both the order and payment details to the merchant along with the customer's digital certificate. The order confirms the purchase transaction with reference to the items mentioned in the order form. The payment contains credit card details. However, the payment information is so encrypted that the merchant cannot read it. The customer's certificate assures the merchant of the customer's identity.

The Merchant Requests Payment Authorization

The merchant forwards the payment details sent by the customer to the payment gateway via the acquirer (or to the acquirer if the acquirer also acts as the payment gateway) and requests the payment gateway to authorize the payment (i.e., ensure that the credit card is valid and that the credit limits are not breached)

The Payment Gateway Authorizes the Payment

Using the credit-card information received from the merchant, the payment gateway verifies the details of the customer's credit card with the help of the issuer, and either authorizes or rejects the payment.

The Merchant Confirms the Order

Assuming that the payment gateway authorizes the payment, the merchant sends a confirmation of the order to the customer

9.3.3 SET Model

SET: Model can refers to Two different things as follows:

- A set model is a mathematical representation of a group of various items. Any type of mathematical object, including numbers, symbols, points in space, lines, other geometric shapes, variables, or even other sets, can be one of the elements or members of a set model. A set with a single element is a singleton, while a set with no elements is an empty set. A set can either be infinite or have a finite number of elements. If two sets contain exactly the same number of elements, they are equivalent.
- A sort of statistical model called a set model is used in machine learning to describe a group of data points as a set of items. The set's components can be any kind of data, including numbers, texts, or pictures. The set model is employed to forecast the likelihood that a brand-new data point will belong to the set.

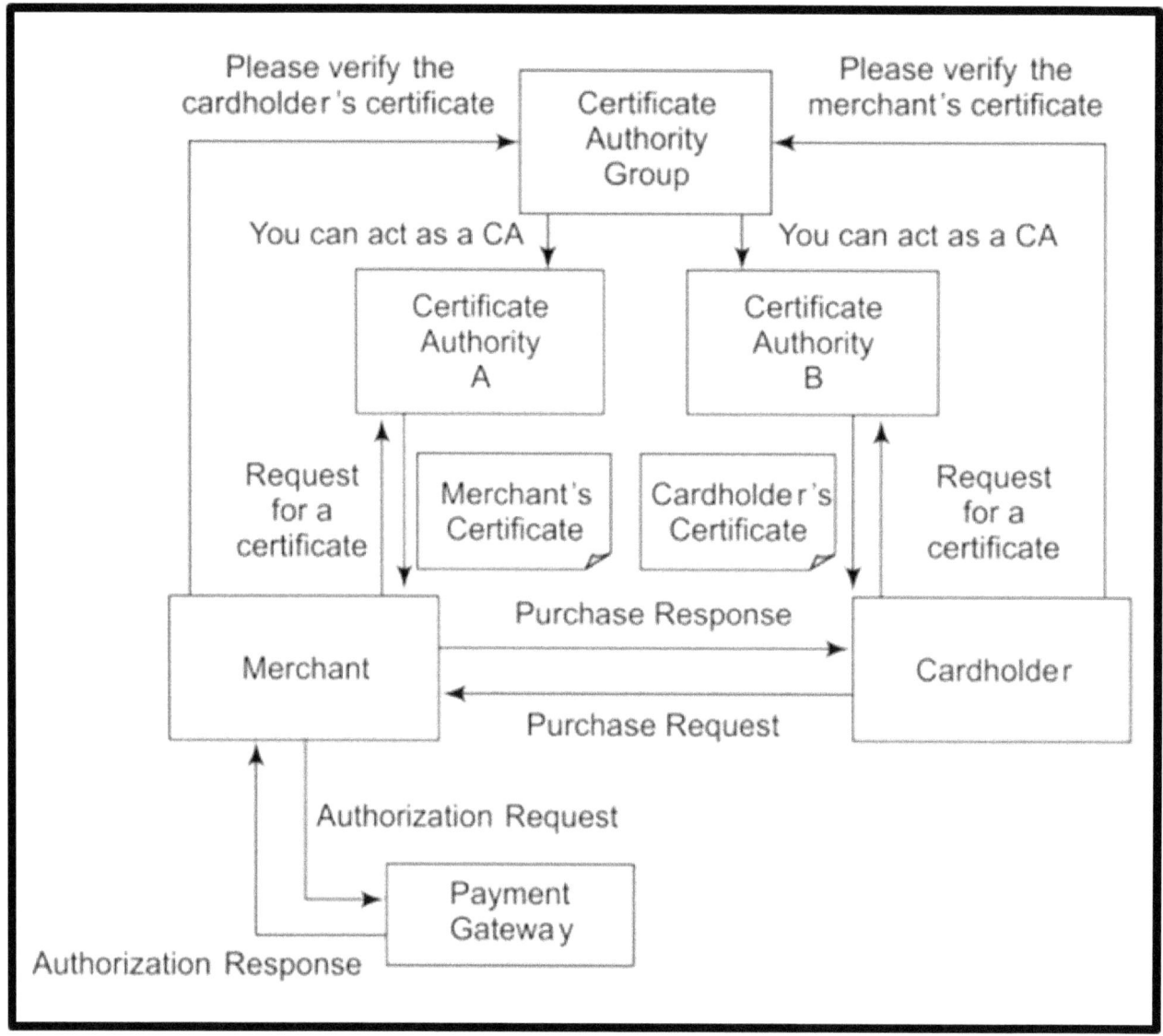

Figure 9.18: SET Model

The phrase "SET: MODEL" refers to a group of items or data points in both situations. The collection in the first instance is abstract and mathematical, whereas the collection in the second instance is tangible and represents actual data.

9.3.4 SSL Versus SET

Data that is communicated over the internet is protected by the security protocols SL (Secure Sockets Layer) and SET (Secure Electronic Transaction). However, they serve various functions and have various strengths and disadvantages as show in below table.

Issue	SSL	SET
Main aim	Exchange of data in an encrypted form	E-commerce related payment mechanism
Certification	Two parties exchange certificates	All the involved parties must be certified by a trusted third party
Authentication	Mechanisms in place, but not very strong	Strong mechanisms for authenticating all the parties involved
Risk of merchant fraud	Possible, since customer gives financial data to merchant	Unlikely, since customer gives financial data to payment gateway
Risk of customer fraud	Possible, no mechanisms exist if a customer refuses to pay later	Customer has to digitally sign payment instructions
Action in case of customer fraud	Merchant is liable	Payment gateway is liable
Practical usage	High	Low at the moment, expected to grow

SSL Versus SET

CHAPTER TEN

Security Features in Operating System

An operating system's (OS) security features are made to guard against unauthorised access, modification, or protection of the system. These qualities may consist of:

- **Authentication**: It verifying a user's identity is done through the process of authentication. The usual method is to ask the user to provide a username and password.
- **Access Control**: It refers to the process of managing who has access to which system resources. Normally, this is accomplished by granting people and groups certain permissions.
- **Auditing**: This is the process of keeping tabs on system user behaviors. This can be used to identify unauthorised modifications or access.
- **Encryption**: Data is encrypted when it is changed into a format that cannot be read without the right key. Passwords and credit card numbers are examples of sensitive data that can be protected in this way.
- **Firewall**: A firewall is a security measure that prevents unauthorised access to a computer network. Incoming or outgoing connections from specified IP addresses are just one example of the kinds of traffic that can be blocked by firewall configuration.
- **Virus Protection**: Software that checks a computer for viruses and other malware is known as virus protection. Infected files can be quarantined by virus prevention software to stop them from propagating.

10.1 System Security Intruders

System security is the protection of computer systems and information from harm, theft, and unauthorized use. It is a broad term that encompasses a wide range of security measures, including:

- **Physical Security**: This includes measures to protect computer systems from physical damage or theft, such as locks, security cameras, and access control systems.
- **Network Security**: This includes measures to protect computer networks from unauthorized access, such as firewalls, intrusion detection systems, and data encryption.
- **Application Security**: This includes measures to protect computer applications from malware, such as code signing, input validation, and sandboxing.
- **User Security**: This includes measures to protect computer systems from unauthorized users, such as strong passwords, multi-factor authentication, and user education.

One of the most publicized attacks to security is the intruder, generally referred to as hacker or cracker. **Three classes of intruders are as follows:**

- **Masquerader** an individual who is not authorized to use the computer and who penetrates a system's access controls to exploit a legitimate user's account.

- **Misfeasor** a legitimate user who accesses data, programs, or resources for which such access is not authorized, or who is authorized for such access but misuse his or her privileges
- **Clandestine User** an individual who seizes supervisory control of the system and uses this control to evade auditing and access controls or to suppress audit collection.

These are just three of the most common types of intruders in computer security. There are many other types of intruders, and the methods that they use to gain access to systems are constantly evolving. It is important to be aware of these threats and to take steps to protect your systems from them.

Tips for protecting your systems from intruders:

- Use strong passwords and change them regularly.
- Keep your software up to date.
- Use a firewall and antivirus software.
- Be careful about what information you share online.
- Educate your employees about security risks.

Passwords and credit card numbers are examples of sensitive data that can be protected in this way. A firewall is a security measure that prevents unauthorised access to a computer network. Incoming or outgoing connections from specified IP addresses are just one example of the kinds of traffic that can be blocked by firewall configuration. Software that checks a computer for viruses and other malware is known as virus protection. Infected files can be quarantined by virus prevention software to stop them from propagating.

10.2 Viruses & Related Threats

A virus is a form of malware, or malicious software, that travels between computers and corrupts software and data. Computer viruses are designed to interfere with systems, lead to serious functional problems, and cause data loss and leakage.

There are several ways that viruses might propagate, including:

- **Email Attachments**, such as Word documents, Excel spreadsheets, or PDF files, may contain viruses. The malware is triggered and can propagate to other systems when the attachment is opened.
- **File Sharing** Networks for file sharing, like LimeWire or BitTorrent, might help viruses proliferate. A virus may be included in a file that a user gets from a file-sharing network and become active when the file is opened.
- **Direct Downloads:** Websites can be used to download viruses. The virus can be downloaded and activated on a user's computer when they click on a link on a website.
- **USB Devices:** USB drives can be used to distribute viruses. The malware enters the computer through a USB device can be activated and spread to other computers.

Other associated dangers that can affect system security exist in addition to viruses, including:

- **Trojan Horses:** Trojan horses are malicious programs that masquerade as legitimate programs. When a user opens a Trojan horse, the malicious code is activated and can steal data, install other malware, or disrupt system operations.
- **Worms:** Worms are self-replicating malicious programs that can spread from computer to computer without user interaction. Worms can use a variety of methods to spread, including email, file sharing, and network vulnerabilities.
- **Spyware:** Spyware is a type of malware that is designed to collect information about a user's activities on their computer. Spyware can be used to track browsing habits, collect personal information, or even steal passwords.

- **Adware:** Adware is a type of malware that is designed to display unwanted advertisements. Adware can be installed on a computer through a variety of methods, including clicking on malicious links, downloading free software, or opening infected email attachments.

To protect systems from viruses and other related threats, including:

- **Install and keep up to date antivirus software**: Antivirus software can help to detect and remove viruses and other malware. It is important to keep antivirus software up to date to ensure that it can detect the latest threats.
- **Be careful about what you open:** Do not open email attachments from unknown senders, and be careful about downloading files from file sharing networks or websites that you do not trust.
- **Use strong passwords:** Use strong passwords for all of your online accounts, and change your passwords regularly.
- **Keep your operating system and software up to date**: Software updates often include security patches that can help to protect your system from viruses and other malware.
- **Be aware of the latest threats:** Stay up to date on the latest threats by reading security blogs and articles.

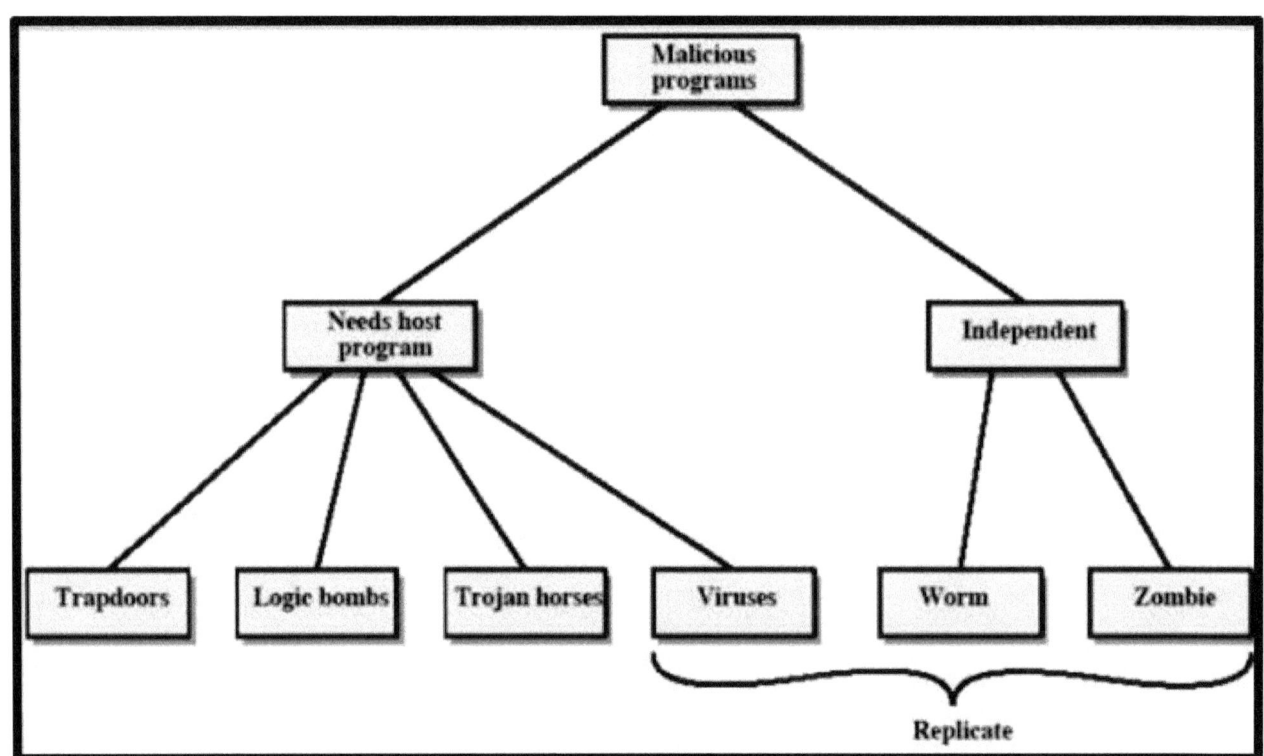

Figure 10.1: Viruses and Related Threats

Most sophisticated types of threats to computer systems are presented by programs that exploit vulnerabilities in computing systems.

10.2.1 Malicious Program

Any software code that is purposely detrimental to a computer, network, or server is referred to as a malicious program or malware. Malware can be created to destroy files, disrupt processes, or steal data. Some typical virus types include. Malicious Program can be divided in two parts as follow,

- Needs Host Program
- Independent

10.2.1.1 Needs Host Program

A host program is a trustworthy program that a malicious program attaches itself to in the context of malware. In order to spread to other computers or execute its harmful payload, the malicious program then makes use of the host program.

For Example, A virus, for instance, might affix itself to a Word document. The virus is active when the document is accessed and can then propagate to more machines connected to the same network. A Trojan horse could also pretend to be a trustworthy program, such a web browser or a PDF reader. The Trojan horse is started when the user launches the application and has the ability to steal data or set up further viruses.

The host program is not necessarily damaged by the malicious program. In fact, the malicious program may not even be detected by the user. However, the malicious program can still use the host program to spread or to carry out its malicious payload.

Needs Host Program form are as follow,

- Trapdoor
- Logic Bomb
- Trojan Horse
- Virus

Trapdoor

A trapdoor is a covert entrance into a computer program or system. An attacker could employ it to get unauthorised access to the program or system. During the development process, programs frequently generate trapdoors that can either be unintentionally left behind or purposefully added as a backdoor.

Logic Bomb

Logic bomb: A logic bomb is a hidden piece of computer code that runs when a certain circumstance is fulfilled. The requirement could be something like a particular day, hour, or event. Logic bombs are frequently used to corrupt or destroy data or to impair a computer system's functionality.

Trojan Horse

Trojan horse: A malicious program that poses as a trustworthy program is referred to as a Trojan horse. The harmful payload of the Trojan horse is executed when it is run, and it may display an obtrusive message or purge the victim's computer of all its files. Many times, rogue websites, file sharing networks, or email attachments are used to propagate Trojan horses.

Virus

A virus is a form of malware that has the ability to replicate itself and propagate from computer to computer. Viruses frequently join themselves to other files, including papers or executable programs. Opening the infected file causes the virus to become active and start reproducing. Numerous issues, including as data loss, system failures, and performance deterioration, can be brought on by viruses.

10.2.1.2 Independent

Malware that can function independently from a host program is known as an independent malicious program. This indicates that malware can spread from computer to computer without the knowledge or involvement of the user.

Independent are categories in two forms as follow,

- Worm
- Zombie

Worm

Malware that can replicate itself and spread from computer to computer without user intervention is referred to as a worm. In order to spread, worms frequently take use of security flaws in operating systems or software program. A worm can exploit a computer's resources to distribute spam, propagate other viruses, or carry out denial-of-service assaults once it has infected the machine.

Zombie

A computer that has been infected with malware and is now controlled by a hacker is referred to as a zombie. The use of zombies for denial-of-service assaults, spam distribution, or cryptocurrency mining is common.

Feature	Worm	Zombie
Self-replication	Yes	No
Spreads without user intervention	Yes	No
Can be used to launch attacks	Yes	Yes
Requires a hacker to control	No	Yes

Worm and Zombie Features

Name	Description
Virus	Attaches itself to a program and propagates copies of itself to other programs
Worm	Program that propagates copies of itself to other computers
Logic bomb	Triggers action when condition occurs
Trojan horse	Program that contains unexpected additional functionality
Backdoor (trapdoor)	Program modification that allows unauthorized access to functionality
Exploits	Code specific to a single vulnerability or set of vulnerabilities
Downloaders	Program that installs other items on a machine that is under attack. Usually, a downloader is sent in an e-mail.
Auto-rooter	Malicious hacker tools used to break into new machines remotely
Kit (virus generator)	Set of tools for generating new viruses automatically
Spammer programs	Used to send large volumes of unwanted e-mail
Flooders	Used to attack networked computer systems with a large volume of traffic to carry out a denial of service (DoS) attack
Keyloggers	Captures keystrokes on a compromised system
Rootkit	Set of hacker tools used after attacker has broken into a computer system and gained root-level access
Zombie	Program activated on an infected machine that is activated to launch attacks on other machines

Viruses Names and Description

During its lifetime, a typical virus goes through the following four phases:

- **Dormant phase:** The virus is idle. The virus will eventually be activated by some event, such as a date, the presence of another program or file, or the capacity of the disk exceeding some limit. Not all viruses have this stage.
- **Propagation phase:** The virus places an identical copy of itself into other programs or into certain system areas on the disk. Each infected program will now contain a clone of the virus, which will itself enter a propagation phase.
- **Triggering phase:** The virus is activated to perform the function for which it was intended. As with the dormant phase, the triggering phase can be caused by a variety of system events, including a count of the number of times that this copy of the virus has made copies of itself.
- **Execution phase:** The function is performed. The function may be harmless, such as a message on the screen, or damaging, such as the destruction of programs and data files.

10.3 Security Features Of Trusted Operating Systems

For sensitive data and applications, trusted operating systems (TOS) are built to offer a high level of security. They provide several security features that are uncommon in standard operating systems, like:

1. User Identification & Authentication
2. Mandatory Access Control
3. Discretionary Access Control
4. Object reuse Protection
5. Complete Mediation
6. Trusted Path
7. Audit
8. Audit Log Reduction
9. Intrusion Detection

User Identification & Authentication

Verifying a user's identity when they want to access a computer system is done through user identification and authentication. The process of giving each user a special identification, such as a username or user ID number, is known as user identification. The act of confirming that a user is who they say they are is known as authentication. This is typically accomplished by requesting a password or some other kind of authentication from the user.

Mandatory Access Control

A security approach known as mandatory access control (MAC) limits access to system resources depending on the user's identification and the sensitivity of the resource. The MAC security approach is effective at preventing unauthorised access to sensitive data.

Discretionary Access Control

A security approach known as discretionary access control (DAC) enables the owner of a resource to grant or prohibit access to other users. Although DAC is more versatile than MAC, it has a poorer security concept.

Object reuse Protection

Object reuse protection (ORP) is a security mechanism that prevents an object from being reused after it has been deleted. ORP helps to protect against malicious software that could be stored in a deleted object.

Complete Mediation

Complete mediation is a security principle that requires all access to system resources to be mediated by the operating system. Complete mediation helps to prevent unauthorized access to system resources.

Trusted Path

A trusted path is a secure communication channel between a user and the operating system. Trusted paths are used to protect sensitive information, such as passwords and cryptographic keys.

Audit

Auditing is the process of tracking and recording system events. Auditing can be used to detect unauthorized access to system resources and to investigate security breaches.

Audit Log Reduction

Reducing the bulk and improving the usability of audit logs involves summarizing and filtering them. Audit log minimization can increase auditing effectiveness and make it simpler to locate pertinent data in audit logs.

Intrusion Detection

Monitoring system activity for indications of unauthorised access or malicious behaviour is the process of intrusion detection. Security breaches can be found and avoided with the aid of intrusion detection systems.

These are only a few of the security measures that operating systems offer. Depending on the security objectives of the operating system and the dangers that it is intended to defend against, different features will be incorporated in different operating systems.

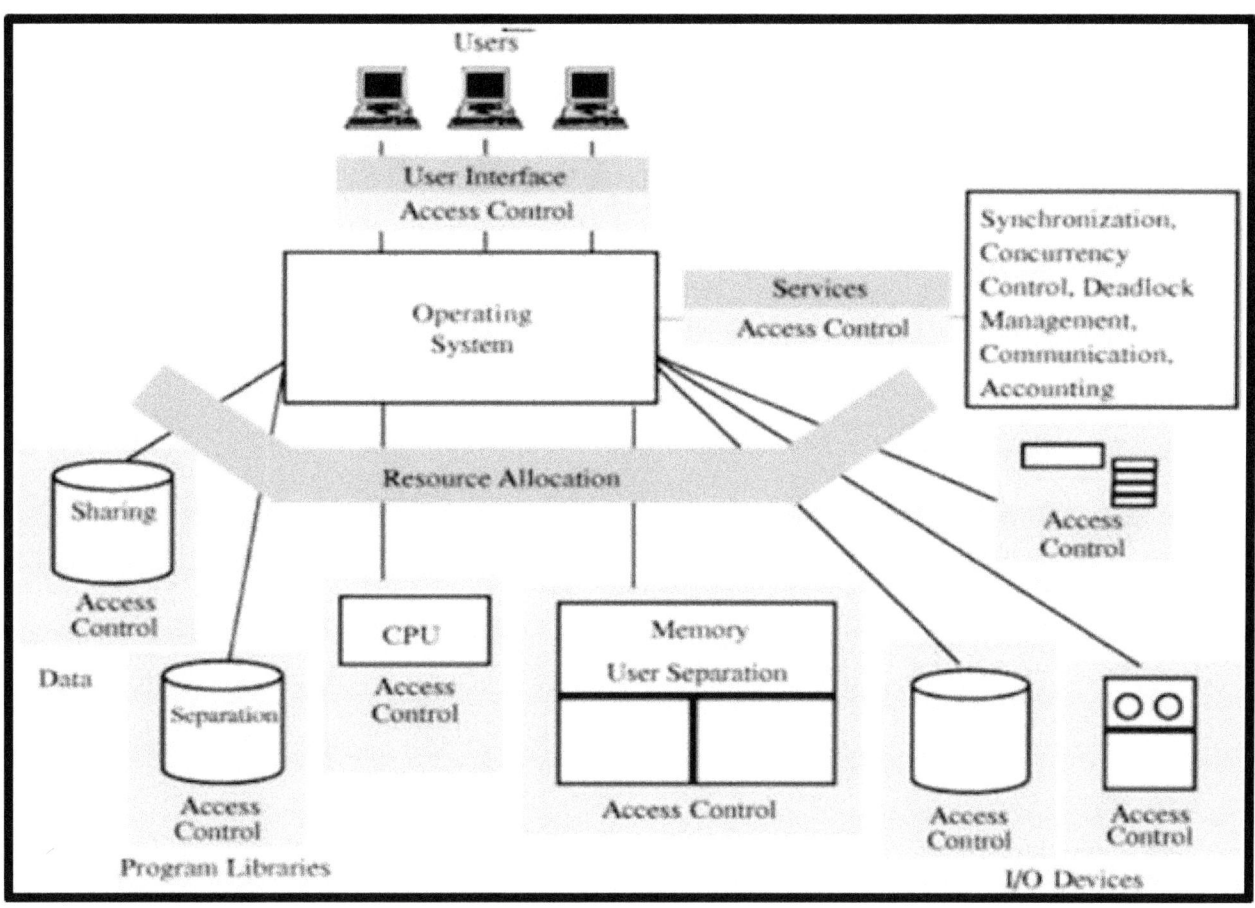

Figure 10.2: Working of Security Features in OS

Demonstrations in SageMath and Other Tools

- Cryptography and Network Security Tools
- SageMath Installation and Configuration
- Linear Algebra, Matrix Multiplication, and Classical Encryption
- Block Cipher and Data Encryption Standard
- Digital Signature
- Public-Key Cryptography and RSA
- Advanced Encryption Standard
- Authentication using Password
- Activation of Firewall on thr System and their Settings
- Detecting Trojans by using -Netstat
- Scanning for Vulnerabilities using Angry IP

CHAPTER ELEVEN

Practical Introduction to Cryptography and Network Security Tools

Two fields that deal with the security of information and communication in computer networks are **cryptography and network security**. The field of **cryptography** focuses on the strategies and procedures used to protect data by converting it into a format that is challenging for unauthorised parties to comprehend or decipher. The practices and policies used to protect computer networks from threats, attacks, and unauthorised access are collectively referred to as **network security**.

Information can be encoded and decoded using cryptography to maintain its confidentiality, integrity, and authenticity. It uses a variety of mathematical formulas and methods to convert plaintext (readable data) into ciphertext (encrypted data) and the other way around. The following are some basic ideas in cryptography:

11.1 Cryptography

Encryption: Using a secret key and an encryption technique, encryption transforms plaintext into ciphertext. Without the accompanying decryption key, the resulting ciphertext cannot be deciphered.

Decryption: Decryption is the opposite of encryption. Using a decryption method and the proper decryption key, ciphertext is converted back into plaintext.

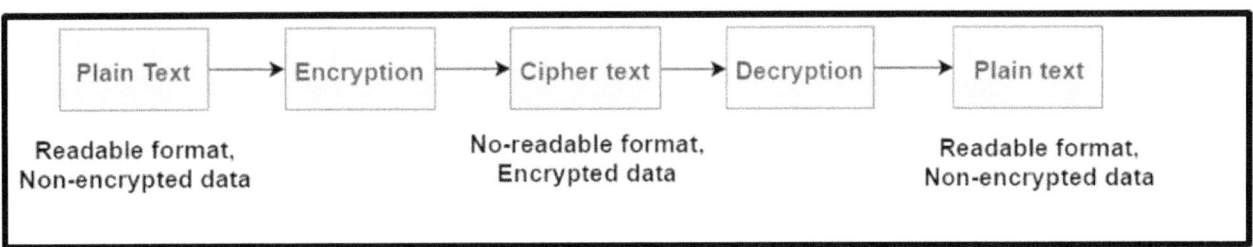

Figure 11.1: Cryptography Basic Flow Diagram

Symmetric Encryption: A single key is used for both encryption and decryption in symmetric encryption. Both the sender and the recipient use the same key. Advanced Encryption Standard (AES) and Data Encryption Standard (DES) are two examples of symmetric encryption methods.

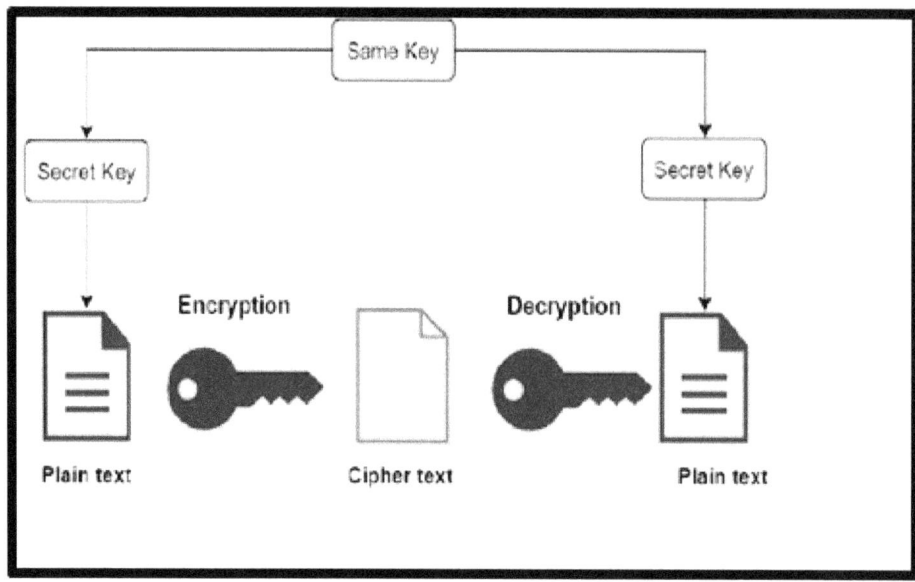

Figure 11.2:Symmetric Encryption

Asymmetric Encryption: Asymmetric encryption uses two keys: a public key for encryption and a private key for decryption. While the private key needs to be kept a secret, the public key can be freely shared. This strategy makes it possible to communicate securely without disclosing the private key. RSA is the most popular asymmetric encryption algorithm.

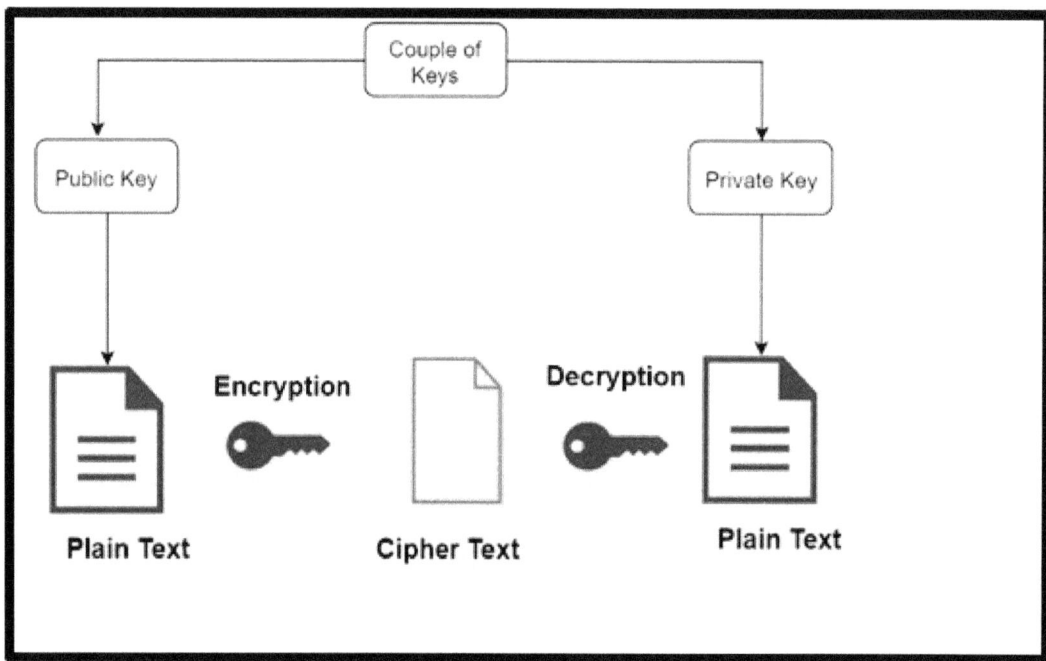

Figure 11.3: Asymmetric Encryption

Hash Function: Hash functions, also referred to as message digests or hash values, are one-way mathematical operations that convert data into fixed-length character strings. Data integrity checks and sender authentication are both done with hash functions. Secure Hash Algorithm (SHA) and Message Digest Algorithm (MD5) are examples of commonly used hash algorithms.

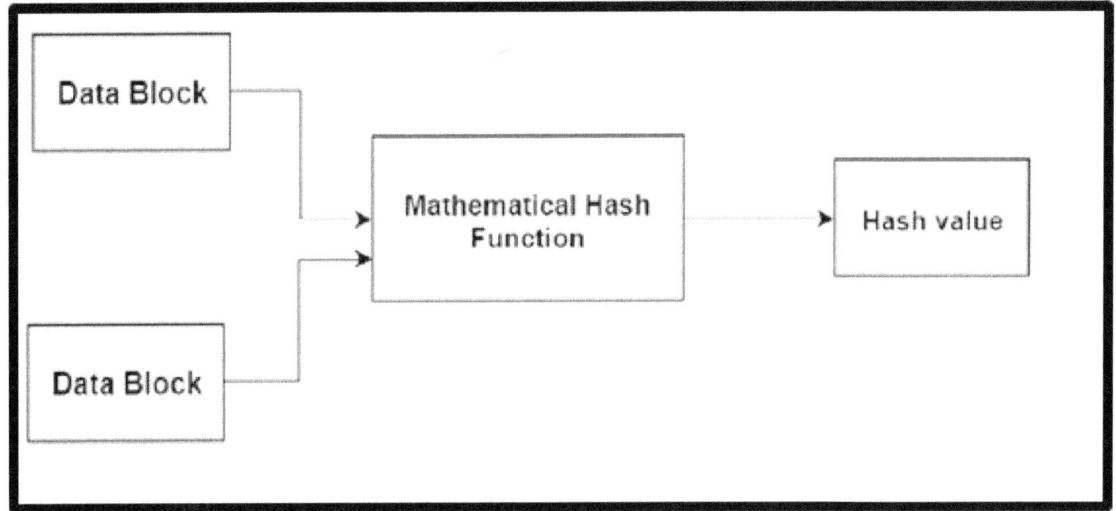

Figure 11.4: Hash Function

Digital Signature: The validity and integrity of digital messages or documents can be confirmed using digital signatures. To link the sender's identity to the message, they use asymmetric encryption. The signature is produced using the sender's private key, and the recipient can validate it using the sender's public key.

11.2 Network Security

To safeguard computer networks against unauthorised access, data breaches, and harmful activity, a variety of procedures and security measures are used. In order to guarantee the confidentiality, integrity, and availability of network resources, both hardware and software solutions are used. The following are some crucial tools of network security:

Firewall: Firewalls are network security tools that regulate and keep track of incoming and outgoing network traffic in accordance with specified security rules. To stop unauthorised access and defend against network risks, they serve as a barrier between internal networks and external networks, such the internet.

Intrusion Detection: Systems for detecting and preventing network attacks and intrusions are known as intrusion detection and prevention systems, or IDPSs.

Virtual Private Network (VPN): Virtual private networks (VPNs) offer private and secure communication over open networks, including the internet. Between remote users and the network, they build encrypted tunnels that provide confidentiality and shield important information from being intercepted.

Authentication and Access Control: Before allowing users or devices access to network resources, authentication systems check their identities. Passwords, biometric information, digital certificates, and multifactor authentication are all examples of this. The actions of users within the network are then subject to limits and permissions enforced by access control systems.

Secure Socket Layer/Transport Layer Security (SSL/TLS): Using SSL/TLS protocols, which stand for Secure Sockets Layer/Transport Layer Security, client and server applications can communicate securely online. To secure critical transactions, financial data, and login passwords while they are being transmitted, they create encrypted connections.

Security Auditing and Incident Response: Regular security audits determine vulnerabilities and gauge the efficiency of network security solutions. Plans for handling security breaches, such as identifying, containing, and lessening the effects of assaults, are outlined in incident response plans.

11.3 Cryptography and Network Security Tools

1. Security Token
2. JCA
3. SignTool.exe
4. Docker

11.3.1 Security Token

A security token is a tangible or digital object that is used to verify a user's identification in the fields of cryptography and network security. To enable strong authentication, security tokens can be used in conjunction with passwords or other authentication elements.

The two primary categories of security tokens are:

- **Hardware Token:** Physical objects known as hardware tokens can create one-time passwords (OTPs). OTPs are brief passwords that are generated at random and only remain valid for a brief duration. Hardware tokens frequently feature a screen where the OTP is displayed, though they can also produce it as sound.
- **Software Token:** Applications that operate on a user's computer or mobile device are referred to as software tokens. Software tokens often offer a challenge-response authentication method or OTP generation.

11.3.2 Java Cryptography Architecture (JCA)

A group of APIs known as the Java Cryptography Architecture (JCA) offer the Java programming language's necessary cryptographic capability. Secure communications, digital signatures, key management, and password authentication are just a few of the uses for it.

- **Independence of Implementation:** Between the cryptographic methods and their implementation, the JCA offers a layer of abstraction. As a result, developers can use the JCA without worrying about how the algorithms will actually be implemented.
- **Algorithm Independent:** Algorithm impartiality The JCA gives programmers the option to select the cryptographic algorithms most appropriate for their application. This means that even if the methods they utilize are no longer regarded as secure, developers may be sure that their programs will be secure.
- **Extensibility:** Because the JCA is extensible, new providers and algorithms can be added to it without disrupting already-running programs. As a result, the JCA is able to stay current with cryptographic advancements.

With the help of the JCA, a number of cryptographic and network security protocols can be implemented. It is a popular option for developers who need to securely and effectively implement various protocols.

11.3.3 SignTool.exe

A command-line tool called SignTool.exe is used to digitally sign files and check their signatures. It is a component of the CryptoAPI (Cryptography API) toolkit, which gives Windows applications access to a number of cryptographic operations.

Digital signatures are used in cryptography to confirm a file's integrity and validity. A hash of the file's contents is encrypted with the use of a private key to produce a digital signature. The hash is a singular value created from the contents of the file, and it is impossible to change it without also changing the contents of the file.

The signature is then decrypted using the signer's public key, and if it is valid, it can be used to confirm that the file has not been altered since it was signed. Files in a number of formats, such as executable files, DLLs, and CAB files, can be signed with SignTool.exe. Additionally, catalogue files, which are used to store the digital signatures of numerous files, can be signed using this method.

Digital signatures can be used in network security to safeguard the confidentiality and integrity of data transmitted over a network. or example, a digital signature can be used to sign a message that is sent over an email or a file that is transferred over a file sharing network. The digital signature can be used to verify that the message or file has not been tampered with since it was sent.

11.3.4 Docker

Although Docker is a well-known technology for containerization that enables effective application deployment and management, it's crucial to remember that Docker does not by default include encryption or security protections for data stored within containers. The application developers and administrators using Docker are in charge of protecting the data. Let's examine a few security and encryption-related issues in relation to Docker:

- **Data encryption:** Data kept in containers is not encrypted by Docker automatically. The application developer is in charge of including encryption measures to safeguard sensitive data. This may involve leveraging encryption tools or libraries offered by the computer language or framework being used to encrypt data both in transit and at rest.
- **Access Control:** To control access to containers and their resources, Docker offers security capabilities. To prevent unauthorised access to containers and the data they store, access control measures can be established, such as user permissions and container isolation. As a result, the containers are protected so that only authorized people or processes can interact with them or access the data they contain.
- **Secure Configuration:** By adhering to best practices, it is essential to configure Docker containers safely. By eliminating pointless services, adopting secure base images, and often patching and updating container images, one can reduce the attack surface. The containers are protected against any flaws and exploits thanks to proper configuration.
- **Network security:** Docker supports networking both with the host system and between containers. It's crucial to establish network settings correctly in order to guarantee network security. To prevent unauthorised access to containerized programs and associated data, this may entail the use of secure network protocols, network segmentation, and the implementation of firewalls or network policies.
- **Security of Container Images:** Docker's container images must be secure. Images ought to come from reliable sources, be updated frequently, and be vulnerability-scanned. For locating known security flaws in container images, Docker offers tools like Docker Security Scanning.

CHAPTER TWELVE

SageMath Installation and Configuration

SageMath is a piece of open-source, free software for mathematic. It is built on top of numerous open-source software programs including, NumPy, SciPy, matplotlib, Sympy, Maxima, GAP, FLINT, R and many more. Access their combined strength through an interface or wrapper, or indirectly through a shared Python-based language.

SageMath is an effective tool for computation, research, and education in mathematics. It can be applied to a wide range of mathematical issues, such as:

- **Algebraic Problems:** solving equations, factoring polynomials, and locating polynomial roots are examples of algebraic problems.
- **Combinatorial Problems:** Counting the number of possible arrangements for an object, determining the maximum flow in a network, and discovering all permutations of a set are examples of combinatorial tasks.
- **Graph theory Problems:** Graph theory issues such determining the network's maximum flow, determining the chromatic number of a graph, and determining the shortest path between two nodes.
- **Numerical Analysis:** difficulties involving numerical analysis, including those involving the solution of differential equations, computing integrals, and fitting data to curves.
- **Number Theory Problems:** Identifying prime numbers, factoring integers, and computing modular functions are examples of number theory difficulties.
- **Calculus Problems:** Problems in calculus that include finding derivatives, integrals, and limits.
- **Statistics Problems:** data fitting to distributions, estimating confidence intervals, and doing hypothesis testing are examples of statistics challenges.

Installation of SageMath

1. Installation of SageMath in Window
2. Installation of SageMath in Mac
3. Installation of SageMath in Linux

Installation of SageMath in Window

- Open PowerShell as runs as administrator
- Enabling Windows Subsystem for Linux (WSL) write command

wsl --install in PowerShell as follow

Figure 12.1: Enabling WSL

Installation of SageMath in Mac

- Open a web browser and go to the official SageMath website: https://www.sagemath.org/
- Click on the "Download" link in the top menu.
- Scroll down to the macOS section and click on the appropriate version of SageMath for your macOS version.
- Once the download is complete, open the downloaded file (e.g., SageMath-X.Y.Z-OSX_10.9-x86_64.dmg).
- In the disk image window that opens, double-click on the "SageMath-X.Y.Z.app" file to start the installation.
- Follow the on-screen instructions to complete the installation process. It may require entering your administrator password.
- After the installation is finished, you can find SageMath in your "Applications" folder. Double-click on the SageMath icon to launch it.

Installation of SageMath in Linux / Ubuntu

The Ubuntu Linux distribution will be installed and the functionalities required to run WSL will be enabled by this command.

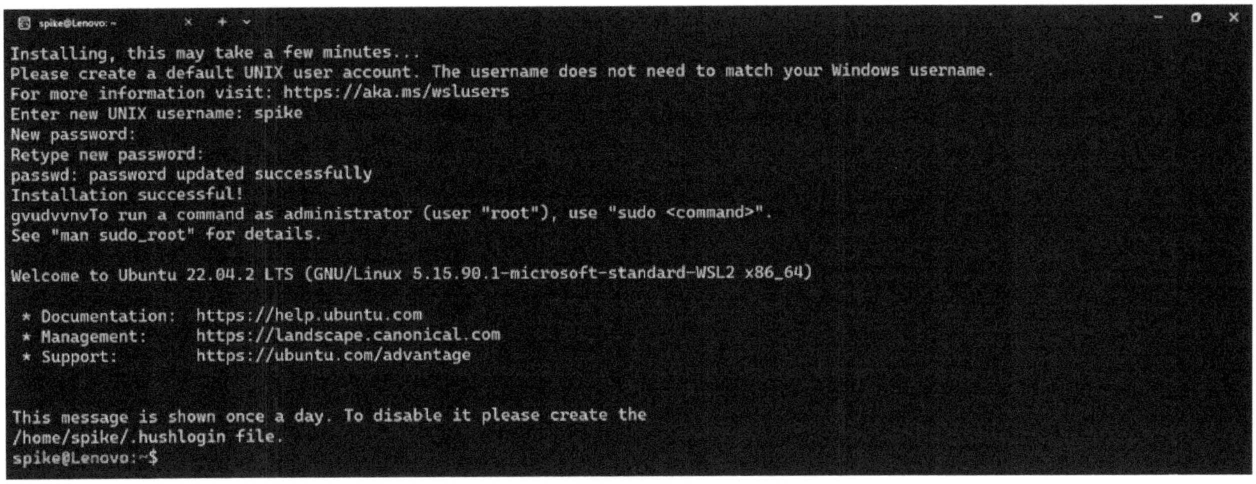

Figure 12.2: Setting up New UNIX Username and Password for Ubuntu

After successful installation of Ubuntu set a new UNIX username as well as password to use it, then use following commands in Ubuntu for installation of SageMath.
sudo apt update

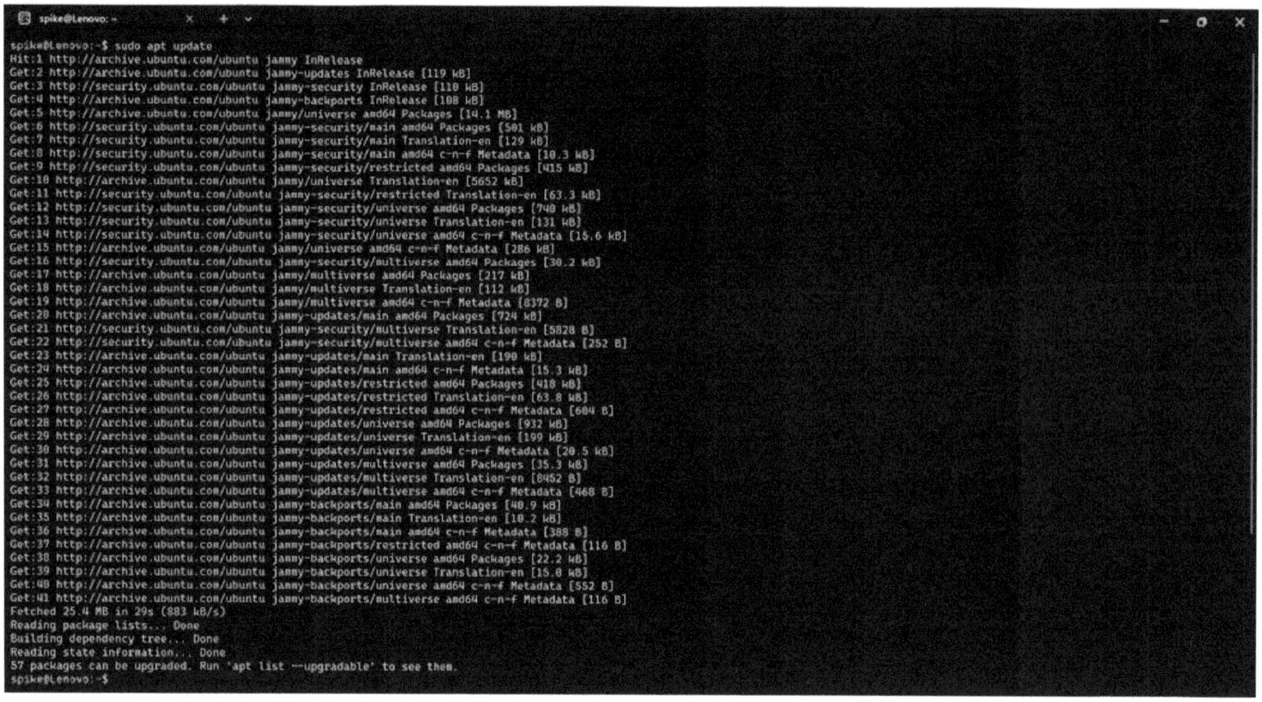

Figure 12.3: Checking up Package Needs to Upgrade

sudo apt update, you ensure that you have the latest information about software packages available in the repositories configured on your system. This is an important step before performing any package installations or upgrades, as it ensures that you have up-to-date information about the packages you can install or update.

sudo apt upgrade

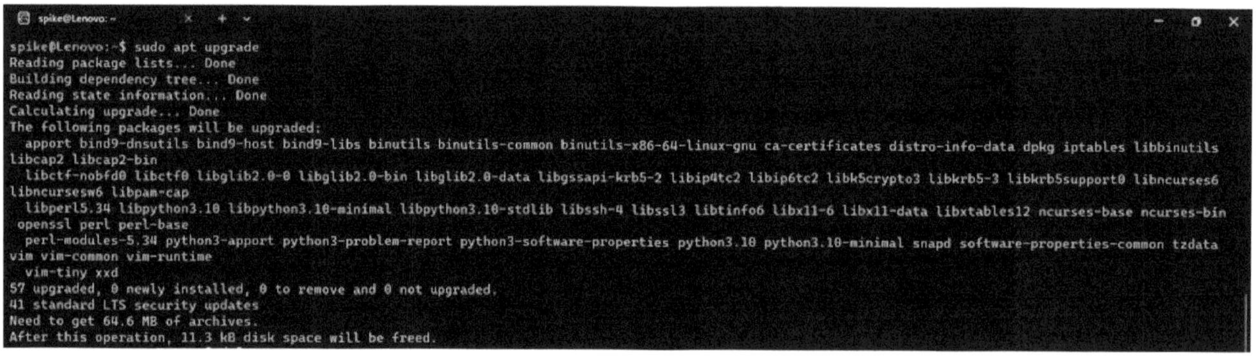

Figure 12.4: Upgrading Packages

sudo apt upgrade ensures that your installed software packages are up to date with the latest versions provided by the repositories configured on your system. It is an important command to keep your system secure and benefit from bug fixes, new features, and performance improvements in the updated packages.

SageMath Installation

Use command ***sudo apt install sagemath*** in ubuntu to install SageMath. Installation process for the SageMath package will be start & apt package manager will download the necessary files for SageMath from the configured software repositories and install them on your system.

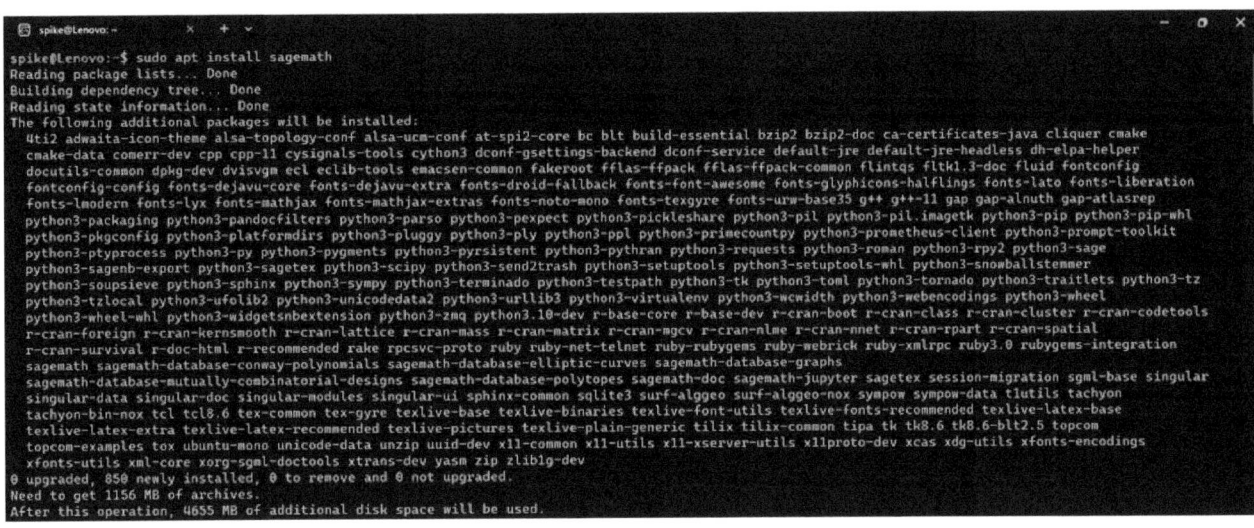

Figure 12.5: Installation of SageMath in Ubuntu using Command sudo apt install sagemath

Jupyter Notebook Installation

Use command **sudo apt install jupyter-notebook** install jupyter-notebook for to write and run program using python language. Then run command sage -n jupyter to launch notebook and jupyter-notebook will open as follow,

Figure 12.6: Jupyter Notebook Interface

CHAPTER THIRTEEN

Linear Algebra, Matrix Multiplication, and Classical Encryption with SageMath

Linear Algebra in SageMath

SageMath has a wide range of features for calculations involving linear algebra. It provides a variety of tools for manipulating matrices, linear transformations, and vectors.

Matrix Multiplication in SageMath

SageMath makes multiplying matrices simple. The matrix function can be used to define matrices, and the * operator can be used to multiply them.

Classical Encryption in SageMath

- SageMath offers a number of mathematical tools and functions that can be used to investigate traditional encryption methods. The Caesar cipher, a straightforward replacement cipher, is a frequently researched method.
- Matrix and linear algebra features are available in Sage. The following illustrates some of the fundamental cryptography functionality.

Linear Algebra & Matrix Functionality

When using Sage, a matrix is specified as a list of lists of numbers that are supplied to the matrix function. like an illustration, try passing a list of integer list like follows

sage: M = matrix ([[1, 3], [7,9]]); M

[1 3]

[7 9]

Passing a list of lists of rational as follows:

sage: M = matrix ([[1/2, 2/3, 3/4], [5, 7, 8]]); M

[1/2 2/3 3/4]

[5 7 8]

Using the IntegerModRing (functionality will be discussed later), you may declare that the input should be decreased by a given modulus.

sage: R = IntegerModRing (100)

sage: M = matrix (R, [[1],[102], [1003]]); M

[1]

[2]

[3]

Or that the input should be taken into account within a finite field (to be further explained).

sage: F = GF (2);

sage: M = matrix (F, [[1, 2, 0, 3]]); M

[1 0 0 1]

Additionally, Sage offers matrix multiplication, addition, and inversion as follows:

sage: M1 = matrix ([[1, 2], [3,4]]);

sage: M2 = matrix ([[1, −1], [1, 1]]);
sage: M1*M2
[3 1]
[7 1]
sage: M1 + M2
[2 1]
[4 5]
sage: M2^−1
[1/2 1/2]
[−1/2 1/2]

Classical Encryption

For examples and exercises involving classical cipher, the following functions are helpful:

en_analphabet = "abcdefghijklmnopqrstuvwxyz"
# This function returns true if and only if the character c is an alphabetic character
def is_alphabetic_char(c):
return (c.lower() in en_alphabet)
# This function converts a single character into its numeric value
def char_to_num(c):
return en_alphabet.index(c.lower())
# This function returns the character corresponding to x mod 26 in the English alphabet
def num_to_char(x):
return en_alphabet [x % 26]

Example 1: Implement Sage encryption/decryption functions that take a key (As an integer in 0, 1, 2, . . ., 25), and a string. The function should only operation the characters 'a', 'b', . . . 'z' (both upper and lower case), and it should leave any other characters unchanged.

Solution:
def CaesarEncrypt (k, plaintext):
ciphertext = ""
for j in xrange(len(plaintext)):
p = plaintext[j]
if is_alphabetic_char(p):
x = (k + char_to_num(p)) % 26
c = num_to_char(x)
else:
c = p
ciphertext += c
return ciphertext
def CaesarDecrypt (k, ciphertext):
plaintext = ""
for j in xrange(len(ciphertext)):
c = ciphertext[j]
if is_alphabetic_char(c):
x = (char_to_num(c) − k) % 26
p = num_to_char(x)
else:
p = c
plaintext += p
return plaintext

Code Explanation:

Each letter in the plaintext is moved a specific number of positions in the alphabet when using the Caesar cipher, which is a substitution cipher. The number of positions to move depends on the key (k). For instance, if k equals 3, the letters "A" and "B" would be encoded as "D" and "E," respectively.

Let's dissect the code and describe each component:

def CaesarEncrypt (k, plaintext):
ciphertext = ""
for j in xrange(len(plaintext)):
p = plaintext[j]
if is_alphabetic_char(p):
x = (k + char_to_num(p)) % 26
c = num_to_char(x)
else:
c = p
ciphertext += c
return ciphertext

This function accepts plaintext and a key (k) as input. The ciphertext is stored in an empty string that is initialised. The plaintext character (p) by character is then iterated over. If the character is an alphabetic character, it uses the char_to_num function to convert it to a numeric value before encrypting it by appending the key (k). The outcome is multiplied by 26 and wrapped around the alphabet. Using the num_to_char function, the resultant numeric value is changed back into a character and appended to the ciphertext string. The ciphertext string is immediately extended if the character is not an alphabetic character. The function then outputs the ciphertext.

def CaesarDecrypt (k, ciphertext):
plaintext = ""
for j in xrange(len(ciphertext)):
c = ciphertext[j]
if is_alphabetic_char(c):
x = (char_to_num(c) - k) % 26
p = num_to_char(x)
else:
p = c
plaintext += p
return plaintext

This function accepts ciphertext and a key (k) as inputs. In order to store the plaintext, it initialises an empty string. The ciphertext's characters (c) are then iterated over. If the character is an alphabetic character, it uses the char_to_num function to transform it to a numeric value before performing the decryption by deducting the key (k). The outcome is multiplied by 26 and wrapped around the alphabet. Using the num_to_char function, the resultant numeric value is changed back to a character and then appended to the plaintext string. The plaintext string is immediately expanded if the character is not an alphabetic character. The function finally returns the plaintext.

Example 2: Implement a function that performs a brute force attack on a ciphertext, it should print a list of the keys and associated decryptions. It should also take an optional parameter that takes a substring and only prints out potential plaintexts that contain that decryption.

Solution:

def BruteForceAttack (ciphertext, keyword=None):
for k in xrange (26):
plaintext = CaesarDecrypt (k, ciphertext)
if (None==keyword) or (keyword in plaintext):
print "key", k, "decryption", plaintext

return

Code Explanation:

BruteForceAttack, this function tries each key (i.e., all 26 possible shifts) to decrypt a given ciphertext before determining whether a supplied keyword (which is optional) is present in the decrypted plaintext.

The ciphertext parameter of the BruteForceAttack function is the encrypted message to be decrypted, and the optional keyword parameter specifies a term that the decrypted message should contain. The xrange function is used to cycle through all conceivable keys (k) from 0 to 25.

It uses the current key (k) to encrypt the ciphertext and calls the CaesarDecrypt function for each key to produce the appropriate plaintext. It is assumed that the CaesarDecrypt function is defined somewhere else because it was not present in the code snippet you submitted.

In the absence of a keyword or if the keyword appears in the plaintext after decryption, the key (k) and the output plaintext are printed.

When the first legitimate decryption is discovered, the function is terminated using the return statement. This suggests that the function will only display and give back the first successful decryption it finds. If the return statement is not included, the function will keep searching all keys until all viable decryptions have been discovered.

Example 3: Show the output of your encrypt function (Example 1) on the following (key, plaintext) pairs:
- k = 16 plaintext = "Get me a vanilla ice cream, make it a double."
- k = 15 plaintext = "I don't much care for Leonard Cohen."
- k = 16 plaintext = "I like root beer floats."

Solution:

sage: k = 6; plaintext = 'Get me a vanilla ice cream, make it a double.'

sage: CaesarEncrypt (k, plaintext)

'mkz sk g bgtorrg oik ixkgs, sgqk oz g juahrk.'

sage: k = 15; plaintext = "I don't much care for Leonard Cohen."

sage: CaesarEncrypt (k, plaintext)

"x sdc'i bjrw rpgt udg atdcpgs rdwtc."

sage: k = 16; plaintext = "I like root beer floats."

sage: CaesarEncrypt(k, plaintext)

'y byau heej ruuh vbeqji.'

Code Explanation:

Sage encrypting three different plaintext messages using a Caesar cipher with different key values (k). Let's analyze each example,

Plaintext for k = 6 is "Get me a vanilla ice cream, make it a double."

The Sage uses a key value of 6 to encrypt the plaintext.

"Mkz sk g bgtorrg oik ixkgs, sgqk oz g juahrk" is the ciphertext that is produced.

Plaintext, k = 15 is "I don't much care for Leonard Cohen,"

The Sage uses a key value of 15 to encrypt the plaintext.

The ciphertext that is produced is 'x sdc'i bjrw rpgt udg atdcpgs rdwtc.'

Plaintext for k = 16 is "I like root beer floats."

The Sage uses a key value of 16 to encrypt the plaintext.

The ciphertext that is produced is "y byau heej ruuh vbeqji."

Each letter in the plaintext is moved a specific number of positions in the alphabet when using a Caesar cipher. The number of shifts is determined by the key value (k). In these instances, the Sage encrypts the data by moving each letter by the appropriate key value. Punctuation and other non-alphabetic characters are left alone.

You would need to utilise the equivalent key value (k) in the Caesar decryption procedure, which entails shifting each letter back by the same number of positions, in order to decrypt the ciphertext.

Example 4: Show the output of your decrypt function (Example 1) on the following (key, ciphertext) pairs:
- k = 12 ciphertext = 'nduzs ftq buzq oazqe.'

- k = 3 ciphertext = "fdhvdu qhhgv wr orvh zhljkw."
- k = 20 ciphertext = "ufgihxm uly numnys."

Solution:

sage: k = 12; ciphertext = "nduzs ftq buzq oazqe."
sage: CaesarDecrypt(k, ciphertext)
'bring the pine cones.'
sage: k = 3; ciphertext = "fdhvdu qhhgv wr orvh zhljkw."
sage: CaesarDecrypt(k, ciphertext)
'caesar needs to lose weight.'
sage: k = 20; ciphertext = "ufgihxm uly numnys."
sage: CaesarDecrypt(k, ciphertext)
'almonds are tastey.'

Code Explanation:

Sage is decrypting three ciphertexts using the CaesarDecrypt function with different key values (k). Let's analyze each example:

Ciphertext for k = 12 is "nduzs ftq buzq oazqe."

Using the CaesarDecrypt function, the Sage decrypts the ciphertext using a key value of 12. "bring the pine cones" is the plaintext that is produced.

Ciphertext k = 3 is "fdhvdu qhhgv wr orvh zhljkw."

With a key value of three, the Sage decrypts the ciphertext. "caesar needs to lose weight.", which is the resultant plaintext.

Ciphertext k = 20 is "ufgihxm uly numnys."

A key value of 20 is used by the Sage to decrypt the ciphertext. "almonds are tasty" is the phrase that is produced.

Example 5: Show the output of your attack function (Example 4) on the following ciphertexts, if an optional keyword is specified, pass that to your attack function:

- ciphertext = 'gryy guru gob tab gb nzoebfr puncry.' keyword = 'chapel'
- ciphertext = 'wziv kyv jyfk nyve kyv tpdsrcj tirjy.' keyword = 'cymbal'
- ciphertext = 'baeeq klwosjl osk s esf ozg cfwo lgg emuz.' no keyword

Solution:

sage: ciphertext = 'gryy gurz gb tb gb nzoebfr puncry.'
sage: BruteForceAttack(ciphertext, 'chapel')
key 13 decryption tell them to go to ambrose chapel.
sage: ciphertext = 'wziv kyv jyfk nyve kyv tpdsrcj tirjy.'
sage: BruteForceAttack(ciphertext, 'cymbal')
key 17 decryption fire the shot when the cymbals crash.
sage: ciphertext = 'baeeq klwosjl osk s esf ozg cfwo lgg emuz.'
sage: BruteForceAttack(ciphertext)
key 0 decryption baeeq klwosjl osk s esf ozg cfwo lgg emuz.
key 1 decryption azddp jkvnrik nrj r dre nyf bevn kff dlty.
key 2 decryption zycco ijumqhj mqi q cqd mxe adum jee cksx.
key 3 decryption yxbbn hitlpgi lph p bpc lwd zctl idd bjrw.
key 4 decryption xwaam ghskofh kog o aob kvc ybsk hcc aiqv.
key 5 decryption wvzzl fgrjneg jnf n zna jub xarj gbb zhpu.
key 6 decryption vuyyk efqimdf ime m ymz ita wzqi faa ygot.
key 7 decryption utxxj dephlce hld l xly hsz vyph ezz xfns.
key 8 decryption tswwi cdogkbd gkc k wkx gry uxog dyy wemr.
key 9 decryption srvvh bcnfjac fjb j vjw fqx twnf cxx vdlq.
key 10 decryption rquug abmeizb eia i uiv epw svme bww uckp.

key 11 decryption qpttf zaldhya dhz h thu dov ruld avv tbjo.
key 12 decryption posse yzkcgxz cgy g sgt cnu qtkc zuu sain.
key 13 decryption onrrd xyjbfwy bfx f rfs bmt psjb ytt rzhm.
key 14 decryption nmqqc wxiaevx aew e qer als oria xss qygl.
key 15 decryption mlppb vwhzduw zdv d pdq zkr nqhz wrr pxfk.
key 16 decryption lkooa uvgyctv ycu c ocp yjq mpgy vqq owej.
key 17 decryption kjnnz tufxbsu xbt b nbo xip lofx upp nvdi.
key 18 decryption jimmy stewart was a man who knew too much.
key 19 decryption ihllx rsdvzqs vzr z lzm vgn jmdv snn ltbg.
key 20 decryption hgkkw qrcuypr uyq y kyl ufm ilcu rmm ksaf.
key 21 decryption gfjjv pqbtxoq txp x jxk tel hkbt qll jrze.
key 22 decryption feiiu opaswnp swo w iwj sdk gjas pkk iqyd.
key 23 decryption edhht nozrvmo rvn v hvi rcj fizr ojj hpxc.
key 24 decryption dcggs mnyquln qum u guh qbi ehyq nii gowb.
key 25 decryption cbffr lmxptkm ptl t ftg pah dgxp mhh fnva.

Code Explanation:

A function called "BruteForceAttack" is being used by the Sage to decrypt some ciphertexts. The ciphertexts are messages that have been encoded using a straightforward Caesar cipher, shifting each letter in the plaintext by a predetermined number of alphabetic places.

Let's see Example:

Ciphertext: "gryy gurz gb tb gb nzoebfr puncry."

Key: 13

Decryption: "tell them to go to ambrose chapel."

The ciphertext is shifted by 13 positions backward in the alphabet to obtain the plaintext message.

Ciphertext: "wziv kyv jyfk nyve kyv tpdsrcj tirjy."

Key: 17

Decryption: "fire the shot when the cymbals crash."

The ciphertext is shifted by 17 positions backward in the alphabet to obtain the plaintext message.

Ciphertext: "baeeq klwosjl osk s esf ozg cfwo lgg emuz."

Key: 0, 1, 2, 3, 4, 5, 6, 7, 8, 9, 10, 11, 12, 13, 14, 15, 16, 17

Decryption: The Sage performs a brute-force attack by trying all possible keys from 0 to 17. The key that results in a meaningful decryption is 0: "baeeq klwosjl osk s esf ozg cfwo lgg emuz."

In a brute-force assault, all potential keys are iteratively tested until the right decryption is discovered. In this instance, it is possible to attempt every key in order to discover the right decryption because there are only 26 potential keys for the Caesar cypher (matching to the 26 letters of the alphabet).

CHAPTER FOURTEEN

Block Cipher and Data Encryption Standard with SageMath

A block cipher is a symmetric cryptographic algorithm that operates on fixed-size blocks of data. It takes a block of plaintext as input and produces a block of ciphertext as output. The block size is typically fixed and commonly used block cipher algorithms have block sizes of 64 or 128 bits.

- Block ciphers use a key to determine the transformation applied to the input plaintext block to produce the corresponding ciphertext block. The same key is used for both encryption and decryption. The security of a block cipher relies on the strength of the encryption algorithm and the secrecy of the key.
- An encryption standard, also known as an encryption algorithm or cryptographic algorithm, is a specific implementation of a block cipher. It defines the exact steps and operations involved in encrypting and decrypting data using the block cipher. Encryption standards are designed to provide confidentiality and data integrity.
-

    Some well-known encryption standards include:

- Data Encryption Standard (DES): DES was developed in the 1970s and became the most widely used encryption standard for many years. It has a block size of 64 bits and uses a 56-bit key. However, due to advances in technology and computational power, DES is no longer considered secure.

- Triple Data Encryption Standard (3DES): 3DES is an enhanced version of DES that applies the DES algorithm three times with different keys to increase security. It provides a higher level of security than DES but is slower due to multiple encryption operations.

- Advanced Encryption Standard (AES): AES is currently the most widely used and accepted encryption standard. It supports block sizes of 128 bits and key sizes of 128, 192, or 256 bits. AES is known for its efficiency and strong security, and it is used in various applications and protocols worldwide.

These encryption standards, among others, form the foundation for secure communication, data protection, and confidentiality in various domains, including network security, e-commerce, and data storage.

Example 1: This example implements simplified DES.

```
# The Expansions/Permutations are stored as lists of bit positions
P10_data = [3, 5, 2, 7, 4, 10, 1, 9, 8, 6];
P8_data = [6, 3, 7, 4, 8, 5, 10, 9];
LS1_data = [2, 3, 4, 5, 1];
LS2_data = [3, 4, 5, 1, 2];
IP_data = [2, 6, 3, 1, 4, 8, 5, 7];
IPinv_data = [4, 1, 3, 5, 7, 2, 8, 6];
```

```
EP_data = [4, 1, 2, 3, 2, 3, 4, 1];
P4_data = [2, 4, 3, 1];
SW_data = [5, 6, 7, 8, 1, 2, 3, 4];
# SDES lookup tables
S0_data = [[1, 0, 3, 2],
[3, 2, 1, 0],
[0, 2, 1, 3],
[3, 1, 3, 2]];
S1_data = [[0, 1, 2, 3],
[2, 0, 1, 3],
[3, 0, 1, 0],
[2, 1, 0, 3]];
```

Code Explanation:

The Data Encryption Standard (DES) algorithm is implemented using the given code in its simplest form. The expansions, permutations, and lookup tables used in the method are defined by a variety of data structures that are included in the system. The various components of the code are explained as follows:

Expansions/Permutations:

- P10_data: The list depicts the permutation that was used to create a 10-bit output from a 10-bit input. The bit positions that are chosen from the input are specified.
- P8_data: This list specifies the permutation used to produce an 8-bit output from an 8-bit input.
- LS1_data: It shows where the bits should be rotated one position to the left when creating keys.
- The bits that will be rotated left by two places during key creation are specified in the LS2_data list.
- IP_data: The list specifies the starting permutation used to shuffle the bits of an 8-bit input.
- IPinv_data: This variable represents the initial permutation's inverse, which is utilised to reverse the original shuffle.
- EP_data: The list shows the expansion permutation used to produce an 8-bit output from a 4-bit input.
- P4_data: This list specifies the permutation used to produce a 4-bit output from a 4-bit input.
- The list in SW_data describes the permutation used during the swap operation.

Lookup tables for SDES:

- S0_data: The S0 substitution box is represented as a 4x4 matrix. 2 bits of input are exchanged for 2 bits of output during the encryption process.
- Similar to S1, S1_data is a 4x4 matrix that represents the S1 substitution box used during encryption.

The code offers the definitions and data structures required to implement the streamlined DES algorithm. The actual implementation of the encryption or decryption functions is not included in the code, though. The code sample you offered is deficient and does not contain the actual logic needed to carry out encryption or decryption operations using the specified data structures.

```
def ApplyPermutation(X, permutation):
    """
    This function takes a permutation list (list of bit positions.) And outputs a bit list with the bits taken from X.
    """
    # permute the list X
    l = len(permutation);
    return [X[permutation[j]-1] for j in xrange(l)];
def ApplySBox(X, SBox):
```

r"""

This function Applies the SDES SBox (by table look up)"""

r = 2*X[0] + X[3];

c = 2*X[1] + X[2];

o = SBox[r][c];

return [o & 2, o & 1];

Each of these functions uses ApplyPermutation and a permutation list to perform an SDES Expansion/Permutation

def P10(X):

return ApplyPermutation(X, P10_data);

def P8(X):

return ApplyPermutation(X, P8_data);

def IP(X):

return ApplyPermutation(X, IP_data);

def IPinv(X):

return ApplyPermutation(X, IPinv_data);

def EP(X):

return ApplyPermutation(X, EP_data);

def P4(X):

return ApplyPermutation(X, P4_data);

def SW(X):

return ApplyPermutation(X, SW_data);

def LS1(X):

return ApplyPermutation(X, LS1_data);

def LS2(X):

return ApplyPermutation(X, LS2_data);

#

These two functions perform the SBox substitutions

#

def S0(X):

return ApplySBox(X, S0_data);

def S1(X):

return ApplySBox(X, S1_data);

def concatenate(left, right):

r"""

Joins to bit lists together.

"""

ret = [left[j] for j in xrange(len(left))];

ret.extend(right);

return ret;

def LeftHalfBits(block):

r"""

Returns the left half bits from block.

"""

l = len(block);

return [block[j] for j in xrange(l/2)];

def RightHalfBits(block):

r"""

Returns the right half bits from block.
"""
l = len(block);
return [block[j] for j in xrange(l/2, l)];
def XorBlock(block1, block2):
r"""
Xors two blocks together.
"""
l = len(block1);
if (l != len(block2)):
raise ValueError, "XorBlock arguments must be same length"
return [(block1[j]+block2[j]) % 2 for j in xrange(l)];
def SDESKeySchedule(K):
r"""
Expands an SDES Key (bit list) into the two round keys.
"""
temp_K = P10(K);
left_temp_K = LeftHalfBits(temp_K);
right_temp_K = RightHalfBits(temp_K);
K1left = LS1(left_temp_K);
K1right = LS1(right_temp_K);
K1temp = concatenate(K1left, K1right);
K1 = P8(K1temp);
K2left = LS2(K1left);
K2right = LS2(K1right);
K2temp = concatenate(K2left, K2right);
K2 = P8(K2temp);
return (K1, K2);
def f_K(block, K):
r"""
Performs the f_K function supplied block and K.
"""
left_block = LeftHalfBits(block);
right_block = RightHalfBits(block);
temp_block1 = EP(right_block);
temp_block2 = XorBlock(temp_block1, K);
left_temp_block2 = LeftHalfBits(temp_block2);
right_temp_block2 = RightHalfBits(temp_block2);
S0_out = S0(left_temp_block2);
S1_out = S1(right_temp_block2);
temp_block3 = concatenate(S0_out, S1_out);
temp_block4 = P4(temp_block3)
temp_block5 = XorBlock(temp_block4, left_block);
output_block = concatenate(temp_block5, right_block)
return output_block;
def SDESEncrypt(plaintext_block, K):
r"""
Performs a single SDES plaintext block encryption. (Given plaintext and key as bit lists.)

"""
(K1, K2) = SDESKeySchedule(K);
temp_block1 = IP(plaintext_block);
temp_block2 = f_K(temp_block1, K1);
temp_block3 = SW(temp_block2);
temp_block4 = f_K(temp_block3, K2);
output_block = IPinv(temp_block4);
return output_block;

Code Explanation:

The provided code implements various functions for performing encryption using the Simplified Data Encryption Standard (SDES) algorithm. Here's an explanation of the different parts of the code:

ApplyPermutation(X, permutation):

- This function takes a bit list X and a permutation list as input.
- It applies the permutation to the bits in X according to the specified permutation list.
- The function returns a new bit list with the bits taken from X based on the permutation.

ApplySBox(X, SBox):

- This function applies the SDES SBox using table lookup.
- It takes a bit list X and an SBox (substitution box) as input.
- The function uses the bits in X to determine the row (r) and column (c) in the SBox lookup table.
- It retrieves the corresponding value (o) from the SBox and returns a new bit list with the bits of o.

Permutation functions (P10, P8, IP, IPinv, EP, P4, SW, LS1, LS2):

- Each of these functions takes a bit list as input and applies the corresponding permutation using the ApplyPermutation function.
- For example, P10 applies the P10_data permutation to the input bit list X.
- The functions return a new bit list with the bits rearranged according to the specified permutation.

SBox functions (S0, S1):

- These functions apply the S0_data and S1_data substitution boxes to a bit list using the ApplySBox function.
- They return a new bit list with the substituted bits based on the SBox lookup.

Utility functions (concatenate, LeftHalfBits, RightHalfBits, XorBlock):

- These functions provide utility operations for manipulating bit lists.
- Concatenate joins two bit lists together.
- LeftHalfBits and RightHalfBits extract the left and right halves of a bit list, respectively.
- XorBlock performs the bitwise XOR operation between two bit lists.

SDESKeySchedule(K):

- This function expands an SDES key (bit list) into two round keys.
- It applies the P10, LS1, LS2, and P8 permutations to the key to generate the round keys K1 and K2.
- The function returns a tuple (K1, K2) representing the two round keys.

f_K(block, K):

- This function performs the f_K function using the supplied block and key K.
- It applies the EP, XOR, S0, S1, P4, and XOR operations according to the SDES algorithm.
- The function returns the output block after applying the operations.

SDESEncrypt(plaintext_block, K):

- This function performs a single SDES encryption on a plaintext block using the provided key K.
- It applies the initial permutation (IP), f_K function with round keys K1 and K2, swap (SW), and inverse initial permutation (IPinv) operations.
- The function returns the encrypted ciphertext block.

These functions collectively implement the encryption functionality of the Simplified Data Encryption Standard (SDES) algorithm.

CHAPTER FIFTEEN

Digital Signature with SageMath

Digital signature is a mathematical scheme for verifying the authenticity and integrity of a digital message or document.

- A valid digital signature on a message gives a recipient confidence that the message came from a sender known to the recipient and that the message has not been altered since it was sent.
- Digital signatures are based on public key cryptography. In public key cryptography, each user has two keys: a public key and a private key. The public key is used to encrypt messages, and the private key is used to decrypt them.
- To create a digital signature, the sender uses their private key to encrypt a hash of the message. The hash is a unique value that is generated from the message. The encrypted hash is then attached to the message.

When the recipient receives the message, they use the sender's public key to decrypt the hash. If the hash decrypts successfully, the recipient knows that the message came from the sender and that the message has not been altered since it was sent.

Digital signatures are used in a variety of applications, including:

1. Signing contracts
2. Filing tax returns
3. Signing medical records
4. Verifying software downloads
5. Authenticating email messages

Digital signatures are considered to be a secure way to verify the authenticity and integrity of digital messages and documents. They are also legally recognized in many countries.

Benefits of using digital signatures:

1. They provide a high level of security.
2. They are legally recognized.
3. They are easy to use.
4. They can be used to sign a variety of documents.

Drawbacks of using digital signatures:

1. They can be expensive to set up.
2. They require a certain level of technical knowledge.
3. They may not be accepted by all organizations.

Overall, digital signatures are a secure and convenient way to verify the authenticity and integrity of digital messages and documents. They are a valuable tool for businesses and individuals who need to ensure the security of their electronic communications.

Example 1: Using Sage, we can perform a DSA sign and verify:

sage: # First we generate the domain parameters
sage: # Generate a 16 bit prime q
sage: q = 1;
sage: while (q < 2^15): q = random_prime(2^16)
....:
sage: q
42697
sage: # Generate a 64 bit p, such that q divides (p−1)
sage: p = 1
sage: while (not is_prime(p)):
....: p = (2^48 + randint(1,2^46)*2)*q + 1
....:
sage: p
12797003281321319017
sage: # Generate h and g
sage: h = randint(2,p−2)
sage: h
5751574539220326847
sage: F = GF(p)
sage: g = F(h)^((p−1)/q)
sage: g
9670562682258945855
sage: # Generate a user public / private key
sage: # private key
sage: x = randint(2,q−1)
sage: x
20499
sage: # public key
sage: y = F(g)^x
sage: y
7955052828197610751
sage: # Sign and verify a random value
sage: H = randint(2,p−1)
sage: # Signing
sage: # random blinding value
sage: k = randint(2,q−1)
sage: r = F(g)^k % q
sage: r = F(g)^k
sage: r = r.lift() % q
sage: r
6805
sage: kinv = xgcd(k,q)[1] % q
sage: s = kinv*(H + x*r) % q
sage: s

```
26026
sage: # Verifying
sage: w = xgcd(s,q)[1]; w
12250
sage: u1 = H*w % q; u1
6694
sage: u2 = r*w % q; u2
16706
sage: v = F(g)^u1 * F(y)^u2
sage: v = v.lift() % q
sage: v
6805
sage: v == r
True
sage: # Sign and verify another random value
sage: H = randint(2,p-1)
sage: k = randint(2,q-1)
sage: r = F(g)^k
sage: r = r.lift() % q
sage: r
3284
sage: kinv = xgcd(k,q)[1] % q
sage: s = kinv*(H + x*r) % q
sage: s
2330
sage: # Verifying
sage: w = xgcd(s,q)[1]; w
4343
sage: u1 = H*w % q; u1
32191
sage: u2 = r*w % q; u2
1614
sage: v = F(g)^u1 * F(y)^u2
sage: v = v.lift() % q
sage: v
3284
sage: v == r
True
```

Code Explanation:

The provided code demonstrates an example of generating domain parameters and performing DSA (Digital Signature Algorithm) signing and verification using Sage. Here's an explanation of the different parts of the code:

Generating Domain Parameters:

- The code generates a 16-bit prime number q using the random_prime function.
- It generates a 64-bit prime number p such that q divides (p-1).
- It generates a random value h and calculates g as h raised to the power of (p-1)/q in the finite field GF(p).

Generating User Public/Private Key:

- The code generates a random private key x within the range (2, q-1).
- It calculates the public key y as g raised to the power of x in the finite field GF(p).

Signing and Verification:

- The code generates a random value H.
- For signing, it generates a random blinding value k within the range (2, q-1).
- It calculates r as g raised to the power of k modulo q.
- It calculates s using the formula: kinv*(H + x*r) modulo q, where kinv is the inverse of k modulo q.
- For verification, it calculates w as the inverse of s modulo q.
- It calculates u1 as Hw modulo q and u2 as rw modulo q.
- It calculates v as (g^u1 * y^u2) modulo q.
- Finally, it checks if v is equal to r to verify the signature.

Additional Signing and Verification:

- The code performs another round of signing and verification with a different random value H.
- The process is similar to the previous round, generating a new random blinding value k, calculating r, s, w, u1, u2, and v, and checking if v is equal to r.

The code demonstrates the generation of domain parameters, generation of public/private keys, and the process of signing and verifying using the DSA algorithm.

Example 2: The following functions implement DSA domain parameter generation, key generation, and DSA Signing:

```
# Generates a 16 bit q and 64 bit p, both prime such that q divides p-1
def DSA_generate_domain_parameters():
g = 1
while (1 == g):
# first find a q
q = 1
while (q < 2^15): q = random_prime(2^16)
# next find a p
p = 1
while (not is_prime(p)):
p = (2^47 + randint(1,2^45)*2)*q + 1
F = GF(p)
h = randint(2,p-1)
g = (F(h)^((p-1)/q)).lift()
return (p, q, g)
# Generates a users private and public key given domain parameters p, q, and g
def DSA_generate_keypair(p, q, g):
x = randint(2,q-1)
F = GF(p)
y = F(g)^x
y = y.lift()
return (x,y)
#
# Given domain parameters p, q and g as well as a secret key x and a hash value H
```

```
# this performs the DSA signing algorithm
#
def DSA_sign(p, q, g, x, H):
    k = randint(2,q-1)
    F = GF(p)
    r = F(g)^k
    r = r.lift() % q
    kinv = xgcd(k,q)[1] % q
    s = kinv*(H + x*r) % q
    return (r, s)
```

Code Explanation:

The provided code implements DSA (Digital Signature Algorithm) domain parameter generation, key generation, and DSA signing. Here's an explanation of the different functions:

DSA_generate_domain_parameters():

- This function generates domain parameters for DSA.
- It first generates a prime number q of 16 bits using the random_prime function.
- Then, it generates a prime number p of 64 bits such that q divides (p-1).
- It generates a random value h.
- Finally, it calculates g as h raised to the power of (p-1)/q and returns the values (p, q, g).

DSA_generate_keypair(p, q, g):

- This function generates a user's private and public key pair for DSA, given the domain parameters p, q, and g.
- It generates a random private key x within the range (2, q-1).
- It calculates the public key y as g raised to the power of x in the finite field GF(p).
- Finally, it returns the key pair (x, y).

DSA_sign(p, q, g, x, H):

- This function performs the DSA signing algorithm given the domain parameters p, q, and g, the private key x, and the hash value H.
- It generates a random blinding value k within the range (2, q-1).
- It calculates r as g raised to the power of k modulo q.
- It calculates s using the formula: kinv*(H + x*r) modulo q, where kinv is the inverse of k modulo q.
- Finally, it returns the signature (r, s).

These functions allow for the generation of domain parameters, generation of key pairs, and signing using the DSA algorithm.

CHAPTER SIXTEEN

Public-Key Cryptography and RSA with SageMath

Public Key Cryptography

A pair of keys that are mathematically connected are used in public key cryptography: a public key and a private key. It enables confidential communication between two parties who have never previously exchanged a secret key. Asymmetric cryptography, commonly referred to as public key cryptography, is frequently used for key exchange, digital signatures, and encryption.

RSA (Rivest-Shamir-Adleman):

One of the most well-known and commonly used public key encryption algorithms is RSA (Rivest-Shamir-Adleman). In 1977, Ron Rivest, Adi Shamir, and Leonard Adleman created it. The mathematical challenge of factoring big composite numbers serves as the foundation for RSA.

RSA Algorithm as follow:

1. Choose two large prime numbers, p and q.
2. Calculate n = p * q, which is the modulus.
3. Calculate f(n)= (p - 1) (q - 1), which is the Euler's totient function.
4. Choose an encrypt key, e, that is relatively prime to f(n).
5. Calculate the decrypt key, d, as the multiplicative inverse of e mod f(n).
6. To decrypt a ciphertext, C, raise it to the power of the decrypt key, d.
7. To encrypt a message, M, raise it to the power of the encrypt key, e.

Implementation of RSA Algorithm with example:

1. Select two prime numbers, p = 17 and q = 11.
2. Calculate n = pq = 17 * 11 = 187.
3. Calculate f(n) = (p - 1) (q - 1) = 16 * 10 = 160.
4. Select e such that e is relatively prime to f(n) = 160 and less than f(n); we choose e = 7.
5. Determine d such that de K 1 (mod 160) and d 6 160. The correct value is d = 23, because 23 * 7 = 161 = (1 * 160) + 1; d can be calculated using the extended Euclid's algorithm.

The resulting keys are public key PU = {7, 187} and private key PR = {23, 187}.

The example shows the use of these keys for a plaintext input of M = 88. For encryption, we need to calculate C = 887 mod 187. Exploiting the properties of modular arithmetic, we can do this as follows.

6. To decrypt a ciphertext, C, raise it to the power of the decrypt key, d (C = 887 mod 187)

88 mod 187 = [(88 mod 187) * (88 mod 187) * (88 mod 187)] mod 187

88 mod 187 = 88

88 mod 187 = 7744 mod 187 = 77

88 mod 187 = 59,969,536 mod 187 = 132

1 mod 187 = (88 * 77 * 132) mod 187 = 894,432 mod 187 = 11

7. To encrypt a message, M, raise it to the power of the encrypt key, e.

For decryption, we calculate M = 1123 mod 187:

11 mod 187 = [(11 mod 187) * (11 mod 187) * (11 mod 187) * (11 mod 187) * (11 mod 187)] mod 187

11 mod 187 = 11

11 mod 187 = 121

11 mod 187 = 14,641 mod 187 = 55

11 mod 187 = 214,358,881 mod 187 = 33

11 mod 187 = (11 * 121 * 55 * 33 * 33) mod 187 = 79,720,245 mod 187 = 88

Using Sage, We Can Simulate an RSA Encryption & Decryption

sage: # randomly select some prime numbers

sage: p = random_prime (1000); p

191

sage: q = random_prime (1000); q

601

sage: # compute the modulus

sage: N = p*q

sage: R = IntegerModRing(N)

sage: phi_N = (p-1) *(q-1)

sage: # we can choose the encrypt key to be anything relatively prime to phi_N

sage: e = 17

sage: gcd (d, phi_N)

1

sage: # the decrypt key is the multiplicative inverse of d mod phi_N

sage: d = xgcd (d, phi_N) [1] % phi_N

sage: d

60353

sage: # Now we will encrypt/decrypt some random 7 digit numbers

sage: P = randint (1,127); P

97

sage: # encrypt

sage: C = R(P)^e; C

46685

sage: # decrypt

sage: R(C)^d

97

sage: P = randint (1,127); P

46

sage: # encrypt

sage: C = R(P)^e; C

75843

sage: # decrypt

sage: R(C)^d

46

sage: P = randint (1,127); P

3

sage: # encrypt

sage: C = R(P)^e; C

288

sage: # decrypt

sage: R(C)^d
3

Also, Sage can just as easily do much larger numbers:

sage: p = random_prime (1000000000); p
114750751
sage: q = random_prime (1000000000); q
8916569
sage: N = p*q
sage: R = IntegerModRing(N)
sage: phi_N = (p-1) *(q-1)
sage: e = 2^16 + 1
sage: d = xgcd (e, phi_N) [1] % phi_N
sage: d
237150735093473
sage: P = randint (1,1000000); P
955802
sage: C = R(P)^e
sage: R(C)^d
955802

Code Explanation:

sage: p = random_prime (1000); p
191
sage: q = random_prime (1000); q
601
*sage: N = p*q*
sage: R = IntegerModRing(N)
*sage: phi_N = (p-1) *(q-1)*

In this section, two prime numbers, p and q, are chosen at random from the range [1,000]. In this case, p = 191 and q = 601. After that, p and q are multiplied to determine the modulus N. An integer modular ring with modulus N is allocated to the variable R, and this ring will be utilised for modular arithmetic operations. The Euler's totient function of N, which is (p-1)*(q-1), is used to determine phi_N.

sage: e = 17
sage: gcd (d, phi_N)
1
sage: d = xgcd (d, phi_N) [1] % phi_N
sage: d
60353

The encryption key e is assigned to a specified value in this section, which is in this case 17. The greatest common divisor between d and phi_N is then checked using gcd (d, phi_N). D is currently undefined; hence it will result in an error. It appears that the code has an error. Before d is used in gcd (d, phi_N), it should be declared. Using the extended Euclidean algorithm (xgcd), d is calculated as the modular multiplicative inverse of e modulo phi_N, presuming its definition was correct. D has a value of 60353.

sage: P = randint (1,127); P
97
sage: C = R(P)^e; C
46685
sage: R(C)^d
97

The method of encryption and decryption is shown in this section. First, a 7-digit number P is produced at random from 1 to 127. P is 97 here. The encryption is then carried out by raising P in the modular arithmetic ring R to the power of e. The ciphertext C that is produced is 46685. The original plaintext P, or 97, is obtained by raising C to the power of d in the modular arithmetic ring R, which completes the decryption process. This demonstrates how the encryption and decryption procedures are correct.

sage: p = random_prime (1000000000); p

114750751

sage: q = random_prime (1000000000); q

8916569

sage: N = p*q

sage: R = IntegerModRing(N)

sage: phi_N = (p-1) *(q-1)

sage: e = 2^16 + 1

sage: d = xgcd (e, phi_N) [1] % phi_N

sage: d

237150735093473

sage: P = randint (1,1000000); P

955802

sage: C = R(P)^e

sage: R(C)^d

955802

This section explained how greater prime numbers can be used.

CHAPTER SEVENTEEN

Advanced Encryption Standard with SageMath

In the 1990s, the US Government wanted to standardize a cryptographic algorithm Many proposals were submitted, and after a lot of debate, an algorithm called Rijndael was accepted Joan Daemen and Vincent Rijmen (Belgium) (Rijmen and Daemen). 56-bit keys of DES were no longer considered safe against attacks and the 64-bit blocks were also considered weak.

AES based on 128-bit blocks, 128-bit keys, June 1998, the Rijndael proposal was submitted to NIST as one of the candidates for AES. Out of the initial 15 candidates, only 5 were shortlisted in August 1999.

- Rijndael (From Joan Daemen and Vincent Rijmen; 86 votes)
- Serpent (From Ross Anderson, Eli Biham, and Lars Knudsen; 59 votes)
- Two fish (From Bruce Schneier and others, 31 votes)
- RC6 (From RSA Laboratories, 23 votes), MARS (From IBM, 13 votes)

October 2000, Rijndael was announced as the final selection for AES
November 2001, Rijndael became a US Government standard published as Federal
Information Processing Standard 197 (FIPS 197).

AES MAIN FEATURES:

- Symmetric and Parallel Structure, Adapted to Modern Processors, Suited to Smart Cards.
- Supports key lengths and plain-text block sizes from 128 bits to 256 bits, in the steps of 32 bits.
- Key length and the length of the plain-text blocks need to be selected independently.
- AES mandates that the plain-text block size must be 182 bits, and key size should be 128, 192, or 256 bits.
- Two versions of AES: 128-bit plain-text block with 128-bit key block, and 128- bit
- plain text block with 256-bit key block.
- Commercial standard: 128-bit plain text block and 128-bit key length
- 128 bits give a possible key range of 2^{128} or 3×10^{38} keys
- Even if NSA manages to build a machine with 1 billion parallel processors, each
- being able to evaluate one key per picosecond, it would take such a machine about
- 10^{10} years to search the key space.

AES OF OPERATION:

- Basics of Rijndael are in a mathematical concept called Galois field theory
- Similar to the way DES functions, Rijndael also uses the basic techniques of
- substitution and transposition (i.e. permutation)
- Key size and the plain-text block size decide how many rounds need to be executed. The minimum number of rounds is 10 when key size and the plain-text block size are each 128 bits.

- Maximum number of rounds is 14, One key differentiator between DES and Rijndael is that all the Rijndael operations involve an entire byte, and not individual bits of a byte.
- This provides for more optimized hardware and software implementation of the Algorithm.

Simplified AES

Pass the plaintext and key as a input for encryption purpose, Also be pass the ciphertext and key as a input for decryption purpose.

plaintext= [0,1,2,3,4,5,6,7,8,9,10,11,12,13,14,15,14,13,12,10,9,8,7,6,5,4,3,2,1,0];

K= [0,15,1,5,7,1,12,9,14,8,5,9,0,12,11,7,10,13,13,6,10,15,7,6,7,9,8];

ciphertext= [15,15,0,11,8,4,4,10,0,8,5,3,11,15,7,12,6,9,3,4,10,11,4,3,4,1,4,8,15,11,9];

These structures are the underlying Galois Field and corresponding Vector Space of the field used in the SAES algorithm. These structures allow us to easily compute with these fields.

F = GF(2);
L.<a> = GF(2^4);
V = L.vector_space();
VF8 = VectorSpace(F, 8);

The MixColumns and its Inverse matrices are stored as 2x2 matrices with elements in GF(2^4) (as are state matrices.) . The MixColumns operation (and its inverse) are performed by matrix multiplication.

MixColumns_matrix = Matrix(L, [[1,a^2],[a^2,1]]);
InverseMixColumns_matrix = MixColumns_matrix.inverse();
SBox_matrix = Matrix(L,
[
[1 + a^3, a^2, a + a^3, 1 + a + a^3],
[1 + a^2 + a^3, 1, a^3, 1 + a^2],
[a + a^2, 0, a, 1 + a],
[a^2 + a^3, a + a^2 + a^3, 1 + a + a^2 + a^3, 1 + a + a^2]
]);
InverseSBox_matrix = Matrix(L,
[
[a + a^3, 1 + a^2, 1 + a^3, 1 + a + a^3],
[1, 1 + a + a^2, a^3, 1 + a + a^2 + a^3],
[a + a^2, 0, a, 1 + a],
[a^2 + a^3, a^2, 1 + a^2 + a^3, a + a^2 + a^3]
]);
RCON = [
VF8([F(0), F(0), F(0), F(0), F(0), F(0), F(0), F(1)]),
VF8([F(0), F(0), F(0), F(0), F(1), F(1), F(0), F(0)])
];
def SAES_ToStateMatrix(block):
B = block;
# form the plaintext block into a matrix of GF(2^n) elements
S00 = L(V([B[0], B[1], B[2], B[3]]));
S01 = L(V([B[4], B[5], B[6], B[7]]));
S10 = L(V([B[8], B[9], B[10], B[11]]));
S11 = L(V([B[12], B[13], B[14], B[15]]));
state_matrix = Matrix(L, [[S00,S01],[S10,S11]]);
return state_matrix;
def SAES_FromStateMatrix(state_matrix):

```
output = [];
# convert State Matrix back into bit list
for r in range(2):
for c in range(2):
v = V(state_matrix[r,c]);
for j in range(4):
output.append(Integer(v[j]));
return output;
def SAES_AddRoundKey(state_matrix, K):
K_matrix = SAES_ToStateMatrix(K);
next_state_matrix = K_matrix + state_matrix;
return next_state_matrix;
def SAES_MixColumns(state_matrix):
next_state_matrix = MixColumns_matrix*state_matrix;
return next_state_matrix;
def SAES_InverseMixColumns(state_matrix):
next_state_matrix = InverseMixColumns_matrix*state_matrix;
return next_state_matrix;
def SAES_ShiftRow(state_matrix):
M = state_matrix;
next_state_matrix = Matrix(L, [
[M[0,0], M[0,1]],
[M[1,1], M[1,0]]
]);
return next_state_matrix;
def SAES_SBox(nibble):
v = nibble._vector_();
c = Integer(v[0]) + 2*Integer(v[1]);
r = Integer(v[2]) + 2*Integer(v[3]);
return SBox_matrix[r,c];
def SAES_NibbleSubstitution(state_matrix):
M = state_matrix;
next_state_matrix = Matrix(L,
[ [ SAES_SBox(M[0,0]), SAES_SBox(M[0,1])],
[ SAES_SBox(M[1,0]), SAES_SBox(M[1,1])] ]);
return next_state_matrix;
def SAES_InvSBox(nibble):
v = nibble._vector_();
c = Integer(v[0]) + 2*Integer(v[1]);
r = Integer(v[2]) + 2*Integer(v[3]);
return InverseSBox_matrix[r,c];
def SAES_InvNibbleSub(state_matrix):
M = state_matrix;
next_state_matrix = Matrix(L,
[ [ SAES_InvSBox(M[0,0]), SAES_InvSBox(M[0,1])],
[ SAES_InvSBox(M[1,0]), SAES_InvSBox(M[1,1])] ]);
return next_state_matrix;
def RotNib(w):
```

```
N_0 = L(V([w[j] for j in range(4)]));
N_1 = L(V([w[j] for j in range(4,8)]));
return (N_1, N_0);
def SAES_g(w, i):
(N0, N1) = RotNib(w);
N0 = V(SAES_SBox(N0));
N1 = V(SAES_SBox(N1));
temp1 = VF8( [ N0[0], N0[1], N0[2], N0[3],
N1[0], N1[1], N1[2], N1[3] ] );
output = temp1 + RCON[i];
return output;
def SAES_KeyExpansion(K):
w0 = VF8([K[j] for j in range(8)]);
w1 = VF8([K[j] for j in range(8,16)]);
w2 = w0 + SAES_g(w1, 0);
w3 = w1 + w2;
w4 = w2 + SAES_g(w3, 1);
w5 = w3 + w4;
K0 = [w0[j] for j in range(8)];
K0.extend([w1[j] for j in range(8)]);
K1 = [w2[j] for j in range(8)];
K1.extend([w3[j] for j in range(8)]);
K2 = [w4[j] for j in range(8)];
K2.extend([w4[j] for j in range(8)]);
return (K0, K1, K2);
Encrypts one plaintext block with key K
def SAES_Encrypt(plaintext, K):
# get the key schedule
(K0, K1, K2) = SAES_KeyExpansion(K);
state_matrix0 = SAES_ToStateMatrix(plaintext);
state_matrix1 = SAES_AddRoundKey(state_matrix0, K0);
state_matrix2 = SAES_NibbleSubstitution(state_matrix1);
state_matrix3 = SAES_ShiftRow(state_matrix2);
state_matrix4 = SAES_MixColumns(state_matrix3);
state_matrix5 = SAES_AddRoundKey(state_matrix4, K1);
state_matrix6 = SAES_NibbleSubstitution(state_matrix5);
state_matrix7 = SAES_ShiftRow(state_matrix6);
state_matrix8 = SAES_AddRoundKey(state_matrix7, K2);
output = SAES_FromStateMatrix(state_matrix8);
return output;
Decrypts one ciphertext block with key K
def SAES_Encrypt(plaintext, K):
# get the key schedule
(K0, K1, K2) = SAES_KeyExpansion(K);
state_matrix0 = SAES_ToStateMatrix(plaintext);
state_matrix1 = SAES_AddRoundKey(state_matrix0, K0);
state_matrix2 = SAES_NibbleSubstitution(state_matrix1);
state_matrix3 = SAES_ShiftRow(state_matrix2);
```

```
state_matrix4 = SAES_MixColumns(state_matrix3);
state_matrix5 = SAES_AddRoundKey(state_matrix4, K1);
state_matrix6 = SAES_NibbleSubstitution(state_matrix5);
state_matrix7 = SAES_ShiftRow(state_matrix6);
state_matrix8 = SAES_AddRoundKey(state_matrix7, K2);
output = SAES_FromStateMatrix(state_matrix8);
return output;
```

Output :

SAES_Encrypt(plaintext, K)

[1, 0, 0, 1, 1, 0, 1, 1, 1, 1, 1, 1, 0, 1, 1, 0]

SAES_Decrypt(ciphertext, K)

[1, 1, 0, 1, 1, 0, 0, 1, 0, 1, 1, 1, 1, 1, 1, 1]

Code Explanation:

Bit lists to state matrices conversion

The SAES_ToStateMatrix() and SAES_FromStateMatrix() functions, which convert between bit lists and state matrices, are defined in the first section of the code. A state matrix is a 2x2 matrix made up of Galois field GF(24) elements. While the SAES_FromStateMatrix() function transforms a state matrix back into a bit list, the SAES_ToStateMatrix() function converts a bit list into a state matrix.

AddRoundKey Operation

The SAES_AddRoundKey() function is defined in the second section of the code. This function adds the round key to the state matrix from the input round key and a state matrix. In GF(24), the addition is carried out.

NibbleSubstitution and ShiftRow Operations

The SAES_ShiftRow() and SAES_NibbleSubstitution() methods are described in the third section of the code. Both the NibbleSubstitution and ShiftRow actions are carried out by these functions. Each nibble (4-bit group) in the state matrix is taken out and replaced by the matching value from the S-Box via the NibbleSubstitution operation. The state matrix's rows are moved one position in a cyclical manner by the ShiftRow operation.

MixColumns Operation

The SAES_MixColumns() function is described in the fourth section of the code. The MixColumns operation, a diffusion operation that mixes the state matrix's columns, is carried out by this function. Each column of the state matrix is multiplied by a fixed matrix during the MixColumns procedure.

Overall, the S-AES encryption technique is implemented in the code. The algorithm has 10 rounds with the following steps in each round:

1. AddRoundKey
2. NibbleSubstitution
3. ShiftRow
4. MixColumns

The MixColumns operation is excluded from the final round.

CHAPTER EIGHTEEN

Password -based Authentication with JAVA

A java program for demonstrating authentication Using Password. Java program to illustrate how user authentication is performed based on entered username and password. Both strings are matched against given username and password. If it matches then authentication is successful or else authentication fails.

Code
```java
import java.util.Scanner;
public class User_Authentication
{
public static void main(String args[])
{
String username, password;
Scanner s = new Scanner(System.in);
System.out.print("Enter username:");//username:user
username = s.nextLine();
System.out.print("Enter password:");//password:user
password = s.nextLine();
if(username.equals("user") &password.equals("user"))
{
System.out.println("Authentication Successful");
}
else
{
System.out.println("Authentication Failed");
}
}
}
```

Code explanation:

First, we import the Scanner class for Scan the input from user then we write a class name as User_Authentication. This class will be public class then we write a main function declared the username and password as a string. Then Scan the username from user. A Scanner class is used using System.in object stored the result in S. Similarly we Scan the password from the user stored result in S passes the value in password.

Next will be write a if-else for checking the condition Authentication is Successful or not. Inside if username are equals "user" passes parameter and condition. Same password equals "user" then condition is a fulfill then print the message Authentication Successful. Otherwise, condition will be false, the print message is a Authentication Failed.

Output:
$ javac User_Authentication.java
$ java User_Authentication
Enter username:user
Enter password:user

Authentication Successful
Enter username:abcd
Enter password:1234
Authentication Failed

CHAPTER NINETEEN

Activation of Firewall on Windows Operating System

Firewall is network security device which is used to manage and filter the incoming and outgoing Network Traffic between private and public network. The main function of firewall of firewall is to manage the unwanted access over a network and also out the unfaith traffic from the network. Firewall exist since 1980's filter the packet over the network. There are many types of firewall.

- Packet filtering
- Proxy services
- Stateful inspection
- Next generation firewall

Working of firewall:

- Firewall Basically work to filter the traffic
- Remove the Malicious activity.
- It blocks Malicious access over a network.
- It senses quickly and detect the outside attack & also notify the legitimate user over a network.
- Especially next generation firewalls, Focus on blocking malware and application-layer attacks.
- Network layer and Application layer inspection

Network layer or packet filters inspect packets at a relatively low level of the TCP/IP protocol stack, not allowing packets to pass through the firewall unless they match the established rule set where the source and destination of the rule set where the source and destination of the rule set is based upon internal protocol (Ip) addresses and ports.

Firewall that do network layer inspection perform better than similar devices that do application layer inspection. The downside is that unwanted application or malware can pass over allowed port. E.g, outbound internet traffic over web protocols HTTP and HTTPs, port 80 & 443 respectively.

Firewall & Network Protection

There are many types of firewalls:

Packet filtering:

Packet filtering is a firewall technique used to control network access by monitoring outgoing and incoming packets and allowing them to pass or halt based on the source and destination Internet Protocol (Ip) addresses , protocols and pair.

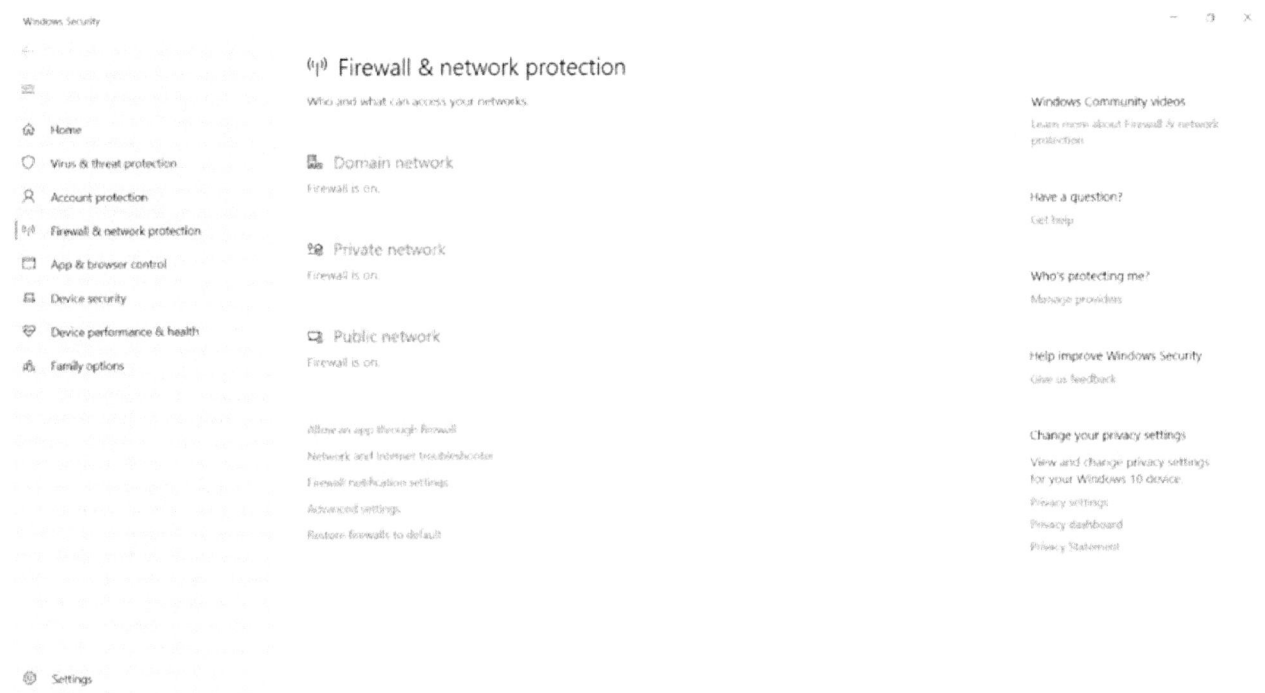

Proxy services:

A proxy firewall is a network security system that protects network resources by filter messages at the application layer.

State full inspection:

In Computing a state full firewall is a network-based firewall that individually tracks session of network connections traversing it. State full packet inspection, also refer to bee dynamic packet filtering is a security feature often used in non-commercial & business network.

Next Generation Firewall:

A next- generation firewall (NGFW) is a network security device that provides capabilities beyond a traditional state full firewall.

Activation of firewall on the windows 10 & their settings:

1. Select the start Button > setting > update & security > windows security and then Firewall & network protection open windows security settings.
2. Select a network profile: Domain network private network or public network.
3. Under Microsoft Defender firewall, switch the setting to on if your device is connected to a network, network policy settings might prevent you from completing these steps for more info contact your administrator.

Allow an app through firewall

There are two ways to allow an app through windows Defender firewall Both are risky

i. Add an app to the list of allowed apps (less risky).
ii. Open a Port (riskier).

Network and Internet troubleshooter:

This firewall is a network security device that works to monitor incoming and outgoing network traffic and makes decision in terms of allowing or blocking determined traffic based on a set of security rules.

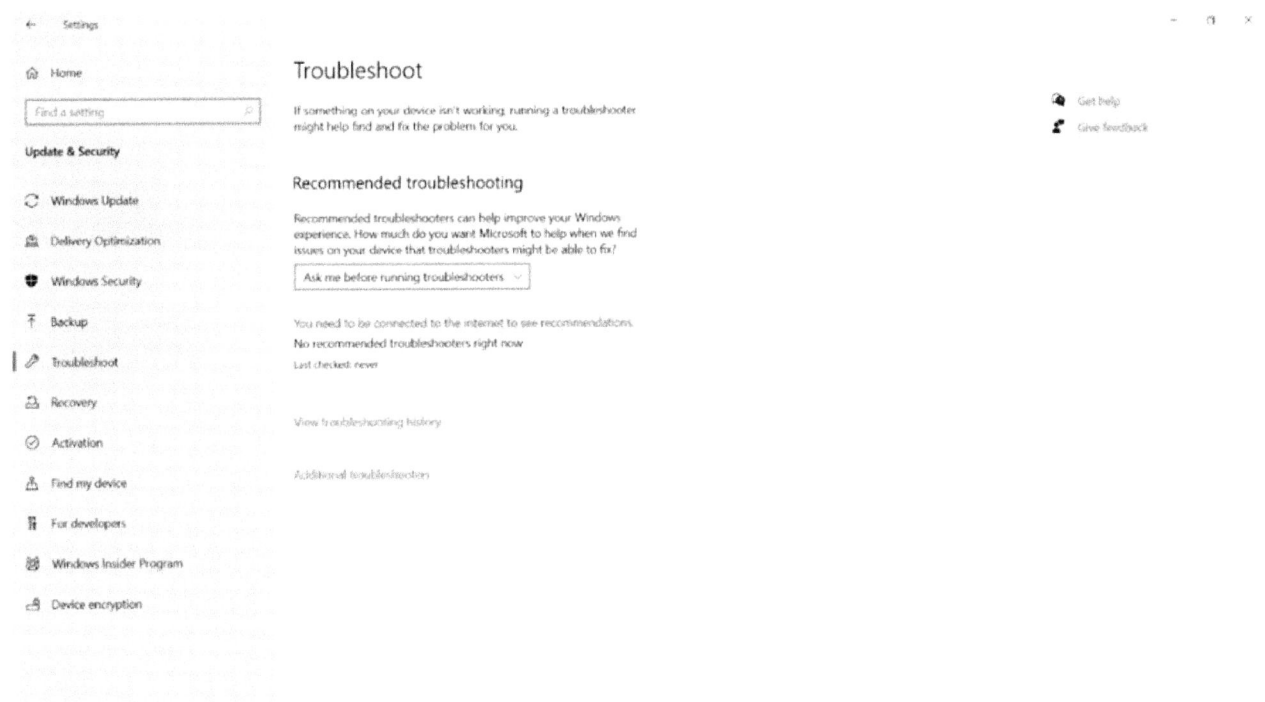

Network and Internet troubleshooter Restore Firewalls to default:

Restoring default settings will rename all windows defenders firewall settings that you have configured for all network locations. This might cause some apps to stop working.

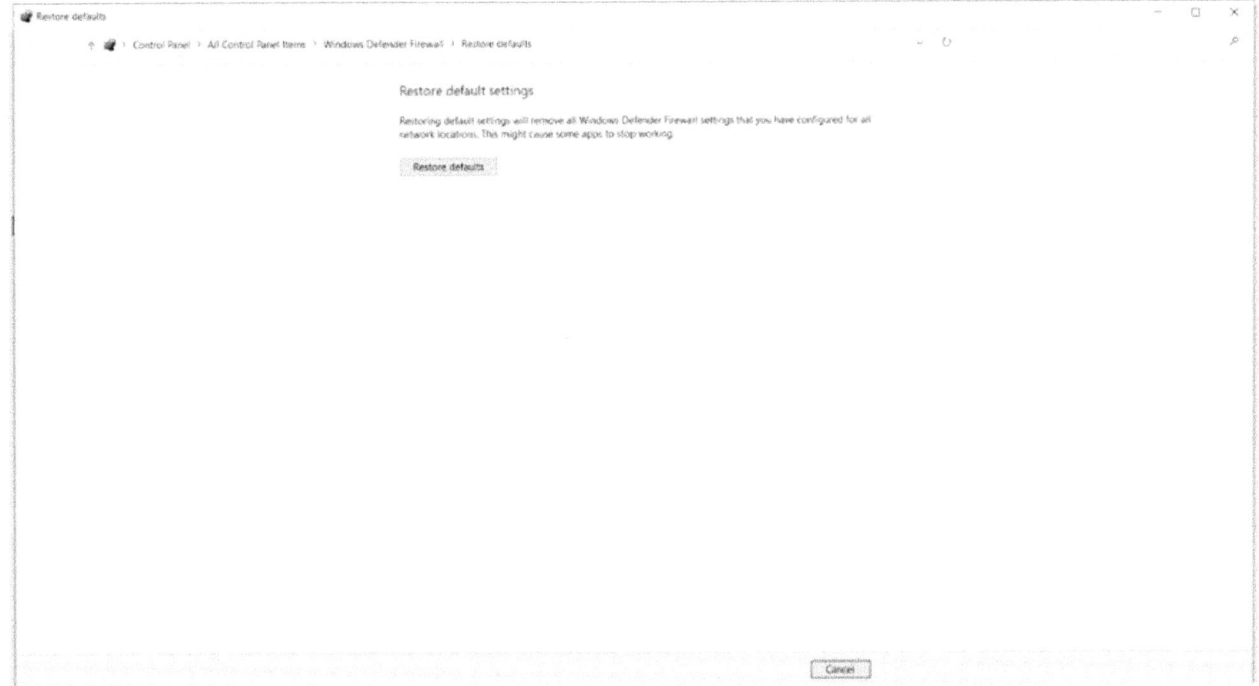

Restore firewall to default Firewall notification settings:

Manage your security providers and notification settings manage the apps and services that protects your device choose the notification you receive from windows security.

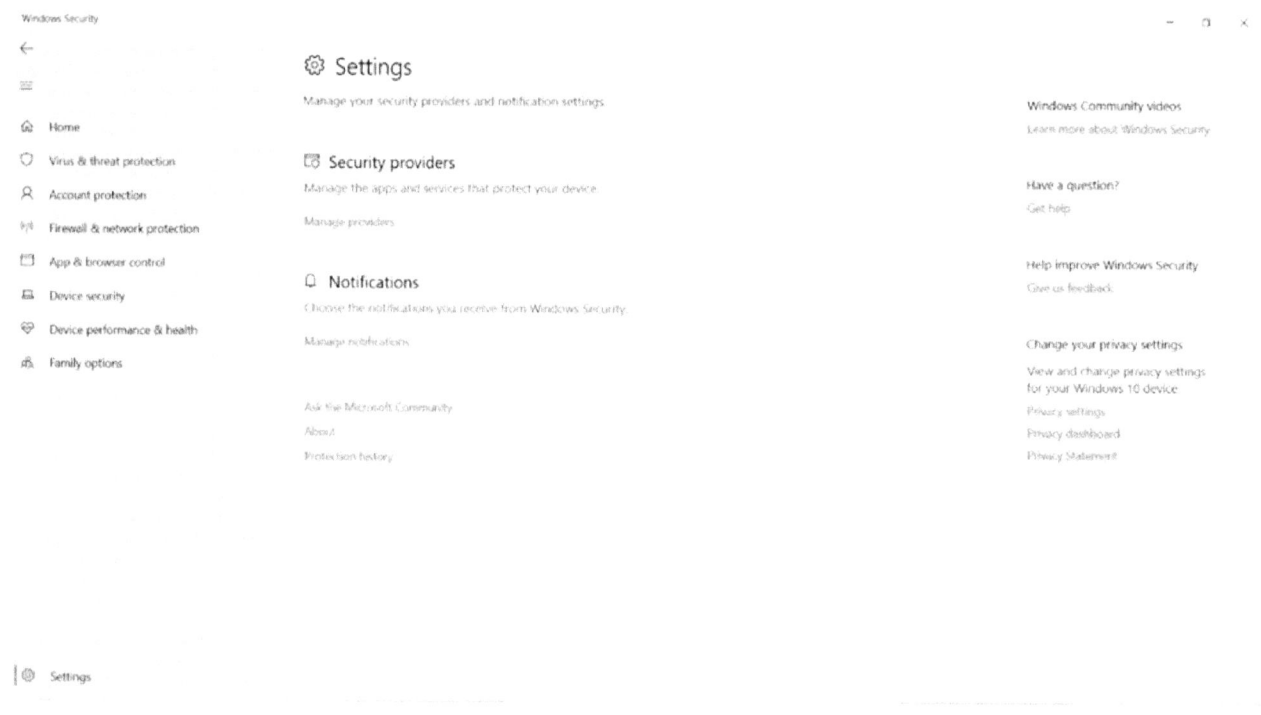

Firewall Notification Setting Advanced setting:
Windows Defends firewall with advanced security on local computer.
There are four types of manage a advanced security such as ,

i. Inbound rules
ii. Outbound rules
iii. Connection security rules
iv. Monitoring

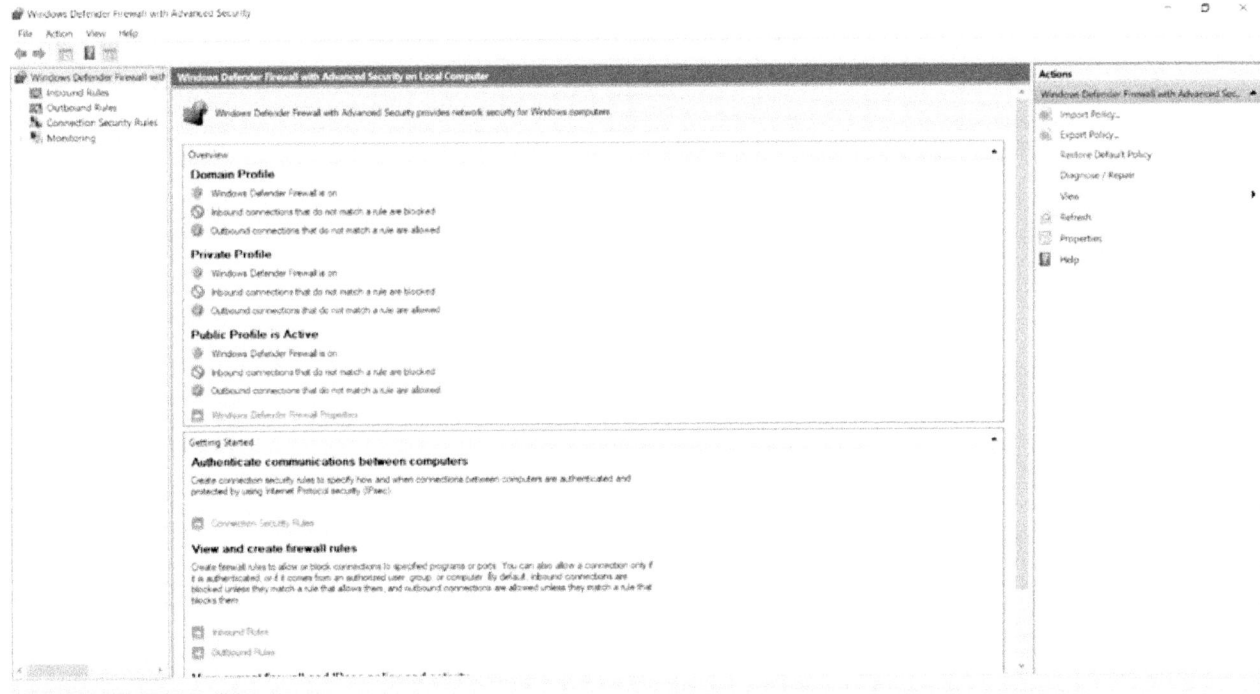

CHAPTER TWENTY

Detecting Trojans by using -Netstat and TCP view

The name of the **Trojan Horse** is taken from a classical story of the Trojan War. It is a code that is malicious in nature and has the capacity to take control of the computer. It is designed to steal, damage, or do some harmful actions on the computer. It tries to deceive the user to load and execute the files on the device. After it executes, this allows cybercriminals to perform many actions on the user's computer like deleting data from files, modifying data from files, and more. Now like many viruses or worms, Trojan Horse does not have the ability to replicate itself.

For example: there is a direct action Trojan name Js. ExitW. It can be downloaded from many malicious sites. The effect of the Js. ExitW is to make the computer fall into a never-ending loop of start and shutdown. The Trojan does not do any damage which could be considered dangerous. But we should be aware that there are many Trojans that are far more dangerous.

Some features of the Trojan horse are as follows :

- It steals information like a password and more.
- It can be used to allow remote access to a computer.
- It can be used to delete data and more on the user's computers

Advantage of the Trojan Horse:

- It can be sent as an attachment in an email.
- It can be in some pop-up ads that we find on the web page.

Disadvantages of the Trojan Horse:

- It can't manifest by itself. It requires the implementation of the .exe files.
- It remains undetected and starts its execution when the user is doing any online transaction activity.

The most basic prevention method: –

1. Do not download anything like the images, and audios from an unsecured website.
2. Do not click on the ads that pop up on the page with advertisements for online games.
3. Do not open any attachment that has been sent from an unknown use.

The user has to install the anti-virus program. This anti-virus program has the capacity to detect those files which are affected by a virus.

20.1 Netstat

You can use the netstat command to monitor and troubleshoot many network problems, and in this guide, you'll get the knowledge to get started with the tool on Windows 10.

On Windows 10, netstat (network statistics) has been around for a long time, and it's a command-line tool that you can use in Command Prompt to display statistics for all network connections. It allows you to understand open and connected ports to monitor and troubleshoot networking problems for system or applications.

When using this tool, you can list active networks (incoming and outgoing) connections and listening ports. You can view network adapter statistics as well as statistics for protocols (such as IPv4 and IPv6). You can even display the current routing table, and much more.

How to use netstat on Windows 10 :-

1. Open **Start**.
    2. Search for **Command Prompt**, right-click the top result, and select the **Run as administrator** option.
    3. Type the following command to show all active TCP connections and press **Enter** :- netstat

4. Type the following command to display active connections showing numeric IP address and port number instead of trying to determine the names and press **Enter** :- netstat -n

5. Type the following command to refresh the information at a specific interval and press **Enter** :- netstat -n INTERVAL In the command, make sure to replace **INTERVAL** for the number (in seconds) you want to redisplay the information. This example refreshes the command in question every five seconds :- netstat -n 5 **Quick note:** When using the interval parameter, you can terminate the command using the **Ctrl + C** keyboard shortcut in the console.

• 183 •

```
C:\Windows\system32>netstat -n 5
Active Connections

  Proto  Local Address          Foreign Address        State
  TCP    10.1.4.119:53643       52.230.222.68:443      ESTABLISHED
  TCP    10.1.4.119:54175       40.90.23.208:443       TIME_WAIT
  TCP    10.1.4.119:54177       205.185.216.42:80      TIME_WAIT

Active Connections

  Proto  Local Address          Foreign Address        State
  TCP    10.1.4.119:53643       52.230.222.68:443      ESTABLISHED
  TCP    10.1.4.119:54175       40.90.23.208:443       TIME_WAIT
  TCP    10.1.4.119:54177       205.185.216.42:80      TIME_WAIT

Active Connections

  Proto  Local Address          Foreign Address        State
  TCP    10.1.4.119:53643       52.230.222.68:443      ESTABLISHED
  TCP    10.1.4.119:54175       40.90.23.208:443       TIME_WAIT
  TCP    10.1.4.119:54177       205.185.216.42:80      TIME_WAIT
  TCP    10.1.4.119:54186       10.1.4.101:52323       SYN_SENT
  TCP    10.1.4.119:54187       10.1.4.101:52323       SYN_SENT

Active Connections
```

Once you execute the command, it'll return a list of all active connections in four columns, including :-

- **Proto:** Shows the connection protocol (TCP or UDP).
- **Local Address:** Shows the computer's IP address followed by a semicolon with a port number of the connection. The double-semicolon inside brackets indicates the local IPv6 address, and "0.0.0.0" refers to the local address too.
- **Foreign Address:** Lists the remote device's IP (or FQDN) address with the port number after semicolon port name (for example, https, http, Microsoft -ds, wsd).
- **State:** Indicates where the connection is active (established), the local port has been closed (time_ wait), and the program hasn't closed the port (close_ wait). Other status include, closed, fin_wait_1, fin_wait_2, last_ ack, listen, syn_ received, syn_ send, and timed_ wait.

How to use netstat parameters on Windows 10

The tool also includes several parameters that you can use in Command Prompt to display different information about the network connections.

netstat -a command displays all active and inactive connections, and the TCP and UDP ports the device is currently listening.

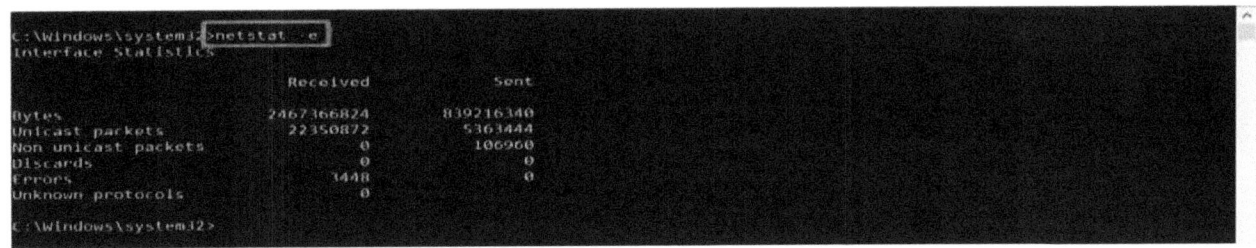

netstat -b command lists all the executables (applications) associated with each connection. Sometimes, applications may open multiple connections.

netstat -e command generates a statistic of the network interface, which shows information like the number of bytes, unicast and non-unicast sent and received packets. You can also see discarded packets and errors and unknown protocols, which can you troubleshoot networking problems.

netstat -f command shows the fully qualified domain name (FQDN) for foreign addresses. For example, "server-54-230-157-50.otp50.r.cloudfront.net:http" instead of "server-54-230-157-50:http" or "54.230.157.50".

netstat -n command displays the addresses and ports in numerical form. For example, 54.230.157.50:443.

netstat -o command shows all active TCP connections like Enter: netstat , but with the difference that adds a fifth column to display the Process ID (PID) for each connection. The processes available in this view are the same in the "Details" tab of Task Manager, which also reveals the application using the connection.

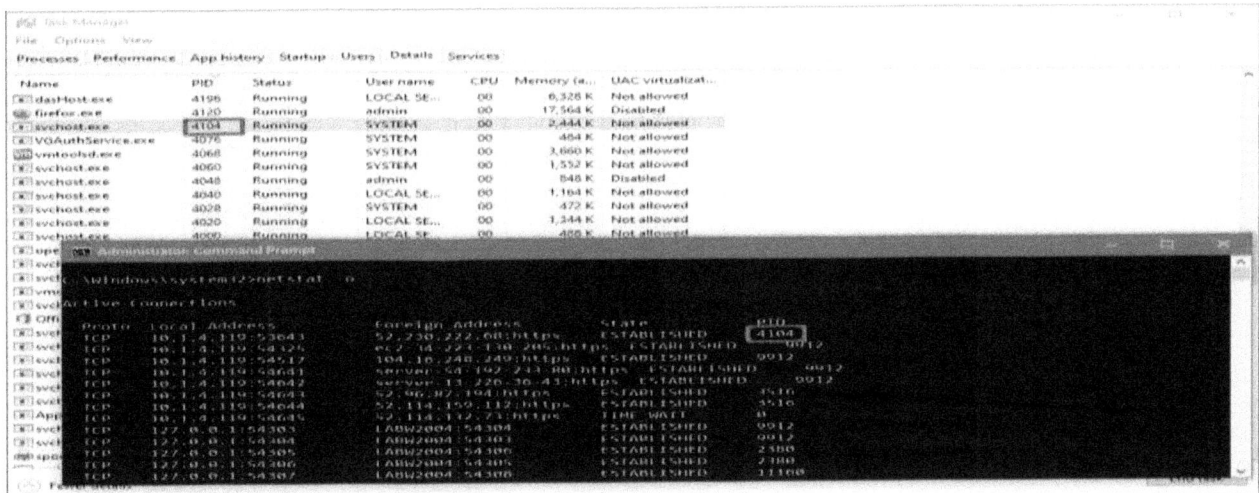

netstat -p can be used to display connections per-protocol that you have to specify using tcp , udp , tcpv6 , or udpv6 next to the command. For example, you can use the netstat -p tcp to view a list of TCP connections.

netstat -q commands can produce a list of all the connections with the listening and bound non-listening ports.

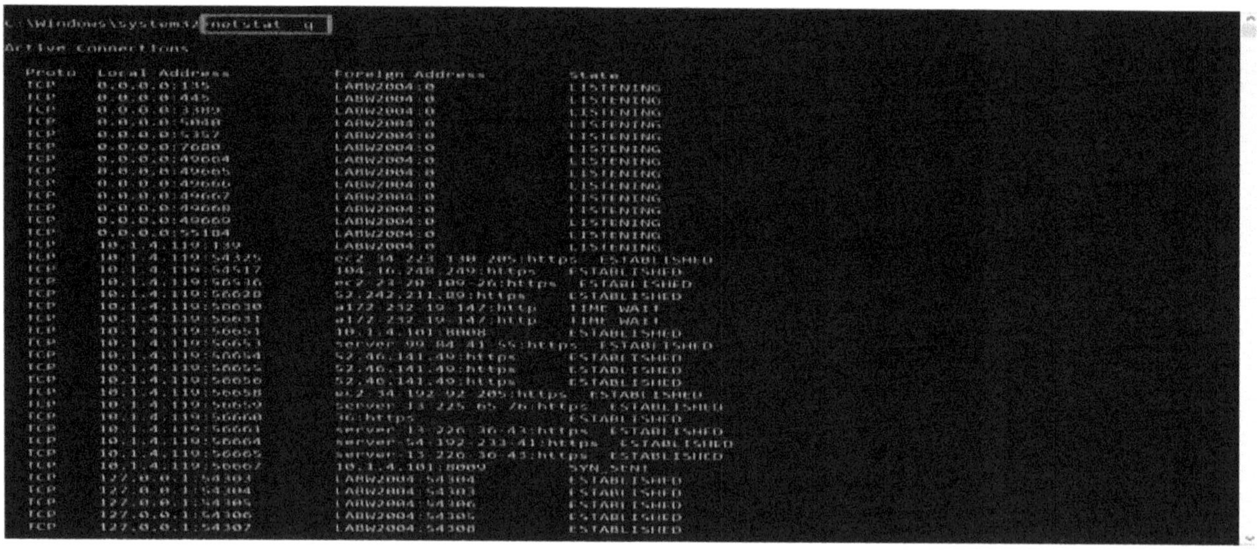
netstat -q
Active Connections
Proto Local Address Foreign Address State

netstat -s shows network statistics for all available protocols, including TCP, UDP, ICMP, and IP protocols (version 4 & 6).

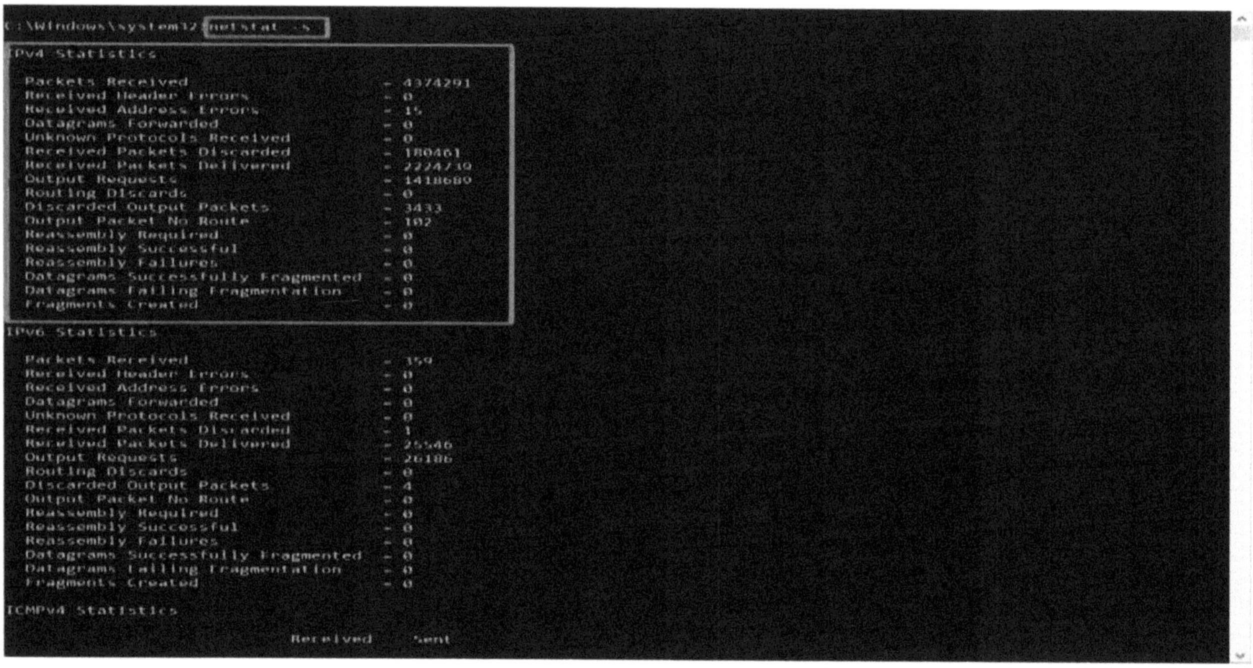
netstat -s
IPv4 Statistics
IPv6 Statistics
ICMPv4 Statistics
Received Sent

netstat -r command displays the current network routing table that lists all the routes to destinations and matric known by the device, for IP version 4 and version 6 (if applicable). If the returned information looks familiar, it's because you can also output the data using the

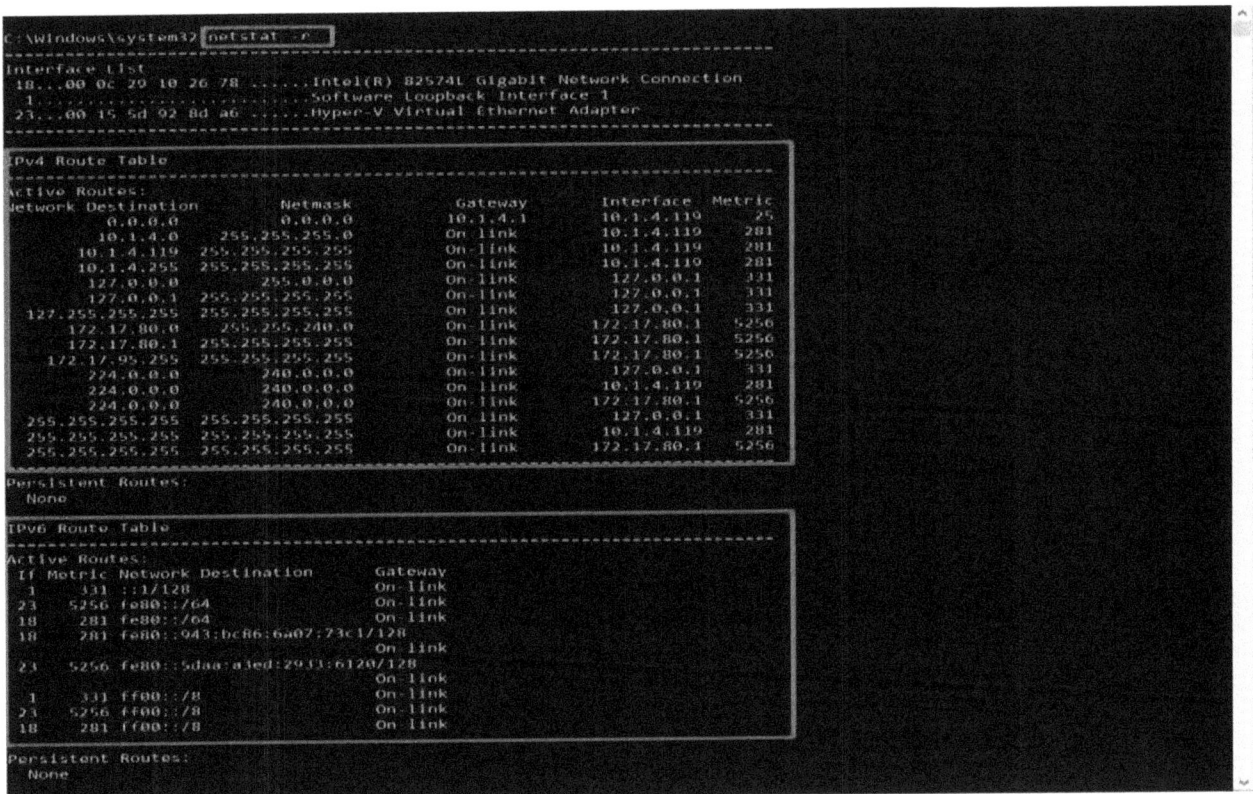

netstat -t command generates a list of the current connection offload state. The offload state refers to the TCP Chimney Offload(opens in new tab), which is a feature that transfers the network workload from the processor to the network adapter during data transmissions. The "In Host" value indicates that offloading isn't enabled, and the "Offload" means that the feature is transferring the workload to the network adapter. (This feature is only present on supported network adapters.)

netstat -x is another supported command on Windows 10, and it produces a list of Network Direct connections, shared endpoints, and listeners.

Network Direct (opens in new tab) is a specification for Remote Direct Memory Access (RDMA), which is a process that allows fast data transfers using the network adapter, freeing up the processor to perform other tasks. Usually, you'll never use this command unless you're using the server version of Windows or a high-performance application with a network adapter that supports this feature.

Show connection template

netstat -y command displays TCP connections templates for all connections.

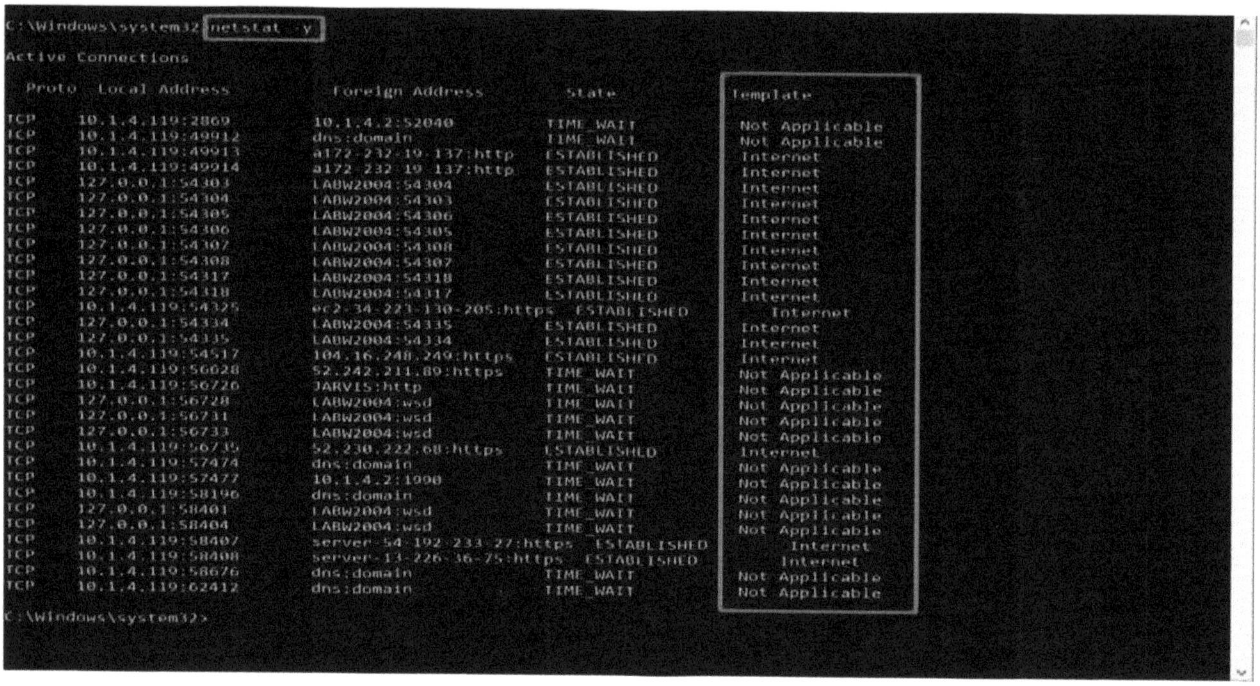
C:\Windows\system32>netstat -y
Active Connections
Proto Local Address Foreign Address State Template
TCP 10.1.4.119:2869 10.1.4.2:52040 TIME_WAIT Not Applicable
TCP 10.1.4.119:49912 dns:domain TIME_WAIT Not Applicable
TCP 10.1.4.119:49913 a172-232-19-137:http ESTABLISHED Internet
TCP 10.1.4.119:49914 a172-232-19-137:http ESTABLISHED Internet
TCP 127.0.0.1:54303 LABW2004:54304 ESTABLISHED Internet
TCP 127.0.0.1:54304 LABW2004:54303 ESTABLISHED Internet
TCP 127.0.0.1:54305 LABW2004:54306 ESTABLISHED Internet
TCP 127.0.0.1:54306 LABW2004:54305 ESTABLISHED Internet
TCP 127.0.0.1:54307 LABW2004:54308 ESTABLISHED Internet
TCP 127.0.0.1:54308 LABW2004:54307 ESTABLISHED Internet
TCP 127.0.0.1:54317 LABW2004:54318 ESTABLISHED Internet
TCP 127.0.0.1:54318 LABW2004:54317 ESTABLISHED Internet
TCP 10.1.4.119:54325 ec2-34-223-130-205:https ESTABLISHED Internet
TCP 127.0.0.1:54334 LABW2004:54335 ESTABLISHED Internet
TCP 127.0.0.1:54335 LABW2004:54334 ESTABLISHED Internet
TCP 10.1.4.119:54517 104.16.248.249:https ESTABLISHED Internet
TCP 10.1.4.119:56028 52.242.211.89:https TIME_WAIT Not Applicable
TCP 10.1.4.119:56726 JARVIS:http TIME_WAIT Not Applicable
TCP 127.0.0.1:56728 LABW2004:wsd TIME_WAIT Not Applicable
TCP 127.0.0.1:56731 LABW2004:wsd TIME_WAIT Not Applicable
TCP 127.0.0.1:56733 LABW2004:wsd TIME_WAIT Not Applicable
TCP 10.1.4.119:56735 52.230.222.68:https ESTABLISHED Internet
TCP 10.1.4.119:57474 dns:domain TIME_WAIT Not Applicable
TCP 10.1.4.119:57477 10.1.4.2:1990 TIME_WAIT Not Applicable
TCP 10.1.4.119:58196 dns:domain TIME_WAIT Not Applicable
TCP 127.0.0.1:58401 LABW2004:wsd TIME_WAIT Not Applicable
TCP 127.0.0.1:58404 LABW2004:wsd TIME_WAIT Not Applicable
TCP 10.1.4.119:58407 server-54-192-233-27:https ESTABLISHED Internet
TCP 10.1.4.119:58408 server-13-226-36-75:https ESTABLISHED Internet
TCP 10.1.4.119:58676 dns:domain TIME_WAIT Not Applicable
TCP 10.1.4.119:62412 dns:domain TIME_WAIT Not Applicable
C:\Windows\system32>

If you want to see all the available parameters and additional help, you can always use the netstat /?

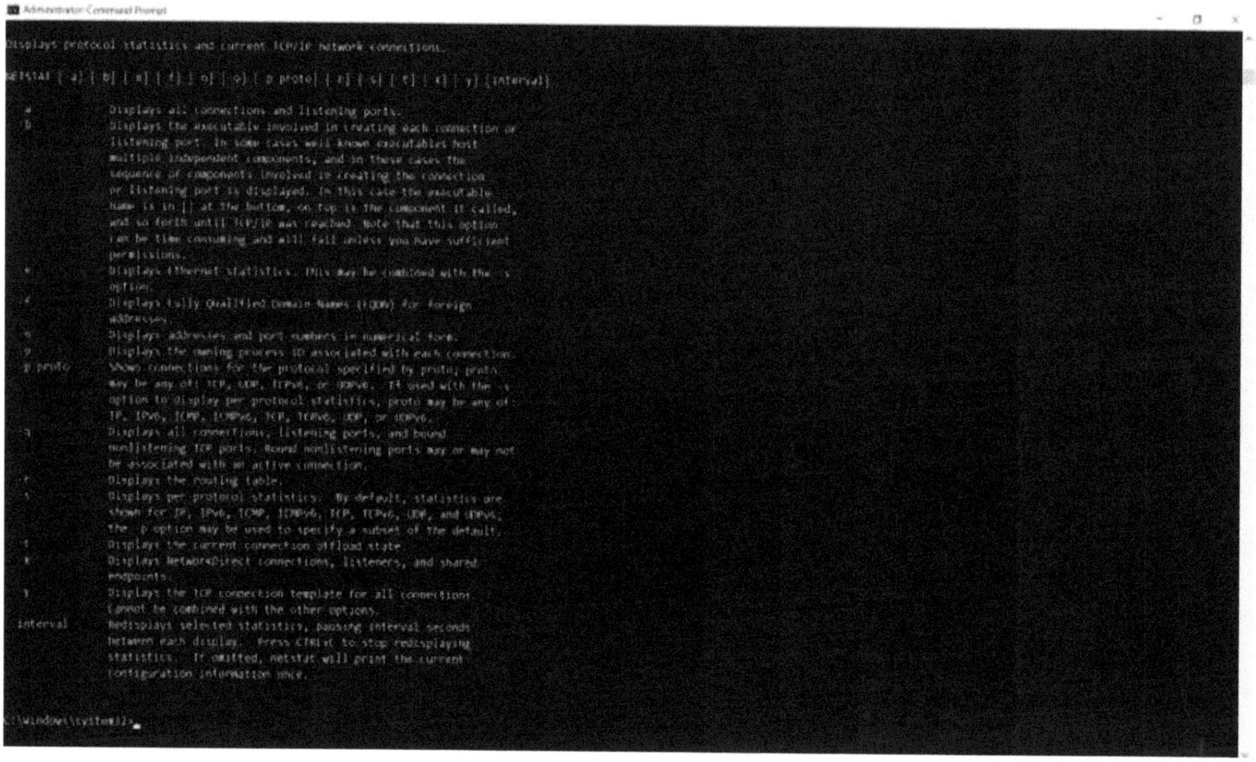

Using Tcpvcon :- Tcpvcon usage is similar to that of the built-in Windows netstat utility:
Usage:- tcpvcon [-a] [-c] [-n] [process name or PID]
Parameter Description

-a Show all endpoints (default is to show established TCP connections).
-c Print output as CSV.
-n Don't resolve addresses.

Identifying TCP Port and Endpoint Issues with TCP View

Conflicts between applications demanding the same TCP/IP port are frustrating, especially if you're working on a system shared with other development teams. Inter-team communication might be lacking, and teams might not clearly lay out their configuration requirements. The same thing happens all too frequently in production systems, where administrative staff miss application requirements or misconfigure the applications.

Tracking down these conflicts can be an irritating task, unless you have Sysinternals's TCP View to ease the way. TCP View shows all TCP communications to and from a particular system. It lets you immediately identify port conflicts and isolate which processes are demanding those ports. TCP View can also help you identify unexpected TCP communications, such as those on a system infected with a Trojan virus.

CHAPTER TWENTY-ONE

Scanning for Vulnerabilities

Vulnerability scanning, also commonly known as 'vuln scan,' is an automated process of proactively identifying network, application, and security vulnerabilities. Vulnerability scanning is typically performed by the IT department of an organization or a third-party security service provider. This scan is also performed by attackers who try to find points of entry into your network.

The scanning process includes detecting and classifying system weaknesses in networks, communications equipment, and computers. In addition to identifying security holes, the vulnerability scans also predict how effective countermeasures are in case of a threat or attack.

A vulnerability scanning service uses piece of software running from the standpoint of the person or organization inspecting the attack surface in question. The vulnerability scanner uses a database to compare details about the target attack surface.

The database references known flaws, coding bugs, packet construction anomalies, default configurations, and potential paths to sensitive data that can be exploited by attackers.

After the software checks for possible vulnerabilities in any devices within the scope of the engagement, the scan generates a report. The findings in the report can then be analyzed and interpreted in order to identify opportunities for an organization to improve their security posture.

Network Vulnerability Scan Categories

Network vulnerability scans can be categorized based on their use-cases:

- Intrusive and non-intrusive methods
- External vulnerability scan
- Internal vulnerability scan
- Environmental scan
- Scanning Methods

Scanning Types: -

External vulnerability scans target the areas of an IT ecosystem that are exposed to the internet, or not restricted for internal use. These areas can include applications, ports, websites, services, networks, and systems that are accessed by external customers or users.

With **internal vulnerability scans**, the primary target of the software is the internal enterprise network. Once a threat agent makes it through a security hole, the threat agent can leave enterprise systems prone to damage. These scans search for and identify the vulnerabilities inside the network in order to avoid damage, as well as to allow organizations to protect and tighten systems and application security that are not exposed by external scans.

Environmental vulnerability scans are based on the specific environment of an enterprise's technology operations. These vulnerability scans are specialized and are available to deploy for multiple technologies, such as IoT devices, websites, cloud-based services, and mobile devices.

Scanning for vulnerabilities using Angry IP:

- Angry IP scanner is a freely available IP address and port scanner known for its ease of use, simplicity, and speed. Angry IP scanners can scan IP addresses in any range and their ports. It was designed to be cross-platform and very lightweight.
- Operating Angry IP is simple but comprehensive. Angry IP scanner pings each IP address to check the status and then optionally resolves its hostname, determines the MAC address, scans ports, and more. Furthermore, the amount of gathered data about each host can be extended with additional functionality through plugins.
- Angry IP scanner has additional features to include NetBIOS information (computer name, workgroup name, and Windows user currently logged in), specified IP address ranges, web server detection, customizable openers, and more.
- Angry IP scanning saves results in many file formats, including CSV, TXT, XML, or IP-Port list files. Through the extended functionality of available plugins, Angry IP Scanner can gather a wide variety of information about scanned IP addresses. Basic Java coding skills are required to write plugins and extend the functionality of Angry IP Scanner.
- Because performance is essential for any scanner, the Angry IP scanner utilizes a multithreaded approach, creating a separate scanning thread for each scanned IP address.

Angry Ip Download for Windows: -

Visit on side https://angryip.org/ which is the official side of Angry IPScanner

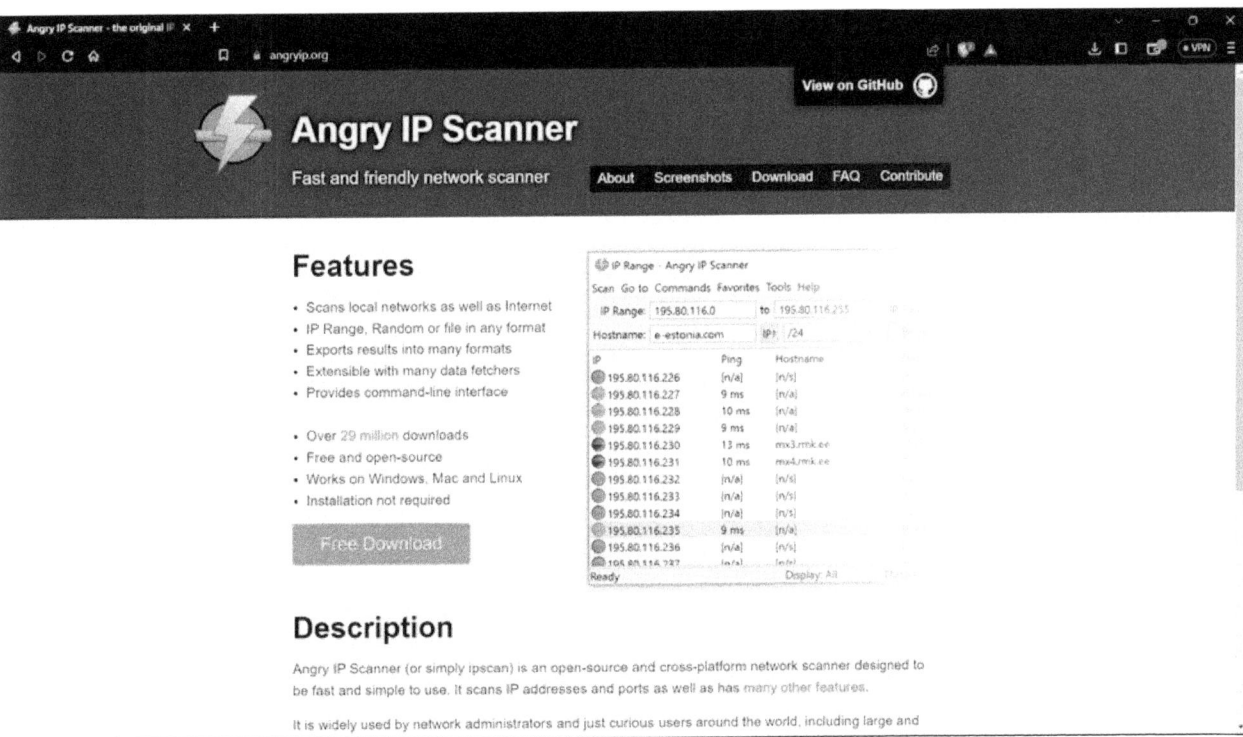

Angry Ip Working: -

1. Open the Angry Ip Scanner & Run as Administrator
2. In Angry Ip many options are available scan, go to, commands, favorites, tools & help this are used to manage the Angry Ip Scanner.

There are three way to find our current IP in our system such as –

1. IP Range
2. Random
3. Text File

We will select Ip Range in my system 192.168.250.0 to 192.168.250.255 Then we write our Hostname, my system hostname is Asus. next we select the IP Netmask. Then we start the Scanning process, there are four columns filed that are scan first we Ip in this filed we scan the current Ip run our system, Ping it is nothing but Packet Internet or Inter-Network Groper, it is a basic Internet program that allows a user to test and verify if a particular destination IP address exist.

Next will be Hostname and last port

Scanning completed Status will be display: - In this status report display the Total time for scanning are 27.72 sec, Average time per host are 0.44 sec. then display the Ip range 192.168.250.0 – 192.168.250.63, Hosts scanned 63 and Hosts alive will be 12.

www.ingramcontent.com/pod-product-compliance
Ingram Content Group UK Ltd.
Pitfield, Milton Keynes, MK11 3LW, UK
UKHW060214240426
12048UKWH00031BB/1722